Indian Integration in Peru

Indian Integration in Peru

A Half Century of Experience, 1900-1948

by

Thomas M. Davies, Jr.

UNIVERSITY OF NEBRASKA PRESS • LINCOLN

Portions of Chapters 5 and 6 have previously been published, in different form, in "The *Indigenismo* of the Peruvian Aprista Party: A Reinterpretation," *Hispanic American Historical Review* 51, no. 4 (November 1971): 626-45, and of Chapters 2-6 in "Indian Integration in Peru, 1820-1948: An Overview," *The Americas* (October 1973).

Publishers on the Plains

UNP

The publication of this book was assisted by a grant from The Andrew W. Mellon Foundation

To Tita

Without whose aid and encouragement
this book could not have been written.

Contents

MAPS

Preface

This work focuses on efforts by the Peruvian government to integrate its large Indian population, from the first decrees of José de San Martín in 1821 through the administration of José Luis Bustamante y Rivero (1945-48). Treatment of the Spanish colonial period has, for the most part, been excluded. An attempt to deal adequately with that three-hundred-year period would require more than one additional volume. Moreover, Spanish attempts to deal with the Indian population were politically, economically, and legally distinct from those of the republican era. Measures developed to maintain colonial status were different from those formulated by an independent nation seeking to unite itself.

The year 1948 was selected as a terminal date for similar reasons. Between 1821 and 1948, Indian integration and the legal relationship of the Indians to the nation was a purely domestic problem. Neither the Indians nor the national government received any outside assistance. The administration of Manuel A. Odría (1948-56), however, marked the beginning of large-scale projects involving international organizations and private foundations. The now famous Peru-Cornell project at Vicos in the Callejón de Huaylas is a prime example of cooperation between the Peruvian government, Cornell University, and the Ford Foundation. Numerous other projects in the sierra received financial and technical assistance from the United Nations, the Organization of American States, and various private foundations. Though these projects varied, they all represent a sharp departure from past Indian programs. Moreover, while the projects did involve government agencies as well as Peruvian scholars and technicians, much of the impetus and funding was provided by foreigners. It would require a completely different frame of reference to evaluate Peruvian government actions in 1955 or 1960 for comparison with those of 1860 and 1920.

For the period selected, I sought to correlate the actions of the president, the Congress, and political parties with their respective programs, promises, and platforms, establishing when possible the success or failure of the numerous Indian laws. Though extremely difficult to document, I also attempted to evaluate the sincerity of a given leader or administration. The criteria I employed included not only their success or failure in implementing Indian reform laws, but also their overall attitude toward the problem. For example, did a president or political leader merely pay lip service to Indian reform in his writings and speeches, or did he strive to move beyond pure rhetoric and attempt to effect change? Likewise, did members of Congress actively fight for proposed legislation, or did they speak on its behalf and then quietly allow it to fail? Though cognizant of the dangers involved in such analysis, I feel that besides offering a compilation of concrete data, a researcher has the obligation to confront such intangible problems as sincerity and motivation.

Thus, old interpretations and myths regarding Indian legislation and the role of political parties and politicians were reexamined and analyzed. My conclusions on the contributions of José de San Martín and Símon Bolívar as well as many nineteenth-century presidents are orthodox, but I have taken exception to previously held opinions on the twentieth-century experience. Along with questioning the sincerity and success of such presidents as Augusto B. Leguía, Luis M. Sánchez Cerro, Oscar R. Benavides, and José Luis Bustamante y Rivero, I have also attempted to place in perspective the ideology and actions of such political thinkers as Manuel González Prada, José Carlos Mariátegui, and Víctor Raúl Haya de la Torre, viewing their *indigenismo* within the context of the contemporary political climate. In so doing, I have reached conclusions which challenge the interpretations of such scholars as Harry Kantor, Fredrick Pike, and Carlos Miró Quesada Laos.

The success or failure of Indian legislation is difficult to demonstrate, but an effort was made to point out repetitious laws, which indicate earlier inefficacy, as well as to analyze the impact which specific laws had on the Indian masses. Since there exist vast cultural differences between the sedentary Quechua- and Aymara-speaking Indians of the sierra and the numerically less significant nomadic tribes of the jungle, no effort was made to deal with government programs in the Amazon Basin except where such programs, or lack thereof, had a direct bearing on the Indian policies of a party or administration.

It is hoped that this study will prompt scholars to undertake a more detailed study of Indian legislation, particularly on a departmental or regional scale. There is also a need for in-depth studies of the causes and effects of local Indian revolts. An attempt might also be made to analyze the relationship between a president's Indian program and his efforts in other areas of social legislation. This type of analysis is not included here because of the enormousness of such an undertaking.

Indian Integration in Peru

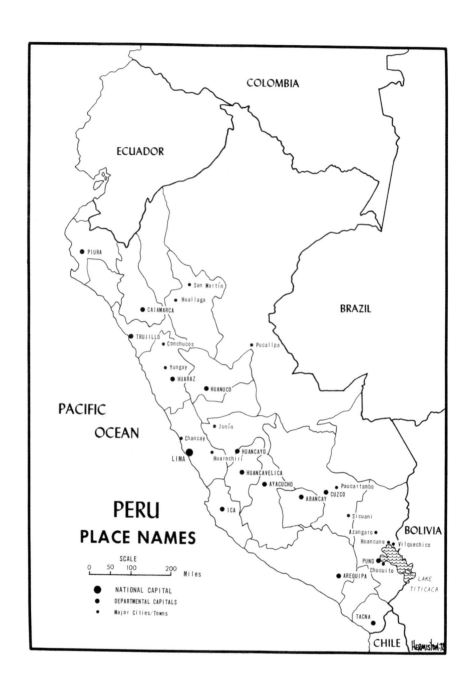

COLOMBIA

ECUADOR

BRAZIL

PACIFIC

OCEAN

• PIURA

• San Martín

• Huallaga

• CAJAMARCA

• TRUJILLO
• Conchucos
• Pucallpa

• Yungay
• HUARAZ
• HUANUCO

• Junín

• Chancay
• HUANCAYO
LIMA
• Huarochirí
• HUANCAVELICA
• AYACUCHO
• Paucartambo
• ABANCAY • CUZCO

PERU

PLACE NAMES

• ICA

• Sicuani

• Azangaro

BOLIVIA

• Huancane • Vilquechico

PUNO
• Chucuito

LAKE
TITICACA

SCALE
0   50   100   200   Miles

● NATIONAL CAPITAL

● DEPARTMENTAL CAPITALS

• Major Cities/Towns

• AREQUIPA

• TACNA

CHILE   HERMISTON 72

1

Introduction

THE LAND AND THE PEOPLE

It is axiomatic when writing about Peru to note that the nation's two most fundamental problems have been geography and the existence of a large, unassimilated Indian population. In practical terms, the two merge to form one giant problem because Peru's extraordinary geographic conditions have served to isolate the largely Indian sierra, or mountain region, from the predominantly Spanish coast. There are hundreds of anthropological studies of Indians in Peru as well as numerous works on Peruvian geography, and while it is not the purpose of this study to summarize that data, a brief overview is necessary to provide a general framework for the discussion of Indian laws and programs which follows.

The flat, dry coast, which is approximately 1,400 miles in length, is extremely narrow, at times dropping to no more than 50 miles in width in the central portion. Although the coast encompasses little more than 10 percent of the nation's area, it contains over 35 percent of the population. It was here that Francisco Pizarro founded his Ciudad de los Reyes (Lima), and it is from here that Peru has been ruled for four centuries. The combination of extremely high mountain ranges to the east and the presence of the arctic cold waters of the Humboldt Current to the west has made the coast a veritable desert, forcing farmers to rely on the scarce water supplies of narrow river valleys.

Over 60 percent of Peru lies east of the Andes mountain chains. Of this about a third is the *ceja de la montaña* (literally, eyebrow of the jungle) stretching from about 4,000 feet up to 11,000. Here the valleys and slopes are extremely fertile, but a near complete lack of access roads has precluded effective settlement. The remainder

1

of the region lies in the largely unexplored and sparsely populated Amazon Basin.

The sierra is characterized by some of the highest peaks in the world (Huascarán is 22,180 feet high and Yerupajá is 21,560). The average altitude of the sierra is about 13,000 feet, and it is here that the great majority of Peru's Indians live, isolated from the rest of the nation by mountains and a lack of transportation facilities.

There is little oxygen at altitudes of 12,000 to 16,000 feet and the unacclimated traveler often falls victim to *soroche*, or mountain sickness. *Soroche* is easy to describe and extremely unpleasant to experience. No amount of clothing keeps out the penetrating cold and it is difficult to breathe even while seated in a car. Minimal exercise is difficult and normal activity is almost impossible. The head begins to throb, accompanied by recurring waves of nausea. While suffering such an attack on the train between Arequipa and Puno, I looked out the window and saw an Indian pedaling a bicycle at high speed. I have also seen soccer games at altitudes of 15,000 feet, which made me feel even more of an outsider in an alien, hostile world.

The coastal dweller, which includes almost all government officials, simply cannot operate effectively at the altitudes of the sierra and they rarely try. One often hears the expression "Lima is Peru and Peru is Lima," and this has been the historical tragedy of the nation. The lack of contact between regions has isolated the Indians and fostered misunderstanding and ignorance about their wants and needs. Although this isolation has been ameliorated somewhat in recent years, Peru still lacks the transportation network necessary to unite the nation.

The physical realities of Indian life have changed very little over the centuries. Most still live on the high, arid, windswept plains (*punas*) of the sierra and in intermontane valleys much in the way as did their Inca ancestors. Since the conquest, Indians have comprised the largest segment in the nation's population. John H. Rowe estimated that at the time of the conquest (1525) the Indian population of the Andean region was about 6,000,000. That figure, however, had been reduced to 1,500,000 by 1571. George Kubler demonstrates that Spanish exploitation and the greed of colonial officials further decimated the Indian population, which fell from 1,200,000 in 1586 to 612,000 in 1754, to 608,894 by 1795.[1]

1. John H. Rowe, "Inca Culture at the Time of the Spanish Conquest," in *The Andean Civilizations,* vol. 2 of *Handbook of South American Indians,* ed. Julian Steward

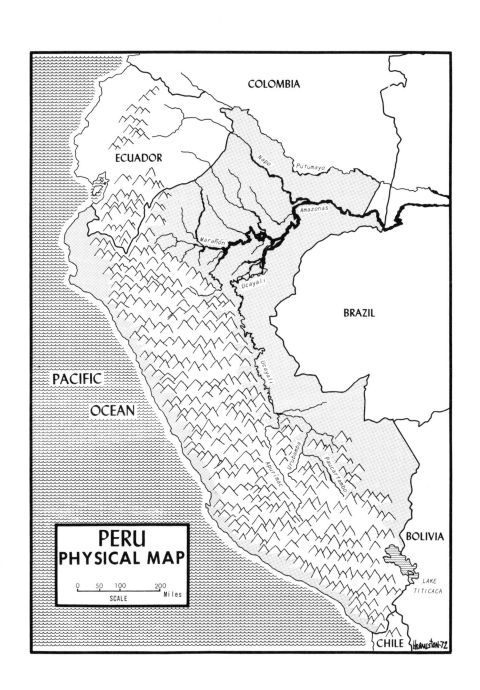

COLOMBIA

ECUADOR

Napo

Putumayo

Amazonas

Marañón

Ucayali

BRAZIL

PACIFIC

OCEAN

Ucayali

Apurímac

Urubamba

Paucartambo

BOLIVIA

LAKE
TITICACA

PERU
PHYSICAL MAP

0   50   100   200
SCALE   Miles

CHILE   HERMISTON-72

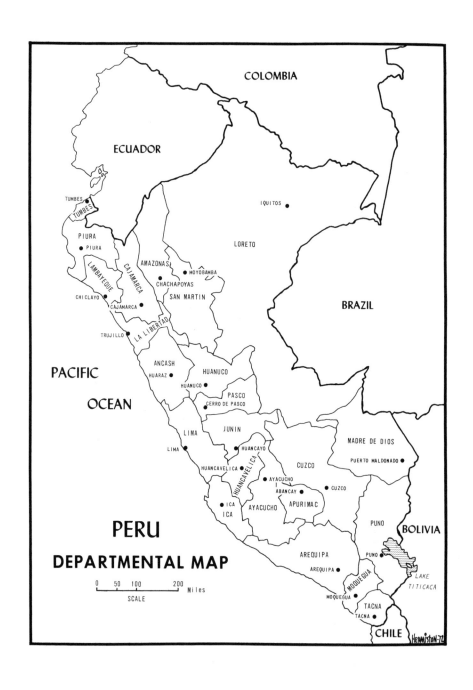

COLOMBIA

ECUADOR

PACIFIC

OCEAN

TUMBES
TUMBES

PIURA
PIURA

LAMBAYEQUE
CHICLAYO

CAJAMARCA
CAJAMARCA

TRUJILLO

LA LIBERTAD

AMAZONAS
CHACHAPOYAS

MOYOBAMBA

SAN MARTIN

IQUITOS

LORETO

BRAZIL

ANCASH
HUARAZ
HUANUCO
HUANUCO

PASCO
CERRO DE PASCO

LIMA
LIMA

JUNIN
HUANCAYO

HUANCAVELICA
HUANCAVELICA

MADRE DE DIOS

PUERTO MALDONADO

CUZCO

AYACUCHO
ABANCAY

CUZCO

PERU

DEPARTMENTAL MAP

ICA
ICA

AYACUCHO

APURIMAC

PUNO

BOLIVIA

AREQUIPA
AREQUIPA

PUNO

LAKE
TITICACA

MOQUEGUA
MOQUEGUA

TACNA
TACNA

CHILE

Hemmiston-72

0   50   100   200   Miles
SCALE

Population data for the republican era are sketchy and often un-reliable. The censuses of 1836 and 1850 were incomplete and contained no information on Indians. The first semireliable census was taken in 1876. It showed a total population of 2,699,106, of which 1,554,678, or 57.6 percent were Indians. The 1940 census revealed a total population of 7,023,111, with Indians numbering 2,847,196, or 40 percent, a decline of some 17 percent.[2]

The reader is warned, however, to treat these figures as rough estimates. The censuses were not conducted scientifically and thousands of Indians were undoubtedly uncounted. Moreover, whereas the census of 1876 listed only Indians and non-Indians, that of 1940 created a separate category for mestizos. Owing to their historical distrust and fear of government officials, many Indians probably avoided the census takers, while others sought to be counted as mestizos in an effort to enhance somehow their economic and social status. Nor is it even known what criteria were supposed to be used to define *Indian* and *mestizo*. Nevertheless, these figures do provide a general picture of Peru's racial composition.

An awareness of Indian population distribution is important for an understanding of Indian legislation. According to the 1940 census, nine of Peru's twenty-three departments had Indian majorities, while in eight others Indians comprised between 25 and 50 percent of the total. The departments containing the highest percentage of Indians are located in the central and southern regions of the sierra, from north-central Ancash (55.8 percent) through Huánuco (63.4 percent), Huancavelica (78.6 percent), Ayacucho (75.9 percent), Cuzco (71.7 percent), to Puno (92.3 percent) in the south. Linguistic figures are also revealing. In the department of Huancavelica, with a population of 203,128 persons, 200,587 spoke Quechua, and in Puno 427,101 out of 463,080 spoke Quechua or Aymara.[3]

(Washington, D.C.: Government Printing Office, 1946), pp. 184-85; and George Kubler, "The Quechua in the Colonial World," in *The Andean Civilizations*, p. 334. See also Kubler's masterful study, *The Indian Caste of Peru, 1795-1940: A Population Study Based upon Tax Records and Census Reports* (Washington, D.C.: Government Printing Office, 1952).

2. See Kubler, *The Indian Caste of Peru;* and Bernard Mishkin, "The Contemporary Quechua," in *The Andean Civilizations*, pp. 411-14.

3. See Mishkin, "The Contemporary Quechua," p. 412; and Atilio Sivirichi, *Derecho indígena peruano: Proyecto de código indígena* (Lima: Ediciones Kuntur, 1946), p. 47.

In these departments of central and southern Peru, where the Indians have constituted a majority of the population, they also have been the most exploited. The majority of Indian uprisings have occurred in the departments of Ancash, Cuzco, Huánuco, and particularly in Puno, which was wracked by some of the most serious revolts of the nineteenth and twentieth centuries. When a government official or legislator spoke of the Indian problem or of the Indian danger, he generally was referring to conditions in this region of the country.

All responsible Peruvians have recognized that the non integrated Indians posed a myriad of economic, social, and political problems for the nation, and references to it are many. When someone spoke of the Indian danger, however, he was verbalizing a deep-seated fear held by most white and mestizo Peruvians—the fear that the Indians would rise up and initiate a series of racial massacres. The bloody revolt of Tupac Amaru II in 1780 has served for almost two centuries as an example of what could happen. Subsequent, though smaller, revolts merely deepen that fear.[4]

Conditions of Life

Indian demographic patterns did not cause revolts. They were spontaneous outbursts of primary violence directed against the ghastly conditions under which Indians had to live and the shocking oppression which they suffered. As one author has stated:

> Peru groans under the weight of oppressive economic slavery and anachronistic personal servitude. In the sierra, along the valleys and hills, humans live under the double burden of exploitation and oppression. There

---

4. The literature on the revolt of Tupac Amaru is extensive, but the reader is directed particularly to the following works: Jorge Cornejo Bouroncle, *Tupac Amaru: La revolución precursora de la emancipación continental*, 2d ed., enlarged (Cuzco: Editorial H. G. Rozas, 1963); Boleslao Lewin, *La rebelión de Túpac Amaru y los orígenes de la emancipacion americana* (Buenos Aires: Librería Hachette, 1957); Inca Juan Bautista Tupac Amaru, *Las memorias de Tupac Amaru* (Lima: Fondo de Cultura Popular, 1964); Daniel Valcárcel, *La rebelión de Tupac Amaru* (Mexico, D.F.; Fondo de Cultura Económica, 1965); and Juan José Vega, *José Gabriel Tupac Amaru* (Lima: Editorial Universo, 1969). Except for the revolt of Tupac Amaru, Indian uprisings in Peru have been inadequately studied. In large part this is due to a paucity of data on the various revolts and to actual suppression of such data by local *hacendados* and government officials. Some very preliminary work has been done by Peruvian historian Jorge Basadre and by French sociologist Jean Piel, but much more is needed if we are to understand the dynamics and history of Indian movements and revolts in the nineteenth and twentieth centuries.

are souls there, whites or Indians, but souls nevertheless. Souls with whips they crack on the bloody backs of the Indian slave. Men of the noose and knife who decide the fate of their servants. The Indian doesn't live. The Indian vegetates; the Indian dies.[5]

The diet of Peruvian Indians must rank among the worst in the world. The average caloric intake in Peru in 1947 was 2,062 per day, falling to 1,970 by 1959. This is the national average; most Indians consume far less, with a diet almost devoid of proteins. Small Andean potatoes, often freeze-dried into *chuño*, constitute the basic staple. Meat, eggs, and milk are rare and it is not uncommon to see Indian women still nursing nearly grown children (six to ten years old).[6]

Basic sanitation methods are almost unknown and diseases such as typhoid, diphtheria, and tuberculosis are pandemic. Because of both ignorance and lack of money, Indians rarely visit doctors, relying instead on the local *curandero* (curer) or on myths such as that the best way to cure venereal disease is to pass it on to another. Animals and humans share the same drinking water and living space—the *choza*. One author described the sierran *choza* as follows:

> The *choza* or *chujlla* on the *puna* is constructed of sod, cut in the form of adobe.... According to the weather, the wind cries, blasphemes, and curses. Dirt permeates everything. The stench impregnates the pores. Flies and mosquitos, according to the climate, live tranquilly in this propitious atmosphere, incubating and propagating the epidemics that periodically and infallibly level the *campesinos*. Inside the *choza* or *chujlla,* the Indian procreates, is born, and dies. In this meager living space he has his dining room, bedroom, grain bin, raises *cuyes* [guinea pigs], dogs, cats, sheep, birds, and even his pigs, all of which live together in an indescribable mess with household goods and tools.[7]

5. Manuel A. Capuñay, *Lequía: Vida y obra del constructor del gran Perú* (Lima: Compañía de Impresiones y Publicidad, Enrique Bustamante y Ballivián, Sucesor, 1952), p. 125.

6. For statistics on diet, see: Carlos Malpica S. S., *Crónica del hambre en el Perú* (Lima: Francisco Moncloa Editores, 1966); and Virgilio Roel Pineda, "La agricultura en la economía peruana," in Sebastián Salazar Bondy et al., *La encruci jada del Perú* (Montevideo, Uruguay: Ediciones ARCA, 1962), pp. 34-37.

7. J. Guillermo Guevara, *Rijchari Perú; despierta Perú* (Lima: C.I.P., 1965), pp. 11-12. The best available studies of health and hygiene conditions among Peruvian Indians are those of Máxime H. Kuczynski Godard. See particularly: *La condición social del indio y su insalubridad: Miradas sociográficas del Cuzco* (Lima: Ministerio de Salud Pública y Asistencia Social, 1945); and with Carlos Enrique Paz Soldán, *Disección del indigenismo peruano: Un examen sociológico y médico social* (Lima: Instituto de Medicina Social, 1948).

Altitude also has played an important role in the life and health of the sierran Indian. As Carlos Monge Medrano has shown, water boils at a very low temperature at high altitudes, invalidating sterilization processes, breaking down chemical compounds, and affecting the degree to which food is cooked.[8] In addition, extreme altitude restricts the physical exertions of a person, even the most acclimated. This fact, together with the lack of proper diet and chronic hunger, has led to the widespread use of and reliance upon coca. It is from the leaf of the coca plant that cocaine is derived, and these leaves are chewed extensively by Peruvian Indians. Coca chewing deadens the stomach nerves and relieves hunger pains, so children are started on it at a very young age. It increases the heart rate, arterial blood pressure, and respiratory functions, and serves as a stimulus to the nervous system, thereby increasing powers of endurance. While chewing coca, a man with a heavy load can trot long distances at high altitudes without suffering from fatigue.

Nevertheless, the coca chewer *(coquero)* suffers great physical and mental damage from an overuse of the drug. One study of *coca* use in Peru concludes:

> Coca chewing produces two types of disturbances of mental activity, acute and chronic. The acute disturbances (present during the period of coca chewing) are states of mental hyperexcitability, in particular alterations of perception, affectivity, and thought.... The chronic disturbances are persistent alterations, independent of coca-chewing periods.... The chronic effect of coca leaves is a serious impairment of intelligence, memory, and personality.... Coca chewing favors introversion and the development of autistic thought. The addicts become out of touch with reality and their social adaptability is impaired.... Experimental chronic intoxication affects the liver (fat degeneration and other anatomical lesions). Lesions of the adrenals and the pancreas have been observed.[9]

There is no doubt that coca consumption is debilitating, but one must always remember why it is so extensively used. Gastric ulcers are not pleasant, but then neither is chronic hunger. There are periodic campaigns to eradicate coca addiction among Indians, but while applauding such efforts, one remembers the faces of hungry Indian children. Perhaps one foreign observer summed it up best when she wrote:

8. Carlos Monge Medrano, *La vida en las altiplancies andinas: Procesos ecológicos* (Lima: Ministerio de Trabajo y Asuntos Indígenas, 1963), p. 3.

9. Carlos Gutiérrez-Noriega and Vicente Zapata Ortiz, *Estudios sobre la coca y la cocaína en el Perú* (Lima: Ministerio de Educación Pública, Ediciones de la Dirección de Educación y Extensión Cultural, 1947), pp. 132-34.

Reformers insist that *coca* should be taken from the Andean Indians, but I remember the strain of great altitudes upon the physical system. Even bodies with a lung capacity and heart muscles developed through the centuries in adaptation to altitude must to some extent feel that strain. And I remember also the hard terms of Indian life, and I think no comfort, however dubious, should be removed unless at the same time some improvement in conditions is substituted for it.[10]

Many Peruvian scholars have also attacked the extensive use of alcohol which is prevalent among the Indians. There is no doubt they are correct, particularly when referring to alcoholic abuses at fiestas, but the fiesta is a brief moment in time when the Indian can escape the drudgery and oppression of his daily life. It is one of his few pleasures.

THE INDIANS AND THE LAND

A description of Indian culture falls outside the scope of this study, but there is one socioeconomic-political institution, the *comunidad,* which requires some treatment. The Indian *comunidad* has its origins in the Inca communal landholding system, the *ayllu.* Although the structure varied slightly from region to region, most of the *ayllus* were composed of an extended family which worked the land communally.

The Spanish conquest interrupted normal Indian life and with it the structure of the *comunidad.* The Spanish appropriated Indian roads, irrigation systems, and the land itself and forced the *comuneros* to work in the mines and fields and to grow certain crops in order to pay tribute. The *Laws of the Indies* stated

that it is just and reasonable that the Indians who have been pacified and reduced to obedience and vassalage should pay tribute in recognition of our dominion and contribute service such as subjects and vassals owe, for they have also among themselves the custom of paying tribute to their *tecles* and leaders. It is ordered that the Indians be persuaded for this reason to agree to some tribute of a moderate quantity of the fruits of the soil.[11]

Nevertheless, hundreds of *comunidades* survived because the Crown allowed the Indians to retain some of their lands and pastures in particularly inhospitable areas. In addition, thousands of new ones were created on the lands given to Indian *curacas,* or

10. Blair Niles, *Peruvian Pageant: A Journey in Time* (New York: Bobbs-Merrill Company, 1937), p. 173.
11. Quoted in Hildebrando Castro Pozo, "Social and Economico-Political Evolution of the Communities of Central Peru," in *The Andean Civilizations,* pp. 491-92.

chiefs, by the king, and their structure followed that of the old *ayllu.*

In many instances, the Crown actually tried to protect the *comunidad* and its inhabitants while at the same time submitting them to royal control. The *Laws of the Indies* took cognizance of the existence of the *comunidades* and strove to incorporate them into the Spanish administrative structure.

Two governing bodies dominate the internal affairs of the *comunidad.* The general assembly is made up of all *comunidad* members, with the exception of women and children in some cases, and holds its deliberations in public. The council is composed of *personeros,* or agents, who are elected for one year to take charge of a particular aspect of *comunidad* life such as land distribution, tax collection, and organization of fiestas for patron saints. These two bodies act also in a judicial capacity, settling all internal disputes such as those caused by the destruction of crops by animals or disputes over land distribution.[12]

Until very recently, *comunidad* agricultural methods had not altered greatly since preconquest days. The basic tools are still the *chaquitaclla,* or digging stick; the *taclla,* or hoe; a clod crusher; and a sickle. As Bernard Mishkin notes: "Plow agriculture is practiced in the valleys and sporadically in all parts of Quechua territory, but is primarily an aspect of mestizo and *hacienda* agriculture."[13] Two forms of collective labor are practiced in the *comunidad.* The first is the *ayni,* which is an exchange of services between individuals to work their personal parcels. The other is the *minka,* which requires the labor of all *comunidad* members and is used to

12. Hildebrando Castro Pozo, *Nuestra comunidad indígena* (Lima Tipografía "El Lucero," 1924), pp. 34-37; and Cirilio A. Cornejo, *Visión objectiva del problema indígena: Planteamiento y solución inmediata* (Lima: Ediciones Continente, 1959), pp. 44-46. The historical literature of the *comunidad* is extensive, and almost all works dealing with Indians and Indian integration in Peru devote some attention to it. Most of these works are cited above and below, but for the most complete analyses of the *comunidad indígena* and *Del ayllu al cooperativismo socialista* (Lima: P. Barrantes Casworks: José María Argüedas, *Evolución de las comunidades indígenas* (Lima: C.I.P., 1957), and *Las comunidades de España y del Perú* (Lima: Imprenta de la Universidad Nacional Mayor de San Marcos, 1968); Ricardo Bustamante Cisneros, *Condición jurídica de las comunidades de indígenas en el Perú* (Lima: Tesis, Universidad Nacional Mayor de San Marcos, Facultad de Jurisprudencia, 1918); Castro Pozo, *Nuestra comunidad indígena* and *Del ayllu al cooperativismo socialista* (Lima: P. Barrantes Castro, 1936); Jorge Cornejo Bouroncle, *Las comunidades indígenas: La explotación del trabajo de los indios* (Cuzco: H. G. Rozas Sucs., 1948); and Carlos Valdez de la Torre, *Evolución de las comunidades indígenas* (Lima: Editorial Euforion, 1921).

13. Mishkin, "The Contemporary Quechua," p. 418.

work communal lands, clean irrigation ditches, and repair roads, churches, and schools. Failure to fulfill the obligation of the *minka* may result in the forfeiture of that person's right to work part of the *comunidad* lands.[14]

It should be noted here that Western European concepts of private landownership were alien to the American Indians. For them the land was owned by everyone together or by no one. Agricultural endeavors and indeed the sacred nature of the land itself constituted the basis of Indian life. Not infrequently, a man was born, lived, and died on the same land worked by his ancestors, so that land became part of his primordial value system. Each family was allotted a plot of land according to its needs, but that plot was to be used, not owned. The cultural and religious meaning of land could not be translated into paper titles, and thus Indians often sold or traded their deeds during the republican period without understanding the legal significance of the act.

Since Indians could not comprehend private landownership for themselves, they likewise failed to realize the import of acquisitive Spanish demands for more and more land. This basic philosophical difference between conqueror and conquered fostered the growth of the *comunidad*'s historical enemy — the hacienda, or *latifundio,* as large estates are known in Peru. The process of *comunidad* despoilment began with the first grants of land to Spanish soldiers. Often these grants encompassed several Indian *comunidades,* as did the *latifundio* Lauramarca in the department of Cuzco.[15] *Latifundio* expansion increased during the colonial period, particularly with the awarding of new land grants, and thousands of free Indians were transformed into servants and slaves.

The winning of independence did not impede this process of encroachment; on the contrary it increased. A major difficulty encountered by *comunidades* was that the Spanish government never carried out a careful land survey. Units of measurement were vague and natural landmarks were open to challenge. In addition, Peru maintained no national registry of titles, relying instead on local *notarios* (notaries). The notary, who was a private businessman dependent upon local good will, would never contest the claims of a large landowner and in general favored the interests of all whites and mestizos over those of illiterate Indians. Thus,

---

14. Ibid., pp. 418-20; and Luis E. Valcárcel, *Ruta cultural del Perú,* 4th ed. (Lima: Ediciones Nuevo Mundo, 1966), pp. 112-13.

15. Roberto Mac-Lean Estenós, *Indios de América* (Mexico, D.F.: Universidad Nacional Autónoma de México, Instituto de Investigaciones Sociales, 1962), p. 333.

the unfortunate *comunidades* invariably lost all land disputes.[16]

Hacendados enjoyed other advantages in their relations with Indian *comunidades*. Because of their overwhelming economic and social power, *hacendados* controlled all the principal administrative and judicial positions in their department or province. When these positions were not actually filled by the *hacendado* himself or by members of his family, they were given to local politicians who depended upon the *hacendado* for their future livelihood. Throughout the nineteenth and most of the twentieth century, this rural oligarchy also controlled the national Congress, and *hacendados* from one region usually cooperated with those of another in order to preserve the existing system. Besides actual land takeovers, *hacendados* used the usurpation of scarce water resources as a means of containing and exploiting Indian *comunidades*.[17]

INDIAN LABOR EXPLOITATION

Contrary to the white stereotype of the Indians as lazy, shiftless, dishonest semisavages, Peruvian Indians are extremely hard-working. One *indigenista* author has written:

> Across the centuries, the Indian has not lost his fundamental love of work. He enjoys rural labor; it is for him not only a pleasure, but a sacred rite. ... If he has to irrigate his fields at midnight, he will work tirelessly. For him there is no sacrifice, no displeasure in doing his job, but only when the work is for himself or for his family. He doesn't have nor can he have that same dedication when his efforts benefit a man who oppresses and exploits him.[18]

There are dozens of labor systems with regional variations which were and are used to exploit the Indians of Peru. These systems function to provide the *hacendados* with a cheap and secure supply of workers. In the past, the payment of salaries in cash was almost nonexistent. Instead the *hacendado* allowed the Indian worker to

16. For a succinct discussion of this problem, see: Henry F. Dobyns, *The Social Matrix of Peruvian Indigenous Communities,* Cornell Peru Project Monograph (Ithaca, N.Y.: Cornell University, Department of Anthropology, 1964), pp. 33-35. See also: Ulrich Peter Ritter, *Comunidades indígenas y cooperativismo en el Perú* (Bilbao, Spain: Ediciones Deusto, 1965), pp. 29-30; and Louis Faron, "La formación de dos comunidades indígenas en un valle de la costa peruana," in Luis E. Valcárcel et al., *Estudios sobre la cultura actual del Perú* (Lima: Universidad Nacional Mayor de San Marcos, 1964), pp. 37-63.

17. Mario C. Vásquez, *Hacienda, peonaje y servidumbre en los andes peruanos* (Lima: Editorial Estudios Andinos, 1961), pp. 37-41; and Mishkin, "The Contemporary Quechua," p. 417.

18. Valcárcel, *Ruta cultural del Perú,* p. 112.

utilize a small parcel of land or, if necessary, paid him in coca or alcohol. Much of the Indian legislation of the twentieth century was directed toward improving Indian labor conditions.

One of the best-known systems is that of *yanaconaje,* or share-cropping, which is still practiced in Peru today. Under the Inca Empire, the social position of the *yanacona* fell between that of the Inca nobility and that of the common man and was usually reserved for prisoners of war. During the Spanish colonial period, the *yanacona* was a landless semislave who worked for his Spanish masters in return for food and shelter. During the republican period, the *yanacona* remained a landless Indian who belonged to no *comunidad* and who was forced to work for some landowner as a tenant. The tenant, or *yanacona,* was given a piece of land by the owner, told what crops to plant, and supplied with the seeds, fertilizer, animals, and tools necessary for production. Traditionally, the *yanacona* had to sell his produce to the landowner at a predetermined price, usually well below the current market price. His share of the crop was also predetermined, and was a fixed amount rather than a percentage. If the crop failed, the *yanacona* was still held responsible for the cost of the seed, fertilizer, and tools, as well as other expenses such as housing, food, and clothing which had been advanced by the landowner. The *yanacona* was given irrigation water only at the sufferance of the owner and usually after the owner had utilized all he wanted. He was forced to perform various forms of free labor on the *hacienda.* Contracts were rarely written, and the owner could terminate the contract at any time. The *yanacona,* rarely the gainer, is usually the victim of severe exploitation, and efforts were made in the 1930s and 1940s to relieve his plight.[19]

Two labor systems even more exploitive than *yanaconaje* are *aparcería* and *colonaje.* The *colono* is perhaps the lowest worker of all. He resides on the hacienda and is in effect part of it. He is allowed to utilize a small parcel of land in return for which he works four to six days per week for the *hacendado.* Half of all production from his own parcel, including animal offspring, must be given to the *hacendado.* Until very recently, hacienda for sale ads always

19. For descriptions of *yanaconaje,* see: Castro Pozo, *Del ayllu al cooperativismo,* pp. 215-17; Cornejo, *Visión objetiva,* pp. 86-88; Víctor Graciano Maita, *Política agraria: Bases para una ley agraria y un estatuto de comunidades indígenas* (Lima: Librería y Editorial Mario Campos y Campos, 1963), pp. 118-19; and Thomas R. Ford, *Man and Land in Peru* (Gainesville: University of Florida Press, 1955), pp. 86-87.

listed the number of *colono* families which came with the land purchase. Under *aparcería* the *hacendado* supplied the land, but the
aparcero, unlike the *yanacona,* supplied the necessary seeds, fertilizers, and tools as well as his labor. The *hacendado* received at
least 50 percent of the production, but took even fewer risks than
he would have with *yanaconaje.*[20]

Under all the above systems, the *hacendado* requites more of the
Indians than just a percentage of the crop, and it is these extra
services which make the exploitation so extremely onerous. The
most widespread form of service is that of *pongaje,* whereby the
Indians and their families *(pongos)* are required to work free in the
hacendado household as maids, butlers, chauffeurs, cooks, and general handymen. The Indians receive no payment for these services
and are even required to travel to the *hacendado*'s urban residence
in order to fulfill their obligation. In addition, the *hacendado* can
rent his *pongos* to the local judge, priest, prefect, or neighboring
hacendados, with rent money being paid to the *hacendado* and not
to the Indian. Since many of these Indians are the sons and grand-
sons of *pongos,* one could argue that they are in fact slaves of the
hacendado.[21]

Other exploitive labor requirements are those of *pastoreo, portador,* and *cargador.* The *pastoreo* alternates with other Indians in
caring for the *hacendado*'s livestock. Not only is there no remuneration, but the *pastoreo* is held personally responsible for any losses
incurred while he is on the job. The death of one animal through
accident or disease can put an Indian in debt for the remainder of
his life. The *cargador* is responsible for the transportation of all
merchandise needed by the hacienda and of all products grown
there. In many cases, the absence of roads forces the Indians to
carry the items on their backs, placing them on a level little better
than that of pack animals. The *portador* is like a personal errand
boy for the *hacendado,* delivering mail and personal messages long
distances on foot. In addition to maintaining contact with neigh-

20. Mac-Lean Estenós, *Indios de América,* pp. 311-12; Graciano Maita, *Política
agraria,* pp. 119-20; and Hildebrando Castro Pozo, "Las comunidades indígenas del
Perú," in Darío Sainte Marie S., ed., *Perú en cifras, 1944-1945* (Lima: Talleres de la
Empresa Gráfica Scheuch, 1945), pp. 172-74.
21. Jorge Cornejo Bouroncle, *Tierras ajenas: Estampas de la vida andina* (Cuzco:
Ediciones Inca, 1959), pp. 141-45; Cornejo, *Visión objetiva,* pp. 96-97; and F. Cossio
del Pomar, "Apuntes sobre el indio peruano y su vida," *Cuadernos Americanos* 18,
No. 6 (November-December, 1944): 172.

boring towns and haciendas, the *portadores* are also required to act as *cargadores* for small items.[22]

The extent of exploitation of Indians by *hacendados* is difficult to imagine. The owner of the land is the *tai tai*, or *patrón*, and he literally has powers of life and death over his workers. Hacienda work requirements are so heavy that the Indians can hardly devote sufficient time to their own plots. Fines and penalties for such infractions as absence due to sickness, failure to obey orders, or breaking a tool are levied to keep the Indians in perpetual debt peonage, a condition which is usually passed down from father to son. Since the *hacendados* control all local offices and hold an influential position in the national society, the Indians have no recourse except to rebel. These rebellions are brutally suppressed and the Indians are oppressed even further. The *hacendado* lives in splendor on the free labor of the Indians and for this reason is often referred to in Peru as a *gamonal*, or parasite.

In addition to private exploitive Indian labor systems, there were also public government systems which are less well documented. The *mita*, or forced Indian labor draft so prevalent during the colonial period, was continued during the republican period under the name *faena*. Indians owed so many days of service to the local governments for the construction and maintenance of public buildings, roads, and other public works. The conditions of work and payment were stipulated by law, but more often than not the regulations were ignored. Moreover, local government and Church officials often forced Indians to work as their personal servants, usually without remuneration. There were even cases of government officials renting out "their Indians" to private individuals or putting the Indians to work in their private business ventures. The extent of public and Church exploitation of Indians became evident in the early twentieth century when laws were introduced in the Congress to prohibit such practices.

Peruvian writers have long asserted that discrimination in the nation is predicated upon economic status rather than skin color, but that is simply a myth. Pejorative expressions such as "el es muy oscuro" (he is very dark), "muy cholo" (very mestizo looking), or "tiene cabello crespo" (he has kinky hair) are hardly eco-

---

22. Cornejo, *Visión objectiva*, pp. 94-96. For descriptions of these and other forms of labor, see: Vásquez, *Hacienda, peonaje y servidumbre*, pp. 26-31; and Castro Pozo, *Del ayllu al cooperativismo*, pp. 215-22.

nomic in nature. Lima has long prided itself on its "whiteness." As one foreign observer wrote in 1910: "Indeed pallor is considered a mark of beauty among Lima ladies. It denotes a minimum, or lack of the aboriginal strain in the owner's composition; for distinctions of caste are strong, and the dwellers of coast cities profess to look down upon the Serranos or dwellers of the upland regions."[23] With few exceptions, white and mestizo Peruvians look down on the Indians and point to their degraded state as proof of inferiority. Given this racial climate, it is easy to understand how *hacendados* and others could oppress the Indians with little fear of societal reaction. Racism has served to reinforce the patterns of exploitation and oppression.

The Heritage of the Colonial Period

The pattern of relationships between white and Indian was established during the colonial period and has continued to plague Peru until the present. Extensive Indian legislation issued during the colonial period, particularly that found in the *Recopilación de Leyes de los Reynos de las Indias,* failed to integrate the Indians into the society. Spanish was the official language of the viceroyalty of Peru, but Indians continued speaking Quechua or Aymara. In spite of assiduous missionary work by priests and various colonial officials, the Indians were barely Christianized and usually still practiced their former religion.

Although Spain officially encouraged Indian private enterprise and private ownership, restrictions placed on such ownership negated the policy. An Indian chief might accumulate sufficient wealth to purchase material goods such as horses and firearms, but a viceregal decree restricted his ownership of draft animals to one horse or one mule per man and firearms were outlawed altogether. Indians in actuality were relegated to the status of an inferior caste. One writer has asserted that the Indian was "converted into a nearly irrational being with a standard of living lower than that of work animals and only a little higher than that of the llama, the beast of burden."[24] Thus the Indians were robbed of their culture without being provided with a new one. Generally they learned neither to read nor to write.

23. C. Reginald Enock, *Peru: Its Former and Present Civilization, History and Existing Conditions, Topography and Natural Resources, Commerce and General Development* (London: T. Fisher Unwin, 1910), p. 132.

24. Castro Pozo, "Social and Economico-Political Evolution," p. 495. See also: Kubler, "The Quechua in the Colonial World," p. 374.

This system was designed to prevent the Indians from developing new needs, thereby reducing the danger of revolt. In reaction, they adopted the protective mechanism of unresponsiveness and became servile. The Indian's only concern became self-preservation, that is to say, the survival of his family.

The inability of Spanish policy-makers to cope with the Indian problem was but a prelude to the difficulties faced by republican leaders. There are politicial, economic, social, and educational facets to the problem, but the principal consideration remains cultural. The conquest of Peru did not represent the victory of one Western European nation over another, but rather the subjugation of a totally alien indigenous culture. Spanish options were few. They were a foreign minority trying to govern a vast Indian empire, and they demanded total Indian obedience instead of seeking to work through the process of acculturation. The *Laws of the Indies* offered some protection for the Indians, but in the final analysis, Spanish policy was aimed at domination, not cooperation.

Republican leaders, on the other hand, had a greater range of options, but they also faced greater responsibilities in that their ultimate goal was the creation of a united, integrated nation, not the development of an efficient imperial administration.

At least three options were open to politicians in the early years of the republic. First, they could have tried to integrate the Indians forcibly by systematically destroying their institutions and culture, thereby converting them into dark-skinned copies of their former masters. Many Peruvians felt this to be the only answer, but the Spanish had undertaken similar programs and failed because of Indian resistance and a lack of both material and manpower resources. Similar republican attempts were likewise doomed to failure for the same reasons. The stoic Indians passively resisted all such efforts.

A second option would have been for the government to leave the Indians completely alone or even to segregate them on reservations as was done in the United States and Chile. This procedure was never considered except by a few *indigenistas* in the twentieth century. Since the entire Peruvian agrarian structure depended upon the existence of a steady Indian labor supply, such a solution would have required a total alteration of the existing economic and social structure.

The third option would have been to allow the Indians to integrate themselves peaceably, if they so chose, while at the same time providing government protection for their lands and culture through national legislation. This was and is the most equitable solution, but most Peruvian legislators conceptualized the problem much more narrowly. They felt that with the passage of certain Indian legislation the Indians would discard their way of life and be miraculously integrated into the society. They failed to realize both that Indians were usually prevented from exercising their rights under the law and that many simply did not wish to do so. Furthermore, since the laws were rarely if ever enforced, the Indians enjoyed no protection whatsoever to develop their culture and adapt it to changing conditions.

Those who would argue that modern man has no right to impose his life style on another people are only partly correct. To be sure, no group should be forced to abandon its culture completely, but one must remember that the preservation of Indian culture as it now exists in Peru also means preserving the illiteracy, the hunger, and the exploitation. Peruvian legislators have grappled with this problem for 150 years with very limited success. The history of their efforts is chronicled below.

2

The Nineteenth-Century Experience in Indian Affairs

The critical postindependence nineteenth-century period in Peru has been inadequately studied. The precursors of independence, the movement itself, and its leadership have all received extensive attention, but there remain serious gaps in our knowledge of the years which followed. It was a confusing period, characterized by rampant militarism, conflicting ideologies, and, at times, extreme economic and political instability. Despite these uncertainties, Peru endured as a nation and developed the core of political, social, and economic beliefs and doctrines which were to direct and to influence subsequent attitudes and actions of the nineteenth and twentieth centuries.

The nineteenth century was an exciting and seminal period in Peruvian national development, and this was particularly true of the body of doctrines and legal precedents created to deal with Indian integration. During this time, the crucial issue of how to deal with hundreds of thousands of Indians affected every government action and decision in the realms of politics, economics, and law. Although some politicians and jurists sought to relegate the Indian problem to a position of low priority and others evaded the question by asserting that the Indian was an incompetent savage, most politicians and administrators were forced to come to grips with it in one way or another.

Throughout the century there were several recurring themes in Indian legislation, but there was no continuous pattern of development or progress in any area because of the severe instability of the government, which led to a plethora of conflicting laws and constitutions. In the period 1823-1900, Peru lived under nine different constitutions (1823, 1826, 1828, 1834, 1839, 1856, 1860, 1867, and 1879). In addition, hundreds of laws and constitutional amendments were enacted, adding further confusion to the legal picture. Peruvian legal history in the nineteenth century was like a kaleidoscope and Indian legislation was no exception.

Indian tribute was abolished by the Liberators, reestablished in 1826, abolished by Ramón Castilla, and then reestablished by Mariano Ignacio Prado in the 1860s. There was a continuous conflict betwen those who wanted to end the Indian tax on moral and humanitarian grounds and those who wished to retain it for revenue purposes. In some cases, a leader such as Castilla might offer contradictory legislation from both motives.

Another area of massive confusion was that of Indian voting rights. Peru adopted universal male suffrage immediately following independence and Indians were given the right to vote. Subsequent legislation, however, excluded landless and illiterate persons. Each new government and constitution sought to redefine voting regulations, some of which benefited Indians while others did not. The result was an incredibly confused pattern of conflicting legislation which afforded *hacendados* and local officials the opportunity to disenfranchise Indians. During those periods when Indians were legally eligible to vote, it is doubtful that they were aware of their rights, much less allowed to exercise them.

The legal status of Indian *comunidad* lands was another common theme in the period. Thousands of *comunidades* survived the colonial period, but the various republican governments failed to formulate a clear, consistent *comunidad* policy. Many responsible leaders, who believed private property was a vital prerequisite for progress, favored the abolition of communal landownership. Others held that the *comunidad* structure protected the Indians and sought to retain the *comunidades*. Large landowners viewed them as obstacles to their own expansion. This combination of differently motivated opinions produced a myriad of conflicting laws which demanded protection of *comunidades* one year and their abolition the next. Government indecision and contradiction virtually guaranteed the success of *hacendado* expansionism.

Indian education was another issue which attracted some politicians. Presidents Ramón Castilla and Manuel Pardo both sought to use education as a vehicle for Indian integration. Indeed, education has been touted as a panacea throughout history. The problem in Peru was particularly difficult because of language barriers and strong opposition led by the Catholic Church and by *hacen-dados* and local officials who feared the loss of their control and power. Moreover, since the national government lacked the revenues necessary even to build enough schools for white and mestizo children, Indian education was doomed from the outset.

As is demonstrated below, most of the early attempts at Indian integration were poorly conceived and all were unsuccessful. The experimentation of those Peruvian leaders who sought to rectify the inequities and failures of the colonial regime often resulted in the repetition of previous errors and the creation of new ones. Nevertheless, the conceptualizations of the problem and the various solutions proposed were to endure and to be repeated for over a century. Laws first put forward by Simón Bolívar in the 1820s were passed in the 1920s and 1930s, often with the same unfortunate results. However, the nineteenth century also produced men who offered alternative opinions about Indians and Indian integration, many of which also endured and had great impact on reform-minded elements in the twentieth century.

THE LIBERATORS

The Wars of Independence were not social movements, and the severing of ties with Spain had no autonomic implications for the Indians living outside colonial economic, social, and political life. With an educational and social level which precluded any understanding of the independence movement, the Indians fought for whatever group pressed them into service, with little or no notion of why they were fighting.[1]

The leaders of the independence movement generally held a simplistic view of the Indian problem. Imbued with the ideals of the French Revolution, they failed to realize that Indian assimilation would require many years. In seeking to give all men political rights, they victimized the Indians more than had been the case in the colonial period.[2]

José de San Martín, whose forces took Lima in July, 1821, was the first leader to misjudge the realities of the situation. In August, 1821, he issued a decree which abolished Indian tribute and made it illegal to collect past taxes, ordering the various government of-

---

1. Castro Pozo, "Social and Economico-Political Evolution," p. 496.

2. Víctor Andrés Belaúnde, *Meditaciones peruanas,* 2d ed. (Lima: Talleres Gráficos P. L. Villanueva, 1963), p. 73.

ficials to send their tribute records to Lima. He also declared the Indian a citizen of Peru and prohibited the legal use of the words *Indios* and *Naturales,* asserting that henceforth Indians should be known as *ciudadanos.* San Martín knew that continued servitude made citizenship an empty gesture, so he then abolished all forms of personal service, specifically the *mita,* or Indian forced labor draft, and the *encomienda,* the colonial practice of entrusting a group of Indians to a Spaniard. Any person, ecclesiastical or secular, who violated the order was to be exiled.[3] These decrees were liberal, even radical, but they were not obeyed. Most members of Peruvian society had been reluctant to end colonial rule and certainly were not prepared to relinquish exploitation of the Indians. Since San Martín's government lacked the means to enforce its decrees, the state of the Indian remained unaltered.

In April of 1824, Simón Bolívar, who had replaced San Martín as ruler of Peru, initiated a policy which, though well intentioned, had disastrous effects for the Indian, actually working to deprive him of his lands. His first decree dealt with new fund-raising methods necessary to continue the independence struggle. Bolívar ordered all state lands and state-owned haciendas sold for one-third less than their assessed value. He appointed special agents in all provinces to assure that the sales were made with exactness. He also gave the Indians title to their lands and made it possible for them to sell or dispose of them in the manner of their choosing. In addition, the *comunidades* were all but dissolved by article three, which ordered the land divided among the members. Bolívar took care to order that each Indian receive his fair share of land in the process.

Since Bolívar was occupied with more pressing matters in 1824, the decree had little effect until after the decisive Battle of Ayacucho in December. On July 4, 1825, Bolívar issued three important decrees. The first attacked the question of Indian personal service. After reviewing the abuses of personal servitude and its unacceptability in a society of free men, Bolívar decreed the following: (1) the state could not require personal service, direct or indirect, without drafting a contract which established the wages of the Indian; (2) provincial officials, judges, Church officials at all levels,

3. This decree has been widely published, as have his other Indian decrees, but the source used here is: Perú, Ministerio de Trabajo y Asuntos Indígenas, Dirección General de Asuntos Indígenas *Legislación indigenista del Perú* (Lima: Talleres Gráficos de la Penitenciaría Central, 1948), pp. 7-9 (hereafter cited as PMTAI, *Legislación*).

hacendados, and mine owners were prohibited from employing Indians against their will; (3) labor drafts for public works had to affect all citizens equally; (4) the supplying of the army could not be confined to the Indian but had to fall on all citizens equally; (5) all work in the mines, haciendas, and other jobs had to be paid for in money unless the employee desired otherwise; (6) article 5 was to be enforced by local and provincial officials; (7) the Church could not charge the Indian more for services than it charged others; (8) the civil authorities were to ensure that the Church did not take advantage of the Indian. That the new decree was issued is an indicator of the failure of San Martín's measure on personal service. The problem remained one of enforcement; and since the government still lacked control in the provinces, the effect of this decree was the same as that of the earlier one.

The second decree of July 4 sought to abolish Indian communal landholding and had a far greater impact than the first. Bolívar believed that the communal system was injurious to the Indians, that agriculture had suffered as a result of it, and that Peru could not progress as a nation until the *comunidad* was broken up. He also felt that the Indian leaders, or *caciques,* had usurped the best lands. Such attitudes reflected Bolívar's nineteenth-century economic liberalism.

All *comunidades* were to be abolished and the land divided among the members. *Cacique* lands were to be divided, except for those held under legitimate, historical claims, and landless *caciques* were to receive five *topos* (an imprecise agrarian division which usually meant enough land to support a man and his wife). Every other Indian, regardless of age or sex, was to receive one *topo* of land in arable regions or two *topos* if the land was relatively unproductive. All Indians who had been robbed of their lands by the Spanish or who had suffered after the abortive revolt of Pumacahua in 1814 were to be compensated with a third more land. The prefect of the departmental junta was to assume the responsibility for surveying, dividing, and selling the *comunidad* lands to ensure honesty and integrity. Finally, to protect the Indians in the early years of private ownership, they could not dispose of land until 1850, nor could it ever become part of an entailed estate.

In the final decree of July 4, Bolívar, maintaining that the constitution of the republic did not recognize inequality among citizens, hereditary titles, or special privileges, abolished the title of *cacique* and all of its concomitant powers. Local authorities were charged with assuming the customary duties of the *cacique*. Former *caciques* merited only the respect due all citizens.[4]

Throughout 1825-27, the government tried to enforce these decrees through circulars from Lima demanding local implementation.[5] Indian personal service was not abolished, but the effects of the decree concerning *comunidades* was enormous. Bolívar's aim in abolishing the *comunidades* had been to make the Indian a yeoman farmer, but as noted earlier, Western European concepts of private landownership were alien to the Peruvian Indian, so if he sold or traded his deed it was usually without thought of the consequences. There are even indications that Bolívar sought to protect the *latifundistas* even though the period of confusion which followed independence would have been the ideal time to institute a land reform program.[6]

Abuses were widespread and Bolívar recognized that his policies were not being implemented. In October, 1826, he prohibited any further granting of land titles, but he never withdrew his original decrees which inadvertently accentuated Indian inequality.

Judges and government officials usually cooperated with the *hacendados* to defraud Indians and mestizos. They changed titles; they substituted imposters in legal proceedings; and they often just disallowed the Indian title. Thousands of individual Indians and hundreds of *comunidades* lost their lands and were absorbed into the larger estates. The situation of the Indians was worse than it had ever been under Spanish rule.[7]

The Indian policies of San Martín and Bolívar have merited them much subsequent criticism, but perhaps they have been judged too harshly.[8] San Martín was only ineffectual while Bolívar was motivated by a desire to end a feudalistic situation and to es-

4. For the text of Bolívar's decrees, see: Comisión de Historia, *Próceres del Perú: Felipe Santiago Estenós* (Buenos Aires: Ediciones del Instituto Peruano de Sociología, 1955), pp. 10-15.

5. For the texts of several of these circulars, see: PMTAI, *Legislación,* pp. 16-19.

6. Juan José Vega, *La emancipación frente al indio peruano; la legislación indiana del Perú en la iniciación de la república, 1821-1830: Contribución al estudio del derecho peruano* (Lima: "Editorial San Marcos," Universidad Nacional Mayor de San Marcos, 1958), pp. 56-57.

7. For an excellent study of one area, see: José Varallanos, *Historia de Huánuco: Introducción para el estudio de la vida social de una región del Perú, desde la era prehistórica a nuestros días* (Buenos Aires: Imprenta López, 1959), pp. 617-18.

8. For one author who believes so, see: Castro Pozo, *Del ayllu al cooperativismo,* pp. 190-91.

tablish private property among the Indians. Imbued with the liberal ideals of the French Revolution and of such leaders as Thomas Jefferson, Bolívar attempted foreign solutions where there was neither the desire nor the machinery to implement them, inadvertently contributing to the deterioration of an already intolerable situation. Nevertheless, the thrust of Bolívar's misguided policies was perpetuated for more than a century.

AFTER THE LIBERATORS

Realities soon forced the Peruvian government to reinstitute Indian tribute. A decree of August, 1826, created the Contribución de Indígenas to help defray government expenses and to pay the salaries of government officials.[9] The amount of the Contribución was lowered later in the year, but it was not abolished until 1854.[10]

In March, 1828, President José de la Mar promulgated an Indian land title law which reaffirmed Bolívar's decree by recognizing the Indians and the mestizos as owners of the land which they occupied and ordering the departmental juntas to assign lands to those Indians who were landless. The principal difference between this law and the preceding ones was that instead of waiting until 1850, those owners who could read and write were allowed to dispose of their lands immediately. Thus, one of the few protective devices which had existed was gone and new haciendas sprang up and old ones were expanded, all at the expense of the Indians.[11]

The constitution of 1828 adversely affected the Indians. Suffrage, which had been universal under the 1823 constitution, was restricted to landowners, those with incomes of at least eight hundred pesos a year, and teachers and professors. Moreover, all voters had to be literate. Although Indians were specifically exempted from these provisions, in practice they were not. The mere existence of restrictions provided many officials with the excuse they needed to disenfranchise Indians.

9. Jorge Basadre, *La Multitud, la ciudad, y el campo en la historia del Perú,* 2d ed. (Lima: Editorial Huascarán, 1947), p. 239. See also Carlos Rodríquez Pastor, "Derecho peruano del trabajo," in *Perú en cifras,* ed. Sainte Marie S., pp. 367-68.

10. PMTAI, *Legislación,* pp. 19-20.

11. Ibid., pp. 21-22. See also: Felipe de la Barra, *El indio peruano en las etapas de la conquista y frente a la república: Ensayo histórico-militar-sociológico y con proposiciones para la solución del problema indio peruano* (Lima: Talleres Gráficos del Servicio de Prensa, Propaganda y Publicaciones Militares, 1948), p. 152; Vásquez, *Hacienda, peonaje y servidumbre,* pp. 16-17; Manuel D. Velasco Núñez, *Compilación de la legislación indigenista concordada* (Lima: Editora Médica Peruana, 1959), pp. xii-xiii; and Cornejo, *Visión objectiva,* pp. 155-56.

Under the section that established departmental juntas, the property, possessions, and income of the Indian *comunidades* were designated for use by the *comunidades* themselves.[12] Since earlier legislation had abolished the *comunidades,* this provision illustrates both the ineffectiveness of previous decrees and the lack of a coordinated government policy toward the Indians.

The 1830s brought little change. By supreme decree of October 14, 1830, the government confirmed Indian landownership in response to a proposal by the subprefect of Conchucos that the lands be protected. With respect to the Contribución de Indígenas, the government made the slight alteration that those Indians who paid the tribute no longer had to pay for small licenses or to buy official paper (*papel sellado*), but the tribute was not abolished. The combination of suffrage restrictions which were in fact applied to the Indians and the continuance of the Contribución reestablished, in effect, the old Indian caste system which had prevailed throughout the colonial period.

Personal service, which had been outlawed several times, was once again confronted in June, 1834, by Circular 285. This document, noting that the practice was still widespread, reiterated the prohibition of either forced or gratis Indian labor and ordered the prefects to "redouble your vigilance of strict enforcement of the circulars of July 13, 1826, and September 3, 1833 . . . and in general of all the remedies that have been dictated with the salutary object of bettering the condition of Indians."[13]

The constitution of 1834 differed so slightly from that of 1828 that one historian has declared it a copy of the earlier document.[14] But there was an important difference; the constitution of 1834 fixed no property and literacy requirements for voting. The only condition for Indian suffrage was payment of the tribute.[15] By the end of the year, however, Congress had passed a law which reinstated the former qualifications.

Throughout the 1830s, there was no coordinated Indian policy. Decrees were rescinded almost as quickly as they were promulgated. As an example of the disorganization, two years after the decree of May 9, 1836, creating the office of Protector of the Indian, President Andrés de Santa Cruz suppressed the institution,

12. PMTAI, *Legislación,* p. 23.
13. Ibid., pp. 26-29.
14. Sivirichi, *Derecho indígena,* p. 114.
15. Belaúnde, *Meditaciones,* p. 75.

arguing that it had not fulfilled the duties envisioned by the government and had actually fostered new abuses. The land and the buildings of the protectorate were ordered returned to the municipal governments.[16]

In the constitution of 1839, only article 8 affected Indians. Asserting that "nobody is born a slave in the republic," it again exempted Indians from the literacy qualification for voting until 1844, but they still had to pay the tribute. It is doubtful whether this exception had any impact on Indian voting rights. The real effect of the article was to remove a key legal obstacle to usurpation of Indian lands. Before, illiterates could not sell their lands. Now, they could sell their lands, and could be sued in court by local *hacendados*. The new article hardly benefited the Indians.[17]

An 1839 law echoed earlier intentions of Símon Bolívar. It liberated all peons and *yanaconas* of the various haciendas, including the Indians of those *comunidades* which were surrounded by hacienda lands. It bestowed citizenship on all Indians and made them legal owners of the lands they worked, whether or not the land was claimed by an *hacendado*. The only condition was that they reimburse the *hacendados* the amount paid for the land. This law was intended to foster the growth of small landholdings at the expense of the haciendas. Although there is nothing revolutionary or even liberal in the law, if implemented, it might have helped to reverse the feudalistic tendencies of the period. Moreover, some advantages might have accrued to the Indians from this law had it been enforced; it never was. The haciendas retained control over the lands of the various *comunidades*.[18]

THE AGE OF CASTILLA

The 1820s and 1830s were chaotic periods in Peruvian history, and the 1840s saw little improvement. Very little Indian legislation was passed, and almost none of it was implemented. One man, Ramón Castilla (president 1845-51, 1855-64), stands out. In 1840, as minister of finance, Castilla sent a circular to the minister of church affairs calling for a reform of Indian education and educational facilities. He explained that abuse in the matriculation of students forced the government to step in, and he prohibited

16. PMTAI, *Legislación,* pp. 31-32.
17. For a succinct analysis of this article, see: de la Barra, *El indio peruano,* p. 153.
18. Cornejo, *Visión objectiva,* pp. 156-57; Rodríquez Pastor, "Derecho peruano," p. 368; and de la Barra, *El indio peruano,* p. 153.

further collection of tuition and other illegal payments.

He ordered the ministry to determine the extent of abuse in each parish and to correct it, and further instructed the ministry to distribute copies of the new regulations to all parishes, particularly those in the interior. He requested a complete census of each parish and Indian *comunidad* and an up-to-date record of all marriages, births, and deaths. These records were needed to prevent educational abuses such as the exclusion of Indian children from schools for failure to pay illegal fees, and would also facilitate government efforts to collect the Contribución.

Castilla viewed education as an indispensable function of government. Throughout his years of service to Peru, he worked diligently for educational reform and expansion, particularly in the sierra, where schools were scarce, disorganized, and largely unattended by Indian children. In many ways, Castilla was ahead of his time in recognizing that Indian education and integration were essential to the creation of a unified country and to its future economic development. Despite his interest and efforts, however, he accomplished very little.[19]

The usurpation of Indian lands continued unabated in the 1840s despite government attempts to halt it. In 1845, the Congress passed a law which declared the Indians in the jungle region of Huánuco owners of their land. Foreigners and nationals had settled the land and had claimed ownership. Many entered as "explorers" and had staked out vast tracts, largely at the expense of the Indian residents.

Not only did the settlers steal land, but they also sought to utilize Indian labor. In the valley of Huallaga, the great landholders raided Indian communities and forced captives into a system of slavery on the coca plantations. The working conditions were inhumane and the Indians often died from disease, overwork, and lack of food. The practice continued and even intensified throughout the nineteenth century, but the government was either unable or unwilling to rectify the situation, thereby demonstrating that the Indian occupied the very lowest position in the economic, political, and social heirarchy.[20]

The degree of Indian land transfer during the 1830s and 1840s

19. For a good statement of Castilla's educational philosophy, see his message to Congress, July 28, 1849, reprinted in: Ramón Castilla, *Ideología* (Lima: Ediciones Hora del Hombre, 1948), pp. 38-39. See also: PMTAI, *Legislación*, pp. 32-33.

20. Varallanos, *Historia de Huánuco*, p. 618.

is indicated by the laws of the 1840s designed to return these lands. The Congress, in August, 1846, ordered all lands alienated during the presidencies of Luis José de Orbegoso and Andrés de Santa Cruz considered for indemnification. Likewise, in 1849, the government declared that *comunidad* land in or near municipalities did not pertain to the municipality, but to the Indians. Though the resolution was aimed at abuses in the province of Huarochirí in the department of Lima, the practice of municipal usurpation was widespread. That this resolution failed to end municipality claims can be seen in subsequent orders and decisions regarding Cuzco and other towns.[21]

The central government also attempted to end forced Indian labor within the government itself. In October, 1845, the administration of Ramón Castilla issued a circular ordering a complete investigation of the practice of prefects, subprefects, governors, and priests of holding Indians in personal servitude in the name of public service. Correctly assessing the situation as a total denial of Indian liberty, the government requested complete data on the extent of Indian service at each level of government and detailed explanations of the origin of the practice in order to provide remedial legislation. A similar investigation of Church use of Indians was ordered.

There was some follow-up. In September, 1850, the executive, by supreme resolution, ordered an investigation of the subprefect of Huancavelica, who was accused of forcing Indians in his jurisdiction to comply with various personal service systems. And in 1857, the prefect of Cuzco was ordered to enforce the law "with greater energy and efficiency to halt the abuse of requiring forced Indian labor." Despite the intent of this order, it reiterated that public service of the Indians was authorized by law and the constitution. This loophole remained sufficient for those who sought to enslave the Indians. In fact, the practice actually intensified in subsequent years.

Regarding Indian citizenship and voting rights, seemingly settled by previous legislation, the Congress felt obliged to enact still another law in 1847. While retaining the tribute requirements, it conferred citizenship on those Indians who were married or twenty-five years of age. This group was given the right to vote whether they were literate or not. The passage of the law once again con-

21. The executive and congressional decrees of the 1840s and 1850s, including Castilla's as minister of finance, can be found in PMTAI, *Legislación*, pp. 26-35.

firms that previous legislation had been neither implemented nor enforced.

The variety of abuses committed against Indians is difficult to imagine. In order to control Indian trade as well as to prevent excessive communication among Indians, which, it was feared, might lead to revolts, Indians were required to have passports in order to travel internally in Peru and had to pay for the use of public roads. Passports were outlawed in April of 1851, but the tolls on the roads remained until 1856.[22]

The promulgation of the Código Civil (Civil Code) of 1852 set up another legal trap for Indians. The code was based upon the principles of Roman and Spanish law and incorporated much of the Napoleonic Code. It reflected the extreme individualistic reaction of the French against the problems of feudalism and therefore ignored the Indian *comunidad,*[23] opening the way to new encroachments by *hacendados.* The code stated that any land could be sold, and did not provide for collective ownership. It also established the legal structure for exploitive labor systems by allowing freedom of contract to all, including illiterate Indians. One could almost say that, owing to the abuses common in labor contracts, the code of 1852 recognized the legality of slavery. Furthermore, the strict interpretation of equality before the law provided the basis for all forms of fraud against the Indians. The section concerning debt was widely used to exploit Indians and to lock them firmly into debt peonage.[24]

The immediate and long-range results of the code were devastating. The process of destruction of *comunidades* was accelerated, and it is a wonder that any survived in some areas of the nation. What legal protection existed continued to be vitiated by the very persons appointed to provide aid for all citizens. The prefect, the subprefect, the judge, and other officials frequently took the side of the *hacendado* in legal disputes.

22. It is interesting to note that the administration of Manuel A. Odría (1948-56) reestablished passport requirements in an attempt to slow and contain internal Indian migration.

23. Jorge Basadre, *Perú, problema y posibilidad: Ensayo de una síntesis de la evolución histórica del Perú* (Lima: Librería Francesa Científica y Casa Editorial E. Rosay, 1931), pp. 117-18.

24. There are several critiques of the effects of this code. For example, see: Velasco Núñez, *Compilación,* p. xiv; Abelardo Solís, *Ante el problema agrario peruano* (Lima: Editorial "Perú," 1928), pp. 59-61; and José Pareja Paz-Soldán, *Geografía del Perú,* 2 vols. (Lima: Librería Internacional del Perú, 1950), 188.

In 1854, Ramón Castilla took an important step in improving the lot of the Indians by abolishing the Indian tribute. There had been several other attempts to end it, none successful. Castilla began his decree: "Independence, won with so many sacrifices, is an empty name for the majority of Peruvians who live under the strictest slavery and most complete debasement." He asserted that the cause of this condition was the Indian tribute and that Providence had provided the natural resource of guano (bird excrement used for fertilizer) so that the hated tax could be rescinded. Tribute was not collected in 1855 and provision was supposed to have been made for paying those officials who had depended upon the tribute for their income.

The abolition of the tribute caused severe dislocations in the Peruvian economy. In order to pay tribute, Indians had raised cash crops, thereby contributing positively to the economy. Without the tribute, this activity ceased and the Indians became more and more isolated from the rest of the country. Government revenues were severely affected, and departmental and municipal governments which had depended upon the tribute for operating expenses now had to look elsewhere.[25] Castilla recognized the problem and ordered that the money be supplied from other sources. The question, however, was what source. The Indian tribute had constituted a basic portion of previous national budgets and the providential revenues from guano had turned out to be insufficient to replace it. The problem was so serious that Castilla himself attempted to reinstate the tribute in 1856, but he failed.[26]

A by-product of the abolishment was the temporary statutory disenfranchisement of the Indians, since the constitution provided that only those Indians who had paid the Contribución could vote. It is improbable, however, that a significant portion of the Indian population was affected.

Castilla, who abolished Negro slavery in addition to ending the tribute, gained the title of "The Liberator" for these actions, but historians have long debated whether he acted out of humanitarian liberalism or political expediency. Certainly there were elements of both in his decision, but a critical factor was that he was in the midst of a revolution in 1854, and sought both black and

25. Fredrick B. Pike, *The Modern History of Peru* (London: Weidenfeld and Nicolson, 1967), pp. 112-13.

26. Basadre, *La multitud,* pp. 242-43. See also: Emilio Romero, *Historia económica del Perú,* 2d ed., 2 vols. (Lima: Editorial Universo, 1968), 2:104-7.

Indian allies for his cause. The explanation of political expediency is enhanced by Castilla's attempt to reestablish the tribute shortly thereafter.[27]

In a circular dated April 16, 1856, Castilla suppressed the practice of charging Indians tolls on national roads and endorsed a law which would have given the vote to the Indians.[28] The franchise was debated by the national convention that drafted the constitution of 1856. Article 37 limited suffrage to those who could read and write, with the exception of small businessmen, property owners, and former soldiers. Since many Indians were members of a landowning *comunidad* and thus theoretically owned land, these exceptions allowed them to vote.[29]

The same provisions were also included in article 38 of the constitution of 1860.[30] Nevertheless, these provisions followed the route of other Indian laws. They looked good on paper and appeared to represent growing liberalism and the development of democratic institutions, but they were ignored. Indians did not vote in 1856 or in 1860 or in subsequent years. Thus, the articles were meaningless in any real political sense.

The end of the Indian tribute continued to place great strains on the fiscal condition of the government, and in 1866, President Mariano Ignacio Prado (1866-68) reimposed the tax. This act, coupled with public and private demands for Indian personal service and free labor, Church taxes, discriminatory Indian levies, and general government oppression of the Indians, provoked an uprising in Huancané in the department of Puno in 1866. According to the government, the rebellion was political in nature and had originated in Cuzco among supporters of Castilla, but as Jorge Basadre notes, the Cuzco rebellion was quashed while the Indians fought on.

The Prado administration dispatched a division of troops to Huancané to quell the Indian revolt and Congress passed a special law (the "Law of Terror") which authorized the army to trans-

27. For a discussion of the historiography of this debate, see: Pike, *Modern History of Peru,* p. 103. See also: Felipe de la Barra, *La abolición del tributo por Castilla y su repercusión en el problema del indio peruano* (Lima: Ministerio de Guerra, Servicio de Prensa, Propaganda y Publicaciones Militares, 1956).

28. Vega, *La emancipación,* p. 35.

29. Belaúnde, *Meditaciones,* pp. 79-80.

30. José Pareja Paz-Soldán, ed., *Las constituciones del Perú (Exposición, crítica y textos): Recopilación y estudio preliminar de José Pareja Paz-Soldán* (Madrid: Ediciones Cultura Hispánica, 1954), pp. 663, 688.

plant inhabitants of troublesome Indian *comunidades* and villages to the jungle regions of Carabaya. The troops were instructed to use any methods necessary to subdue the uprising. In cooperation with mercenaries of the affected *hacendados,* the soldiers defeated the Indians and initiated a series of massacres and repressive measures not only in Huancané, but also in other parts of the sierra. Liberals in the Congress initiated a campaign to stop the terrorism and formed a society called Friends of the Indians, which included several former prefects from Cuzco and Puno. Despite their efforts, however, little was done to stop the terror.[31] The Congress also devoted some attention to Indian land tenure problems, but in the final analysis nothing was accomplished.[32]

THE RISE OF THE CIVILISTAS

Since independence, Peru had been ruled by a bewildering succession of colonels and generals. The army was able to maintain political hegemony because of both its monopoly of the power resources and the default of civilian leaders who were more interested in establishing and expanding their own economic positions than in actually governing the country. In 1872, however, Peru elected its first civilian president, Manuel Pardo (1872-76). Pardo embarked upon a general reform program which included some attention to Indian affairs, particularly in the realm of education.

Pardo wished to establish a free and universal primary education system because he felt that as long as the majority of the population remained illiterate and backward, Peru could not progress.[33] The Congress, however, refused to give Pardo the power necessary to create a centralized school system, and the control of the schools remained in the hands of the local officials, many of whom rejected Pardo's ideas.

Nevertheless, Pardo concentrated on Indian education as a means of incorporating the Indian into Peruvian life. In December, 1872, he established one of the first trade schools in the coun-

---

31. Basadre, *La multitud,* pp. 243-44. See also: Virgilio L. Roel Pineda, *El sendero de un pueblo* (Lima: Editorial "Garcilaso," 1955), p. 98.

32. For a discussion of agrarian legislación in this period, see: Francisco García Calderón, *Diccionario de la legislación peruana. 2a. ed. corr. y aum. con las leyes y decretos dictados hasta 1877,* 2 vols. (Nancy, France: Typographie G. Crepin-Leblond, 1879), 2:1106.

33. For a discussion of Pardo's education goals, see: Pike, *Modern History of Peru,* p. 135. See also: David Cornejo Foronda, *Don Manuel Pardo y la educación nacional* (Lima: Pontífica Universidad Católica del Perú, 1953).

try in Ayacucho. The school, which concentrated on training stonemasons, silversmiths, carpenters, and ironworkers, was designed to develop a skilled Indian work force. Eight scholarships were provided by the government for citizens of several departments.[34] Pardo also sought to end the linguistic isolation of monolingual Quechua Indians. In March, 1874, noting that the government should "facilitate the study of the Quechua language and spread Spanish among those Peruvians of the interior who do not yet possess it," Pardo ordered the state press to print one thousand copies of José Dionisio Anchorena's Spanish-Quechua dictionary.[35]

Church officials fought Pardo's educational policies. Not only were they frightened of losing their historical hegemony in the field of education, but they feared the influx of liberal ideas from Europe and the United States. The education of Indians likewise conflicted with the Church's position that the moral purity of the Indian could only be preserved by preventing his contact with the decadent *criollo* coastal society.[36] Though he failed to institute far-reaching educational reforms, Pardo's attitude indicated that civilian politicians were concerned with the state of the Indian and predisposed to act. One can date civilian Indian programs from the presidency of Pardo.

Nevertheless, government action which increased Indian exploitation continued. In 1876, by supreme resolution, the government reaffirmed the disastrous law of 1828 which had given the Indian the right to sell his land, adding a new proviso that the *comunidad* could take no legal action to halt the process. Thus, the great landowners were all but guaranteed protection in their efforts to chip away at Indian *comunidad* holdings. Despite various government efforts to protect the Indians, fraud did exist and increase.[37]

Throughout the twentieth century, the Indian question has provided politicians with numerous possibilities for opportunism, not because the politicians hoped to garner Indian votes in the manner of their contemporaries in the United States courting the black vote, but because Indian subjugation and segregation was by then generally recognized to be economically injurious to the nation.

34. F. Garcia Calderón, *Diccionario de la legislación,* 1:901.
35. Cornejo Foronda, *Don Manuel Pardo,* p. 185. See also: Evaristo San Cristóval, *Manuel Pardo y Lavalle, su vida y su obra* (Lima: Editorial Gil, 1945), pp. 286-90.
36. Pike, *Modern History of Peru,* pp. 135-37.
37. PMTAI, *Legislación,* pp. 36-37. See also: Magdaleno Chira C., *Observaciones e indicaciones básicas de legislación indígena: Elevadas a la comisión parlamentaria respectiva de la honorable Asamblea Constituyente de 1931 por . . .* (Lima: Imprenta "Hispano-América," 1932), pp. 57-58.

To a lesser degree, there has existed a feeling among some that repression is morally wrong. The roots of exploiting the crowd-pleasing potentialities of the Indian issue lie in the past, however. The 1880 decree of President Nicolás de Piérola (1879-81, 1895-99), creating the Protectorate of the Indian Race, ranks among the worst examples of such political opportunism. The decree, a product of internal political intrigues during the War of the Pacific (1879-83), recognized that the Indians were the object of abuse and asserted that the state of war demanded these abuses cease. Piérola decreed himself Protector of the Indian Race, with the right to intervene personally in situations brought to his attention.

The president stated that individuals or groups of Indians had the right to appeal directly to him any time they suffered injustice, bypassing if necessary the legal hierarchy. He declared every case of private punishment, slavery, or taxes that applied only to Indians illegal and promised to deal summarily with the person responsible.[38]

Nothing was ever done for the Indians by the protectorate. Not only is the sincerity of Piérola open to doubt by some commentators, but others make serious accusations of direct presidential injustices against the Indian population. One anonymous author asserted that Piérola, by ordering the destruction of several *comunidades,* was responsible for numerous Indian massacres. Another argued that in the revolts he initiated, Piérola had "spilled more Indian blood than any other Peruvian politician."[39]

The War of the Pacific (1879-83) was caused by the long-standing boundary disputes between Peru, Chile, and Bolivia over the Atacama Desert and by Chile's desire to maintain a favorable balance of power on the west coast of South America. Both Peru and Bolivia were crushed by Chile. Bolivia lost her seacoast; Peru lost her southern provinces and Lima suffered a two-year occupation by Chilean troops. The war was a watershed in Peruvian economic, political, and diplomatic history, and it also marked the beginning of a new era in Indian affairs.

38. PMTAI, *Legislación,* pp. 37-38; and J. V. Fajardo, *Legislación indígena del Perú* (Lima: Editorial Mercurio, n.d. [1961?], p. 32.

39. Dora Mayer de Zulen, *El indígena peruano a los cien años de república libre a independiente* (Lima Imprenta Peruana de E. Z. Casanova, 1921), p. 56. See also: Moisés Poblete Troncosco, *Condiciones de vida y de trabajo de la población indígena del Perú* (Ginebra: Oficina Internacional del Trabajo, 1938), p. 160; Carlos Miró Quesada Laos, *Radiografía de la política peruana* (Lima: Ediciones "Páginas peruanas," 1959), p. 67; and *El pierolismo y compañia; el gobierno Pardo; la candidatura Lequia* (Lima: Imprenta Prince, 1908), pp. 24-25.

During the war, the Indians did the bulk of the fighting. They performed bravely, and many gave their lives; but in the oft-told story they thought the war was between General Chile and General Peru. They gained nothing tangible from the war. Indeed, in many instances their condition worsened, and their frustrations and hatred finally led to violence. A good example was the bloody uprising in Huaráz, Ancash, in 1885. The Indians, led by Pedro Pablo Atusparia, mounted a revolt against the administration of Prefect Noriega, who had committed extreme abuses against the Indians. They were fined, whipped, and forced to work without compensation on public projects, the material for which was often stolen from them. Noriega reestablished the personal tax on the Indians and issued licenses of occupation of territory, jailing those who failed to apply for or to renew their licenses.

Finally Atusparia presented the prefect with a memorial on behalf of the Indians. He was jailed and whipped, and fourteen mayors who protested received the same treatment. In March, 1885, the Indians marched to Huaráz to ask for the release of the prisoners, but instead of attempting conciliation, the authorities attacked. The Indians succeeded in capturing the city, and the prefect fled to Lima, where he maintained that the riot was a result of his attempts to implant morality in the area. The Indians continued to enjoy success and ultimately took Yungay, the provincial capital.

The Indians were all but unarmed. They possessed a few rifles, but the majority had only machetes and small spears. They sent for reinforcements from the departments of La Libertad and Huánuco, but the government held the preponderance of power. In the end "Indians died like ants. Atusparia, wounded in the leg in the battle of Huaráz, fell and the bodies of his personal guard fell on top of him."[40]

Indian blood again had flowed in an attempt to correct daily abuses, but again the Indians lacked the necessary power. To those in authority in Lima, the revolt was merely another example of the "Indian danger," and nothing was done to prevent further violence. Instead, the government followed the same paths as before. By supreme decree of September 30, 1886, all inhabitants were required "to contribute their personal labor *or the labor of their peons*

40. Francois Bourricaud, *Poder y sociedad en el Perú contemporáneo*, trans. Roberto Bixio (Buenos Aires: Editorial SUR, 1967), pp. 85-86. There are several accounts of this uprising and besides Bourricaud, the best is Basadre, *La multitud*, pp. 244-48.

for the repair of bridges and roads whenever there is a lack of special funds for this type of work."[41] Such laws had caused past problems and had provided the foundation for uprisings like that in Huaráz. The government demonstrated again a notable lack of ability to learn from experience.

In 1890, the Congress reexamined the question of suffrage. Deputy Isaac Alzamora from Lima introduced a bill which would reimpose the qualifications of literacy and payment of the Contribución. He revived the old arguments of conservative cleric Bartolomé Herrera, who had been influential in the late 1840s and early 1850s, asserting that the Indians lacked the capacity to exercise their constitutional rights. Since they were not assimilated into the national life, they could not be treated as equals. Moreover, Alzamora argued, disenfranchisement of the Indians would break the power of those *latifundistas* who used their Indian servants as a power base.[42] Following a short debate, the bill passed Congress. But, as Víctor Andrés Belaúnde demonstrates, the power and influence of the *latifundistas* increased. Although Indians were denied the vote, the apportionment of representatives still reflected their presence, giving the *latifundistas* even greater control in the Congress.

In October, 1893, the Congress passed a legislative resolution declaring again that Indians were the legitimate owners of their lands according to the laws of 1824, thereby increasing the Indians' vulnerability to the *hacendados'* efforts at usurpation.[43] The Indians lost nothing new, but the action indicates the indifferent mood toward Indians which existed in Congress and in the country.

That mood was evident in the pronouncements and actions of the opportunistic Piérola. In the 1889 Declaration of Principles of his Democratic party, greater attention was paid to the need for immigration than to the Indians, who were barely mentioned.[44] In the 1895 civil war between Piérola and General and former

41. Rodríguez Pastor, "Derecho peruano," p. 368. The italics are mine.
42. Belaúnde, *Meditaciones,* pp. 83-85. For a complete treatment of Herrera's theories of public, private, and international law, see: Bartolomé Herrera, *Escritos y discursos,* 2 vols. (Lima: Librería Francesa Científica y Casa Editorial E. Rosay, 1929 and 1934). See also: Jorge Guillermo Leguía, *Estudios históricos* (Santiago de Chile: Ediciones Ercilla, 1939), pp. 63-112.
43. For the text, see: Chira C., *Observaciones,* p. 90. For critical comment, see: Cornejo, *Visión objetiva,* pp. 156-57.
44. Partido Demócrata, *Doctrinas de don Nicolás de Piérola: Declaración de principios, bases de organización del partido, anexo histórico* (Lima: n.p., 1950), p. 7.

President Andrés Cáceres (1886-90), Piérola issued ringing pronouncements promising perfect order in the republic with justice
for all. Since Cáceres had the good will of his Indian troops because he treated them with decency, it appeared that the Indians
might gain no matter which man won. Following the victory of
Piérola, however, it soon became clear that the Indians were great
losers. The *hacendados* moved quickly to despoil Indian lands, and,
in some cases, the armies of Piérola were used to attack Indians.
At the Indian *comunidad* of Chucuito near Lake Titicaca, an entire
battalion assaulted unarmed Indians in order to steal their land.[45]

There were numerous other massacres and land grabs in this
period, and the government did nothing to prevent them. Nor was
anything done to alleviate the Indians' economic situation. Some
have believed that Piérola desired to aid the Indians, and point to
his efforts to modernize the army and halt the practice of kidnap-
ing Indians to fill the ranks. The legislation he introduced requiring military service by all citizens was not implemented, however,
and the army returned to its former practice of rounding up
Indians.[46]

MANUEL GONZÁLEZ PRADA AND THE RISE
OF INDIGENISMO

This last decade of the nineteenth century brought the rise of a
true *indigenismo* (Indianism) which was to have tremendous import
for twentieth-century Peruvian history. Earlier, in the 1870s, many
intellectuals in Peru had adopted Auguste Comte's philosophy of
positivism. As did the *Científicos* of Mexico during the same period,
the positivists of Peru believed that the intellectual elite, using the
tools of scientific investigation, could effect sweeping changes in
the economic and social structures. Influenced as well by social
Darwinism, these men viewed the Indians as inferior beings and
blamed them for the ills of the country. The War of the Pacific
undermined this philosophy because it was difficult for a defeated,
prostrate people to hold the tenets of survival of the fittest.

The philosophy which emerged from defeat, termed neopositivism by one historian,[47] reversed the view of the Indian. Whereas

45. José Frisancho Macedo, *Del jesuitismo al indianismo y otros ensayos* (Lima:
Imprensión y Fotograbados C. F. Southwell, 1928), pp. 35-38.
46. General Juan Mendoza R., "El ejército peruano en el siglo xx," in *Visión del
Perú en el siglo XX*, ed. José Pareja Paz-Soldán, vol. 1 (Lima: Librería Studium, 1962),
pp. 294-96.
47. For an examination of positivism, neopositivism, and the representatives of
these doctrines, see: Pike, *Modern History of Peru*, pp. 159-68.

the Indians and their problems had been neglected and avoided in the universities in the 1870s and 1880s, the faculty and the students now turned to a study of the Indian past and its relevance to contemporary problems. Many intellectuals, including the famous writer Manuel González Prada, believed that if the Indians had been incorporated into the national life, Peru would have won the War of the Pacific.

From the belief that correct treatment of the Indians in the past and their assimilation into society would have won the war followed a conviction that potential for future development and modernization lay with implementing the integration of the Indians. One scholar believes that "the most important contribution of the neopositivists was their refutation of the popular notions of racial determinism and their insistence ... that Peru's future depended upon the assimilation of the Indians."[48] There were many important proponents of the new thesis. Carlos Lissón, dean of the faculty of San Marcos University, asserted that the Indians were not inherently inferior, but victims of oppression. Feeling that the future of Peru lay with the Indian mass, he emphasized the need for education. Sociologist Mariano H. Cornejo, who likewise concentrated on education, rejected race prejudice and demanded the immediate incorporation of the Indians into the society. Professor and politician Manuel Vicente Villarán also argued against prejudice. He asserted that the Indians were the only ones in the country that had not degenerated morally, and thus the existence of racial prejudice was a cruel hoax.[49] Joaquín Capelo, another San Marcos professor, worked diligently as a senator from Junín for the regeneration and assimilation of the Indians. He was particularly active in the early twentieth century, but his efforts in the late nineteenth century formed part of the philosophical base of the new *indigenista* movement.

The most influential of the neopositivists and one of the great literary figures in Peruvian history was Manuel González Prada. According to his principal biographer, González Prada underwent

48. Ibid., p. 168. See also: V. A. Belaúnde, *Meditaciones,* pp. 192-93; Eugenio Chang-Rodríguez, *La literatura política de González Prada, Mariátequi y Haya de la Torre* (Mexico, D.F.: Ediciones de Andrea, Colección Studium 18, 1957), pp. 108-9; and Luis Alberto Sánchez, foreword to Manuel González Prada, *Baladas peruanas* (Santiago de Chile: Editorial Ercilla, 1935), pp. 14-15.

49. See his classic essay, "Condición legal de las comunidades indígenas," in Manuel Vicente Villarán, *Páginas escogidas* (Lima: Talleres Gráficos P. L. Villanueva, 1962), pp. 3-8. Other writings in this work also reflect Villarán's *indigenista* sentiment. For example, see pp. 329-30.

fundamental changes during the War of the Pacific.[50] He had fought in the 1881 Battle of Miraflores which led to the fall of Lima, and after the Peruvian defeat, he simply retired to his house in the capital, there to remain until the end of the Chilean occupation of the city. The war and the occupation altered his life pattern. The quiet poet of 1878 was now a "polemicist and a tireless agitator."[51]

González Prada had seen the Indians fight and die for a country that despised them, and he adopted their cause as his own. In 1888, he delivered a blistering speech in the Politeama Theatre in Lima, attacking the smug *limeños* with the assertion that Peru had no viable political parties but rather three large groups divided into those that govern, those that conspire, and those who are indifferent because of their own egotism, stupidity, or disillusion. There were Indians on the altiplano and in the sierra and mestizos on the coast. With these social and political cleavages, Peru could not hope to win any war in the future.

According to González Prada, the real Peru was not the creoles and foreigners who lived on the coast, but the great mass of Indians who inhabited the sierra. For three hundred years, the Indians had lived in ignorance and slavery, abused and exploited by "that Indian-brutalizing trinity," the judge, the governor, and the priest. He called for the education of the Indians and their incorporation into the national life, asserting that then and only then would Peru recuperate and reenter the world as a proud nation.[52]

Throughout the remainder of his life, González Prada fought the Indian problem with his pen. He seemed to blame the clergy, more than any other group, for the exploitation. He described the archbishop of Puno on a pastoral visit to Chucuito. When the archbishop saw the two Indian schools staffed by Indian teachers, he exploded, telling the Indians they ought to dedicate themselves to working the land instead of attending school because they would fall in with Indians in league with the Devil.[53]

---

50. The best biography of González Prada is still Luis Alberto Sánchez, *Don Manuel,* 3d ed., corrected (Santiago de Chile: Ediciones Ercilla, 1937). This work was reprinted in 1965 by the Universidad Nacional Mayor de San Marcos, but citations here are from the 1937 edition.

51. Sánchez, foreword to González Prada, *Baladas peruanas,* p. 14.

52. Manuel González Prada, *Páginas libres,* 2 vols. (Lima: Fondo de Cultura Popular, 1966), 1:61-63. There are other editions of this work, but this is the most accessible.

53. Manuel González Prada, *Prosa menuda* (Buenos Aires: Ediciones Imán, 1941), p. 80. For other examples, see: ibid., pp. 48-50; Manuel González Prada, "Nuestros tigres," *Horas de lucha* (Lima: Fondo de Cultura Popular, Ediciones "Futura," 1964), p. 145; and idem, "Nuestros inmigrantes," *Horas de lucha,* p. 164.

To González Prada, the countless shifts in power known as revolutions in the history of Peru were not revolutions but barracks revolts which altered nothing. He believed that no one cared about the Indians, who were probably worse off in the republic than they had been during the colonial period. He particularly hated Nicolás de Piérola and often ridiculed him for having the audacity to call himself Protector of the Indian Race. He accused him of having restored the hated *mita* and of being responsible for massacres as serious as those committed by Valeriano Weyler in Cuba and the sultan in Armenia. He bitterly attacked the barbarous behavior of the troops at Chucuito in 1885 as an indication of the venality of the government, the political parties, and mestizos in general in their behavior toward the Indians.[54]

Perhaps González Prada's best *indigenista* essay was "Nuestros Indios" (Our Indians), in which he developed the theme of exploitation. He demonstrated that one or two thousand whites and mestizos had succeeded in subjecting three million Indians by means of an alliance between politicians and the wealthy of both the coast and sierra. Under the republic, the *gobernadores* replaced the colonial *corregidores* while the priests continued their same exploitive practices and the old feudalistic system proceeded with few alterations, except that the Indians lacked some protections imposed during the colonial epoch. Their suffering meant nothing, González Prada argued; they still had no rights, only obligations which were enforced with the whip and starvation. The Indians lived in worse conditions than had their grandfathers or great grandfathers, and any protest or demonstration was met with all the firepower at the government's command.

In González Prada's view, the power structure denied Indians the education supposedly available to all citizens because it viewed them as mere animals, unfit for education and also because education might undermine the systematic oppression perpetrated upon them. Moreover, through judicious use of religious teachings, alcohol, and enforced servitude, the Indians were actually prevented from educating themselves. González Prada's solution was to rid the nation of the exploitive system and incorporate the Indians immediately.[55]

54. Manuel González Prada, *Bajo el oprobio* (Paris: Tipografía de Louis Bellenand et Fils, 1933), pp. 134-36; idem, "Los partidos y la Unión Nacional," *Horas de lucha*, p. 18; idem, *Figuras y figurones: Manuel Pardo, Piérola, Romaña, José Pardo* (Paris: Tipografía de Louis Bellenand et Fils, 1938), pp. 168-69; and idem, *Prosa menuda*, pp. 115-18, 127-29, 155-57.

55. González Prada, "Nuestros indios," *Horas de lucha*, pp. 199-213.

Recognizing that political action would be necessary to accomplish his goals, in 1891 González Prada joined other members of his Literary Circle in forming the National Union party. In May of that year, they issued a Declaration of Principles, which was unlike that of existing parties. It called for the establishment of a federal republic, emphasized the resonsibilities of both the president and the Congress, called for direct and universal male suffrage which included foreigners, outlined reform in the imposition and collection of taxes, and demanded the return of Indian lands that had been illegally seized. The declaration also requested the creation of a civilian militia to replace the army.[56]

Having witnessed so many caudillos and personalist parties in his life, González Prada took pains to prevent the National Union from becoming dominated by one man. He stated: "We don't want men that blindly obey the orders of the group," and "the National Union is not any one man." He even refused to accept the title of Jefe del Partido which many of his followers wished to bestow upon him.[57]

The party lasted until 1902, and many have asserted that it was ineffective and that its short duration was an indication of the weakness of its program and the lack of any true direction or ideology.[58] Yet, although they did not outline in detail every proposal that they made or offer legislation on the Indian question, this small group of men left a lasting imprint on Peruvian history. Jorge Basadre has written: "A small but enthusiastic group of intellectuals from Lima, that quickly found an echo in some sectors of the provincial youth, placed in González Prada their hopes of some day obtaining a total transformation, not only in a cultural sense, but also in a political and social sense."[59]

González Prada initiated a wholly new *indigenismo* in Peru and many followed his lead. A look at his disciples and others influenced by him indicates his importance. In 1885, Mercedes Cabello de Carbonera published an article about an Indian fiesta in which she vehemently attacked the exploitation of the Indians. Three

56. Sánchez, *Don Manuel,* pp. 122-24; and Alfredo Hernández Urbina, *Nueva política nacional* (Trujillo, Peru: Ediciones Raíz, 1962), pp. 66-69.

57. González Prada, "Los partidos y la Unión Nacional," *Horas de lucha,* pp. 24-26. See also: Adriana Verneuille de González Prada, *Mi Manuel* (Lima: Editorial Cultura Antártica, 1947), pp. 338-40.

58. For example, see: Belaúnde, *Meditaciones,* pp. 159-61.

59. Jorge Basadre, *Historia de la república del Perú,* 5th ed., enlarged and corrected, 11 vols. (Lima: Talleres Gráficos P. L. Villanueva, 1961-68), 6:2851.

years later, José T. Itolararres published an *indigenista* novel, *La trinidad del indio o costumbres del interior,* and in 1889, Clorinda Matto de Turner published *Aves sin nido,* which one authority asserts "initiated the *indigenista* novel in America."[60]

The influence of González Prada is shown by Matto de Turner's *indigenismo* and anticlericalism and in her analysis of the exploiters of the Indians. She utilized the "trinity of exploitation" in much the same way as he had. Her triangle was composed of the priest, the governor, and the tax collector; the priest received the brunt of her attack. Her true anticlerical feelings are even more clearly defined in the novel *Indole,* published in 1890.[61] Matto de Turner was raised on an hacienda near Cuzco and thus could draw upon personal experience that González Prada lacked. She carried her memories to Lima, and, like González Prada, was influenced by the War of the Pacific. Although her literary style was undistinguished, this did not diminish the impact her works had on the public.[62]

González Prada's influence was felt far beyond literature, however. The twentieth-century leaders José Carlos Mariátegui and Víctor Raúl Haya de la Torre both acknowledged their indebtedness to the polemicist. He instilled a new patriotism in a country badly discouraged by a disastrous war. An iconoclast who severely criticized Peruvian life and culture without regard for sacred cows or heroes, he aligned himself with the poor and the disadvantaged in the society and believed in man's ability to effect sweeping changes. As a forceful and eloquent supporter of the Indians, he succeeded in pricking the conscience of the apathetic *costeño.* His devastating attacks on the clergy and on the doctrines of the Catholic Church left their mark, particularly in the areas of Indian exploitation and public education.[63]

60. Chang-Rodríguez, *Prada, Mariátegui y Haya,* p. 110. He further asserts: "Aqui el indio deja ser adorno literario para convertirse en protagonista en la literatura americana."

61. See the analysis of Francisco Carrillo, *Clorinda Matto de Turner y su indigenismo literario* (Lima: Ediciones de la Biblioteca Universitaria, Editorial Jurídica, 1967), pp. 28-32, 34-39. See also: Eulogio Tapia Olarte, *Cinco grandes escritores cuzqueños en la literatura peruana* (Lima: Imprenta D. Miranda, 1946), p. 49.

62. For further treatment of the author and her impact, see: Basadre, *Historia de la república,* 6:2961-62; Mario Castro Arenas, *La novela peruana y la evolución social,* 2d ed.; corrected and enlarged (Lima: Talleres Gráficos de Iberia, n.d. [1967?]), pp. 107-12; and Alfredo Yépez Miranda, *Signos del Cuzco* (Lima: Imprenta D. Miranda, 1946), pp. 35-45.

63. For an analysis of these and other points, see: Basadre, *Historia de la república,* 6:2854-55.

González Prada has been attacked as an intellectual fraud, as a man suffering from an inferiority complex, who, in search of a public not likely to attack him, turned to the Indians. He has been accused of adopting a "phoenix" approach to Peruvian politics and of trying to intensify the already existing discord and antagonism between the coast and the sierra, the Indian and the white, the rich and the poor, the satisfied and the desperate, the young and the old, the believer and the atheist, while others have attacked him for his failure to employ scientific method and for his lack of direction and concrete ideas.[64]

Nevertheless, one does not always have to have solutions in hand to be an effective critic, nor is it necessary to paint the good in society while depicting the bad. If González Prada was guilty of excess or of basing his conclusions on superficial evidence or of not writing scientific social and economic studies, these failings do not and cannot detract from his importance as a writer and as a political gadfly. He did not wish to burn Peru, only to repair and to regenerate her. He did not wish to destroy one segment of society, but to uplift another. Though at times discouraging, his writings did not contain gloomy predictions of the coming Armageddon, but concentrated on correctible ills within the culture. Despite shortcomings, he assumed his task with vigor and humanity. He was a diagnostician, not an executioner, and his patient was Peru.

Although González Prada held out a bright new hope for Peru and the Indians, the nineteenth century had offered the Indians very little in the way of alleviation from oppression. Without even the modicum of protection offered by the *Laws of the Indies,* the liberal policies of the Liberators and subsequent officials served progressively to deprive the Indians of their land and their liberty. Emphasis on precepts of equality before the law and protection of private property resulted in subsidization for the landed oligarchy and misery, oppression, and illiteracy for the Indians. National legislation designed to protect the Indians was neither obeyed by the people nor enforced by the government. No coherent Indian policy is evident in the conflicting legislation that characterizes the century.

64. Carlos Miró Quesada Laos, *Pueblo en crisis* (Buenos Aires: Emecé Editores, 1946), pp. 63-65; Pike, *Modern History of Peru,* pp. 178-80; and Belaúnde, *Meditaciones, pp. 148-49, 159-62.*

Peru was not one nation by 1900; it was several. There was no unity of language, custom, economics, or geography. There was an Indian nation and a white nation, a coastal nation and a sierra nation, a nation of those who lived within modern Western culture and those who lived under feudalism. Old problems had not been solved, but new ones had been created. The unfinished work of the nineteenth century was left to the intellectuals, the teachers, and the politicians of the twentieth century. Upon their success or failure would depend the future of Peru.

3

Early Twentieth-Century *Indian* Legislation and the *Rise of* Indigenismo, *1900-1919*

Chronological divisions are useful historical tools with which the steady progression of events can be shown to contain a clear developmental pattern. The danger is to view the transition from one century to another as the watershed in the study of a given topic. For the Peruvian Indians, nothing could have been further from the truth. In the first years of the twentieth century, there was no discernible change in either government attitudes or actions. The political alignments in Congress likewise remained unaltered and the large *hacendados* of the sierra still held a preponderance of power.

This old pattern, however, could not endure. Peru underwent economic and social changes in the first two decades of the century that were to challenge traditional political systems. On the coast there were the beginnings of the great sugar and cotton plantations with their increasingly politicized wage labor force that would be so important in the 1920s and 1930s. In addition, this period witnessed the rise of the urban labor movement, with the concomitant introduction of radical foreign ideologies.

Accordingly, political and economic power began to shift away from the rural *hacendados* of the sierra to owners of industralized plantations on the coast and businessmen and laborers. Both President Guillermo Billinghurst (1912-14) and President José Pardo (1904-1908, 1915-19) in his second term were forced to take cognizance of the new forces and both initiated social and labor legislation. The new government focus on social conditions would also result in some attention to Indian conditions.

There were also new voices in Congress which championed social reform in general and Indian reform in particular. Some of the impetus for the rise of *indigenismo* came from Manuel González Prada and the neopositivists discussed earlier, but much of it came in response to changing conditions in the country. Private pro-Indian groups, such as the Pro-Indian Association, sprang up and influenced government leaders and programs.

Still the movement was largely confined to a few men and did not expand to encompass entire political parties. The *hacendados* retained most of their control, but it was weakening and would begin to disintegrate in the succeeding decades. The achievements of the period 1900-1919 were to be limited in scope, but this can be viewed as a precursory age in the history of modern *indigenismo*.

THE EARLY YEARS

President Eduardo López de Romaña (1899-1903) offered neither attitudes nor programs that constituted any departure from previous government practice. In general, López de Romaña's treatment of the Indians was cursory. His messages to Congress made few references to the Indians, and when he did mention them, he demonstrated a complete failure to understand their problems. In 1900, he attacked the evils of alcohol and the debilitating effects that it had on a large portion of the population. The high incidence of Indian alcoholism was cited, with no indication that López de Romaña realized why Indian alcoholism was so prevalent. He pointed with pride in 1902 to the peaceful suppression of three Indian *communidades* that "twenty years ago had withdrawn themselves from the control of the authorities by occupying rough and almost inaccessible lands."[1] The questionable necessity of such a move, if the Indians were living in peace and not endangering

---

1. Eduardo López de Romaña, *Mensaje del presidente de la república en la instalación del Congreso Ordinario de 1900* (Lima: Imprenta del Estado, 1900), p. viii; idem, *Mensaje del presidente de la república en la instalación del Congreso Ordinario de 1902* (Lima: Imprenta del Estado, 1902), p. 8.

It should be noted at the outset of this chapter that I carefully researched the congressional debates for the period 1900-1948, as is reflected in the treatment of legislative proceedings. No such research was undertaken for the nineteenth century owing both to the enormousness of the task and to the fact that the focus of this work is on the twentieth century and not the nineteenth.

the tranquillity of the nation, apparently did not concern the president.

In 1903 López de Romaña praised the establishment of compulsory military service for all males in the country and predicted that it would terminate the old practice of rounding up all able-bodied men. Describing his program to convert the army into a highly trained, professional body of men, with the barracks becoming veritable schools for the illiterate, he fell into the common trap of assuming that the Indians would learn Spanish and return to their communities with new education and habits.[2] This thesis was not new; the belief that the army constituted one of the principal vehicles of Indian integration was commonly held throughout the nineteenth century, and is still believed today. Most leading *indigenistas,* however, have critically examined and fiercely attacked it. Luis E. Valcárcel has written:

> During the Republic, many hoped that the barracks would become the melting pot in which the Indian soldier would cease to be an Indian and would be completely incorporated into the society. Of the millions of Indians that have passed through military service, there remain scarcely a few thousand who did not return to their native *comunidades.* All the rest returned to their traditional homes in both a physical and a cultural sense. The barracks life had effected no change in them except to impair their health. The panacea of Indian military education has likewise failed to produce favorable results. An incredibly bad educational structure rendered null all efforts at instruction.[3]

The government continued to impede the conduct of the affairs of the Indian *comunidades.* In the Código de Aquas, the water code dealing with irrigation rights, promulgated in February, 1902, the *comunidad* was again treated as a group of individuals rather than a legal entity, with the exception that the *comunidad* could designate one or more representatives to vote on water distribution.[4]

Not only were there no programs to aid the Indian population, but clearly implied in the annual messages of López de Romaña and pronouncements by other government officials was the thesis that immigration would be one of the principal solutions to Peru's problems. Not only was it believed that the presence of more Europeans would help move the country forward, but their admix-

2. Eduardo López de Romaña, *Mensaje del presidente de la república en la instalación del Congreso Ordinario de 1903* (Lima: Imprenta del Estado, 1903), pp. xii-xiii.
3. Valcárcel, *Ruta cultural del Perú,* p. 88. For supporting viewpoints, see: Sivirichi, *Derecho indígena,* pp. 58-59, 468; and Cornejo, *Visión objetiva,* pp. 58-59.
4. PMTAI, *Legislación,* p. 159.

ture into the population was expected to improve the race. The very conceptualization of the situation in these terms precluded substantive attention to the Indian.

In the years following the War of the Pacific, three major political parties were established to compete with the Civilista party, which had been founded in 1871. In 1884, Nicolás de Piérola formed the Democratic party (Partido Demócrata) and Andrés A. Cáceres founded his Constitutionalist party (Partido Constitucionalista). Finally, in 1901, Augusto Durand organized the Liberal party (Partido Liberal). All of these parties, however, neglected the Indians both in their platforms and in their ideologies. Like President López de Romaña, they concerned themselves with non-Indian political reforms and with calls for increased immigration. They never identified themselves with the Indian or his problems.[5]

Despite the lack of general political recognition of the Indian problem, there were some thinkers and officials who demonstrated sympathy with Indian needs. Víctor Andrés Belaúnde, a leading Peruvian intellectual and diplomat, was extremely concerned with Indian problems in the period 1902-1904. He felt that Indians constituted the fundamental social problem of the country and that the uniqueness of their situation required unique solutions. Observing that traditional democratic lines of thinking were insufficient in dealing with the Indians, he urged that Indian institutions be protected while they were being modernized to facilitate Indian integration.[6]

One official, Alejandrino Maguiña, made a real effort to bring about changes in the treatment of Indians. In 1901, representatives of the *comunidad* of Chucuito, in the department of Puno, came to Lima to complain about the continuing abuses committed in their area. The Chamber of Deputies appointed Maguiña head of a

5. See: Víctor de Tezanos Pinto, *Dos necesidades urgentes* (Paris: Imprenta Artística "Lux," 1923), pp. 3-7; and José Varallanos, *El cholo y el Perú: Introducción al estudio sociológico de un hombre y un pueblo mestizo y su destino cultural* (Buenos Aires: Imprenta López, 1962), pp. 216-18. For an analysis of the Partido Liberal and its program, see: Carlos Miró Quesada Laos, *Autopsia de los partidos políticos* (Lima: Ediciones Páginas Peruanas, Imprenta "Minerva," 1961), pp. 328-29. The Partido Civil did devote more attention to the Indians, but it was general and still couched in superior-inferior terms. See: Antero Aspíllaga, *Programa de gobierno presentado a la consideración del país por Antero Aspíllaga candidato proclamado a la presidencia de la república por la asamblea general extraordinaria del Partido Civil, 10 diciembre de 1911* (Lima: Tip. de "El Lucero," 1911), pp. 12-14.

6. Víctor Andrés Belaúnde, *Planteamiento del problema nacional*, vol. 3 of *Memorias* (Lima: Imprenta Lumen, 1962), pp. 9-11.

commission to study these complaints. Unlike many of the goverment officials who had been charged with investigatory duties in the past, Maguiña strove to produce an honest, analytical report.[7]

He asserted that practices such as those he discovered in and around Chucuito had produced Indian revolts in the past. He attacked the governors, the priests, and the justices of the peace, González Prada's "brutalizing trinity," for mistreating the Indians at every turn. Officials demanded free services from the Indians, and the inequitable taxes imposed on the Indians' real property had become a burden comparable to the old Contribución. Labor was recruited under an almost unrecognizable form of the *faena*, the only remuneration being a small quantity of coca or alcohol.

Special tax levies were imposed to pay for monuments and other public works. For example, the cost of constructing the public buildings in the district of Santa Rosa fell upon the Indians, as did the obligation to supply labor. The justices of the peace and the priests also imposed fines at will and required selected Indians to serve as sponsors of religious festivals, a dubious honor since the sponsor had to pay the costs of said festival. In the sale of wool and livestock, commercial entrepreneurs, with the acquiescence or even cooperation of government officials, set prices far in advance of the collection date, forcing the Indians to accept payment calculated without reference to the existing market value. The few men in the region who attempted to defend the Indians were themselves subjected to government persecution.

Maguiña proposed several reforms. He suggested that a permanent commission maintain vigilance over the conditions of life of the Peruvian Indians and urged that it be given the power to correct abuses and transgressions on the spot, avoiding the necessity of the plaintiff's going to Lima. He called for specific legislation to limit the powers of the justices of the peace, the clergy, and local officials and for the complete overhaul of the municipal in-

7. This report is printed in: Perú, Ministerio de Gobierno y Policía, *Memoria que el Ministro de Gobierno y Policía sr. Leónidas Cárdenas presenta al Congreso Ordinario de 1902* (Lima: Imprenta del Estado, 1902), pp. 1-34. See also: Basadre, *Historia de la república,* 7: 3482-83; and Sivirichi, *Derecho indígena,* pp. 142-43. I was greatly aided in my search for the Maguiña report by Sr. Guillermo Rouillon, Jefe del Centro de Información Bibliográfica, and Señorita Mireya Montes de Oca, Asistente-Coordinador, both of the Biblioteca de la Universidad Nacional Mayor de San Marcos. For a succinct view of Maguiña's later ideas on the Indian *comunidad,* see his response to a questionnaire in: Bustamante Cisneros, *Condición jurídica de las comunidades,* pp. 102-5.

stitutions which by their very nature had fostered problems.

In response to Maguiña's report, the government named Juan de Dios Salazar y Oyarzábal as prefect of Puno and ordered him to determine whether the charges were true, and if so to propose legal remedies. Salazar y Oyarzábal concurred with many of Maguiña's conclusions. He condemned the *hacendados,* the clergy, and local officials, particularly the justices of the peace. In an official note to the government in February, 1904, he listed as the principal causes of past revolts and sources of discontent: (1) payment of the land tax; (2) collection of arbitrary boundary delineation taxes; (3) inscription in the military lottery; (4) usurpation of Indian lands; (5) forced Indian labor on public works projects; (6) the practice of setting the prices of wool and livestock far in advance; and (7) free Indian services required by government officials, priests, and private individuals.[8]

These two scathing reports were buried by the Lima bureaucracy and failed to produce any government action. Special investigative committees were appointed in the Senate and Chamber of Deputies, but announced debates on the various proposals were never held and no legislation was introduced.[9] Nor did new uprisings in Chucuito in 1903 and 1905 change the situation. The abuses continued; the guilty went unpunished; the Indians continued to suffer. The concern of a few dedicated men proved again to be insufficient in the face of public and government indifference.

The man who might have altered the situation, President Manuel Candamo (1903), who named a commission to study the Chucuito crisis, died soon after taking office and government concern appears to have died with him. In 1904, Vice-President Serapio Calderón noted that the government had named an investigator to study Indian problems, but admitted that the man had not yet begun work.[10]

Candamo's successor, José Pardo, was not ignorant of Indian needs; however, his solution lay with the extension and improvement of the educational structure, an approach which did little to ameliorate the immediate situation. Echoing his father, Manuel Pardo, Pardo called for a vast educational network that would en-

8. Pedro Yrigoyen, *El conflicto y el problema indígenas [sic]* (Lima: Sanmarti y Cía., 1922), pp. 10-13.

9. Basadre, *Historia de la república,* 7: 3483-84.

10. Serapio Calderón, *Mensaje que el segundo vicepresidente de la república encargado del poder ejecutivo presenta al Congreso Ordinario de 1904* (Lima: Imprenta de Gmo. Stolte, 1904), p. x.

compass all areas and all people.[11] He believed that army service provided an educational experience and expected the universal draft system to contribute "to the great work of popular education."[12] Pardo traveled widely during his first term, but he was more concerned with roads, railroads, and other stupendous public works projects than he was with remedial Indian projects. He visited Puno and listened to Indian complaints, but did nothing to rectify them.[13]

Congressional disinterest in dealing with the Indian question continued. On September 7, 1906, Deputy Alberto Gadea from Puno attempted to win approval for the establishment of a commission to study the situation in Chucuito. After substantial debate, the proposal was rejected. During the debate, one deputy maintained that the blame really lay with an unnamed lawyer in Lima who was working in concert with the Indians to provoke incidents. Others argued that there was no need for a commission because the government had already named one that had not reported yet. That it had not reported did not seem to bother the deputies.[14]

There was an important turning point in the *indigenista* movement during this period. In 1907, Manuel Vicente Villarán published an article entitled "Condición legal de las comunidades indígenas" in which he argued for retention of the Indian *comunidad*. He stated that although the organization of the *comunidad* was not compatible with the realities of modern-day life, it was still the Indians' best protection against the white man and in particular the *hacendado*. Noting that the usurpation of Indian land was continuing, Villarán maintained that the fact the Indians had retained any lands was the result of the protection afforded by the *comunidad*. The article effectively refuted the 1905 doctoral thesis of Francisco Tudela y Varela which held that the *comunidades* were unproductive.[15]

11. Mayer de Zulen, *El indígena peruano a los cien años*, p. 56.

12. José Pardo, *Mensaje presentado al Congreso Ordinario de 1906 por el presidente de la república* (Lima: Imprenta del Estado, 1906), p. xxii.

13. For an account of his proclivity for travel, see: Pedro Dávalos y Lissón, *Diez años de historia contemporánea del Perú, 1899-1908: Gobiernos de Piérola, Romaña, Candamo, Calderón y Pardo* (Lima: Librería y Imprenta Gil, 1930), pp. 206-7.

14. Perú, Congreso, Cámara de Diputados, *Diario de los debates de la H. Cámara de Diputados: Legislatura Ordinaria de 1906* (Lima: Imprenta de "El Comercio," 1906), pp. 573-78. Hereafter, all references to the *Diario* will be cited PDD, followed by the year, the house, the date, and the page number.

15. Villarán, *Páginas escogidas*, pp. 3-8. For a discussion of this article and its place

In the opinion of historian Jorge Basadre, this article constituted the point of awakening in the *indigenista* political movement and subsequent action and opinion can be traced to it.[16] Basadre may overstate the case, but the importance of Villarán's work cannot be passed over, and there was a great deal more action on the *indigenista* front in the next few years.

Several of the principal complaints of the Indians of Chucuito involved government abuses. Finally, the Congress intervened in government oppression of the Indian. In July, 1907, Senator Severiano Bezada from Puno introduced legislation which would impose penalties of up to one year in prison for each infraction of rules governing official conduct. The proposal languished for a year, but in August, 1908, was reintroduced. The debate was spirited, but interestingly enough, there was no opposition to the law itself, only to several defects in wording which some senators said would adversely affect the intent of the law.[17]

Senators Leoncio Samanez from Apurímac and Joaquín Capelo from Junín argued that the restrictions on government officials should not be limited to the *montaña* (the region on the eastern slopes of the Andes), but rather should encompass the entire republic, and the amendment was approved. In the only discussion of the penalty, one senator objected to the fact that it seemed to be limited to subprefects and governors and failed to include the prefect.

The most strenuous objections were provoked by the provision which ordered the executive to draw up regulations to systematize the distribution of certain duties that the Indians would still have to perform for the government. Senator Capelo argued that to retain any specified duties for the Indians would merely serve to perpetuate the old system. In fact, it might result in "more inconveniences than leaving things as they are today."[18] Senator Bezada, though sincerely concerned with the well-being of the Indians, still felt that Indians had certain duties to perform which were actually an honor and ought to be continued. He held that he was only attempting to protect the Indians with reference to these gratuitous

in the *indigenista* legal literature, see: Basadre, *Historia de la república*, 10:4551-52; and Bustamante Cisneros, *Condición jurídica de las comunidades*, pp. 85-86. Francisco Tudela y Varela, *Socialismo peruano: Estudio sobre las comunidades indígenas* (Lima: Imprenta La Industria, 1905).

16. Interview with Dr. don Jorge Basadre, August 16, 1967, Lima, Peru.
17. PDD, Ordinario de 1908, Senadores, August 3, 1908, pp. 31-37.
18. Ibid., p. 35.

services, and not proposing a method for imposing new duties. Senator Capelo pointed out that all free personal services were illegal and had been the basis for four hundred years of abuse on the part of officials and priests. The arguments of Capelo prevailed and the section was rejected.

The law (No. 1183) was approved by Congress and signed by President Augusto B. Leguía in November, 1909. In its final form, it prohibited all government authorities from requiring free services of Indians or peons for either public or private projects and prescribed a penalty of one year in jail for infractions.[19]

That Congress had finally accepted its responsibility to provide protection to the Indian population makes the passage of this law an event of great importance in the development of Indian legislation. But the response to it by advocates of Indian reform has not been completely enthusiastic. Anthropologist Mario Vásquez has objected that such laws did not treat the Indian like any other person with rights to protection of the law, but still as something apart—an Indian.[20] Others attacked the law on the grounds that it solved only part of the problem. Senator Capelo had pointed out during the debate that the law ought to include private individuals, particularly the great landowners who still practiced forms of personal service. *Indigenista* author Magdaleno Chira C., acknowledging the benefits of the new law, commented that perhaps the most serious violation of Indian rights was by the *latifundista,* either through manipulation of existing laws, threats, or overt use of armed force against the lives and property of the Indian.[21] The new law made no mention of overt or covert government acquiescence in the abuses committed on the haciendas or by private companies.

LEGUÍA'S FIRST TERM

Congressional action increased during the presidency of Augusto B. Leguía (1908-12); proposals that had died in the past were now approved. In September, 1909, the Chamber of Deputies exempted several Indian *comunidades* from paying matriculation costs and

19. For the text of this law, see: PMTAI, *Legislación,* pp. 39-40; and José Varallanos, *Legislación indiana republicana: Compilación de leyes, decretos, jurisprudencia judicial, administrativa y demás vigentes sobre el indígena y sus comunidades* (Lima: C.I.P., 1947), pp. 74-75.

20. Vásquez, *Hacienda, peonaje,* p. 37.

21. PDD, Ordinario de 1908, Senadores, August 3, 1908, pp. 33-36; Chira C., *Observaciones,* p. 44.

tuition for the education of their children, because of their low annual income. The Chamber also passed, with no opposition, a resolution calling for the establishment of a special commission to study Indian problems and to draw up a tentative law. The commission was actually named the following day.[22]

This commission was as indifferent and inactive as its predecessors, but, for once, this did not pass unnoticed. In September, 1910, Deputy Francisco Tudela y Varela from Ancash complained that the commission had not met and requested that something be done. The deputies named a new presiding officer and reaffirmed their support of the commission,[23] but nothing more was heard from it.

In 1910, Senator Bezada reintroduced in the Senate a law to establish an Indian trade and agricultural school in the department of Puno which he had proposed before in 1907. Indian children from the ages of six to sixteen would attend the boarding school and study Spanish; military science and physical education; methods to improve agriculture, pastures, and breeding stock; and the trades of pottery making, shoemaking, and weaving. The school was to be financed by the sale of government lands in the department and by appropriations from the national budget.[24]

The proposal sparked a spirited debate which lasted several days. In general, the *indigenista* senators supported the law, but there was much opposition from others. Some charged that separating Indian children from white and mestizo children perpetuated the problems of segregation. Other objections were that there were already sufficient schools in the department and that it was absurd to set up an agricultural school in Puno because of the extreme altitude, which precluded the exercise of normal agricultural activity.[25]

The Senate finally passed the bill in altered form and sent it to the executive branch, where it received little attention. The Chamber of Deputies never dealt with the measure, and so it did not become law. Nevertheless, the pro-*indigenistas* were now on the offensive, and their efforts were soon to prove more fruitful. The old

22. PDD, Ordinario de 1909, Diputados, September 27, 1908, pp. 448-50; and October 5-6, 1909, pp. 522, 535.

23. PDD, Ordinario de 1910, Diputados, September 1, 1910, 1: 165-66, and September 5, 1910, 1:200.

24. PDD, Ordinario de 1910, Senadores, October 7, 1910, pp. 568-69.

25. These debates are found in ibid., pp. 568-78, and ibid., October 12, 1910, pp. 610-25.

arguments of Indian inferiority were still offered, but they were couched in respectable phraseology. Indian schools were created under subsequent administrations and they closely resembled that proposed by Bezada.

Another bill introduced in 1910 by Capelo dealt with the labor system of *enganche* in the coal mines. The system of *enganche* varied slightly in different regions, but basically it permitted an *hacendado* or miné owner (the system was particularly prevalent in mines and on the coastal sugar and cotton plantations) to assure himself of a reliable source of labor. Agents sent to the sierran Indian *comunidades,* usually after the harvest, offered large initial sums to idle Indians and those Indians who were deeply in debt because of crop failure or fiesta expenditures. In return, the Indians signed a labor contract which usually bore no relation to the terms offered orally. The monetary advance was then applied to future wages, as were travel expenses and subsequent food and clothing rations. The result was the Indians found themselves in a state of perpetual debt servitude and were legally prevented from returning home. Capelo's law would have prohibited the use of *enganche* in the mines by stipulating that only those Indians who were paid in money on a daily basis could be employed and that no person could be forced to work in the mines for any reason. Injury and death benefits were to be paid by the mine owners, and violations of the law were to carry stiff fines and up to two years in prison. However, the law did not pass.[26]

This increase in congressional activity was spurred by outside forces which sought to apply pressure and influence the direction of the legislative body. The best-organized and most powerful *indigenista* organization was the Pro-Indian Association founded in 1909 by Pedro S. Zulen. It had as its directors three of the most outstanding *indigenistas* in the country: Zulen, Dora Mayer, and Senator Joaquín Capelo, probably its most powerful and influential member. The nation's press applauded the formation of the group and offered space for its news.[27] *El deber pro-indígena,* a weekly devoted to the work of the association and to Indian problems in general, was published by the association from 1912 to 1917.

As a private body the group was not subject to the official pressures (resulting from pressure exerted by the *hacendados)* that had

26. PDD, Ordinario de 1913, Senadores, August 11, 1913, pp. 67-69.
27. Chang-Rodríguez, *Prada, Mariátequi y Haya,* p. 180.

characterized earlier official and semiofficial organizations. It appointed delegations in all areas of the republic to report abuses committed against the Indian and publicized these injustices in the press and its own publications. Special commissions were sent to investigate uprisings or other disturbances which affected Indians, and a board of lawyers was created to defend without charge all Indians involved in civil and criminal cases. The association began a compilation of all existing Indian legislation (a project never finished) and tried to inform the Indians of their constitutional and legal rights. It promoted public debates as well as publication in its attempt to inform the public and to prod Congress into passing remedial legislation.[28]

Basadre's judgment of the association is that it was like "the voice of the national conscience," but that it was a weak voice which often went unheard and was even derided. Its principal chronicler, Dora Mayer de Zulen, regarded its accomplishments more favorably. She felt that the association succeeded in familiarizing the public with the Indian problem through various publications, and that its pressure on government authorities resulted in a series of laws, decrees, and resolutions aimed at bettering the condition of the Indians and at protecting them against hostile elements. She believed the group also succeeded in partially awakening some Indians to their rights. She regretted that the association never had sufficient funds with which to carry on its work, for she thought that had it lasted ten years instead of seven, it might have done far more toward securing justice for the Indians.[29]

There is no doubt that the association did help to influence government officials. Senator Capelo's untiring support of Indian legislation was a key factor in many Senate debates. He also used his position to denounce public and private abuse of the Indians.[30] Though difficult to prove, it would appear that much of the legislation in the second decade of the twentieth century as well as in the early 1920s was directly or indirectly influenced by this group. The association became a clearing-house for *indigenista* thought and a center for the *indigenista* movement. In this role, it served

28. Dora Mayer de Zulen, *Estudios sociológicos de actualidad* (Callao, Peru: Imprenta Colegio Militar Leoncio Prado, 1950), pp. 101-2.

29. Basadre, *Historia de la república,* 8:3658-59; Mayer de Zulen, *El indígena peruano a los cien años,* pp. 89-95, and *Estudios sociológicos de actualidad,* p. 102.

30. Several of his actions have been cited above. For an example of his attacks on *hacendadoes,* see: Basadre, *Historia de la república,* 8:3660-61.

an important function in the development of a national awareness of the Indians' plight.

Despite a more concerned Congress and the activities of the Pro-Indian Association, the administration of Leguía did not commit itself to furthing the cause of the Indians. One searches in vain for any positive suggestions on the problem in Leguía's annual messages to Congress and other speeches. He was concerned instead with industrialization, economic stabilization, national defense, and international affairs.[31]

The famous scandals of Putumayo illustrate Leguía's failure to regard the Indian problem as a paramount national concern.[32] In 1881, Julio C. Arana, a Peruvian, began to exploit rubber and other jungle products in the Amazon Basin around the Putumayo River. In 1903 he formed the company of Julio C. Arana and Brothers and began to produce rubber on a grand scale. He imported black men from Barbados to work as overseers and laborers and used members of the Huitoto, Bora, Andoque, and Ocainas tribes as the actual rubber gatherers. The job of collecting the rubber was extremely difficult because the rubber trees were scattered over thousands of acres. In 1907, the Peruvian Amazon Company,

31. For an analysis of the objectives of the first Leguía period, see: José Reaño García, *Historia del leguiismo: Sus hombres y sus obras,* ed. Ernesto E. Bacarezo Pinillos (Lima: T. Scheuch, 1928), p. 37.

32. The Putumayo scandals merit a book in themselves. The diplomacy of the incident involved not only the boundary dispute between Peru and Colombia, but also the diplomatic efforts of Great Britain and the United States. The charges and countercharges regarding the alleged massacre of thousands of Huitoto and Bora Indians in the rubber-gathering endeavors are to be found in numerous documentary and secondary sources. The most readily available are: United States Department of State, Serial Files on Peru, National Archives, 823.5048/1—(hereafter cited as D.S., followed by the identification number); W. E. Hardenburg, *The Putumayo, the Devil's Paradise: Travels in the Peruvian Amazon Region and an Account of the Atrocities Committed upon the Indians Therein* (London: Fisher Unwin, 1912); Basadre, *Historia de la república,* 8:3654-58; P. Alberto Gridilla, O.F.M., *Un año en el Putumayo: Resumen de un diario* (Lima: Colección Descalzos, 1943); Hank and Dot Kelley, *Dancing Diplomats* (Albuquerque: University of New Mexico Press, 1950), pp. 203-12; Carlos Larrabure y Correa, *Perú y Colombia en el Putumayo: Réplica a una publicación aparecida, con fecha 27 de mayo de última, en el suplemento sudamericano del Times de Londres* (Barcelona: Imprenta Viuda de Luis Tasso, 1913); Carlos Rey de Castro, *Los escándalos del Putumayo,* 2 vols. (Barcelona, Spain: Imprenta Viuda de Luis Tasso, 1913). There are chon, *En el Putumayo y sus afluentes* (Lima: Imprenta La Industria, 1907); Carlos A. Valcárcel, *El proceso del Putumayo y sus secretos inaúditos* (Lima: Imprenta "Comercial" de Horacio La Rosa & Co., 1915); and Pablo Zumaeta, *Las cuestiones del Putumayo,* 2 vols. (Barcelona: Spain: Imprenta Viuda de Luis Tasso, 1913). There are many other references, but these works constitute a preliminary bibliography.

a British-owned enterprise, began to use Arana's company as their local representatives for rubber gathering.

In September, 1909, in the London magazine *Truth,* W. E. Hardenburg, a United States engineer who had just returned from the region, charged in an article entitled "The Devil's Paradise" that the Indian workers were being exploited, tortured, and killed by the hundreds. The article touched off a storm in England, and in 1910, the British government sent Roger Casement, British consul general at Rio de Janeiro, to check on the veracity of the reports. Casement concluded that the members of the various Indian tribes were indeed slaves of the company and their numbers had been reduced from about fifty thousand to eight thousand through torture and murder. Casement's report was published by the British government. The British sent a list of the charges to the Peruvian government and approached the United States for diplomatic support. When the Peruvians did not act, the British put tremendous diplomatic pressure on them, insisting they take steps immediately to halt the atrocities.[33]

Finally in 1911, the Leguía government, while asserting that it had always enforced the law in that region and would continue to do so regardless of what the British said, set up a judicial district to deal with the charges and to punish the guilty. However, of the 215 persons for whom warrants were issued, only 10 or 12 were captured and tried; the remainder escaped into the jungle or crossed over into Brazil or Colombia.[34]

In all fairness, it should be noted that the region in question was so remote as to be outside the effective administrative sphere of the government. Still, Leguía acted only after the publication of Casement's findings and of a report by the United States consul general at Iquitos, James S. Fuller. It is true that Peru was preoccupied with grave international and national problems, but it is also true that high officials were close to Julio Arana and were hesitant to act against him.[35]

33. For example, see: James Bryce, British Ambassador to Washington, to United States Secretary of State Philander C. Knox, May 8, 1911, D.S. 823.5048/10, and Bryce to Knox, October 16, 1911, D.S. 823.5048/21; and Bryce to Acting Secretary of State Huntington Wilson, February 23, 1912, D.S. 823.5048/29.

34. Augusto B. Leguía, *Mensaje que s.e. el presidente de la república presenta al Congreso Ordinario de 1912* (Lima: Imprenta de "La Acción Popular," 1912), pp. 5-10; Basadre, *Historia de la república,* 8:3657-58.

35. Ibid., 8:3657.

In January, 1911, the Leguía administration issued the only restriction to proceed from the scandals, a supreme resolution which prohibited the use of Peruvian Indians in the *enganche* systems of other countries (referring to Brazil and Colombia) and strictly defining what forms *enganche* could take within the jungles of Peru. The user of such labor had to secure a license and be bonded. He also had to fill out a form for each worker which was to state the circumstances of the *enganche:* the time limit, the salary, the place of origin and destination, and the conditions and rights guaranteed to those under contract. The duration of the contract was not to exceed two years and the men were to be provided with all the necessities of life. Police and local officials were prohibited from contracting such labor, and a strict record of all such contracts was to be maintained by the prefect.[36]

This law sounds as if it were a positive response to the conditions in the Putumayo, but a government which could not enforce or regulate laws that applied to Indians around Lima and the principal cities of the sierra could hardly be expected to enforce laws in the unpopulated jungles of the Amazon. And indeed, despite the Leguía commissions and the continued action of subsequent presidents, the atrocities continued in the Putumayo region.[37] There is not much doubt that the Leguía administration simply could not be bothered with the problem. Under British pressure, it went through the motions, but it was never truly committed to stopping the horror. Further, it should be noted that this resolution made no mention of the *enganche* system either in the mines or on the coastal plantations.

This episode reflects the general attitude of Leguía himself, an attitude which he would again demonstrate in his second term in office. He was a master politician for whom words came easily and it was particularly easy to promise Indian reform and aid. The record shows that such sentiments never progressed beyond words on paper, and the first Leguía period was not characterized by any meaningful government commitment to Indian reform.

36. For the text of the resolution, see: Fernando Luis Chávez León, *Legislación social del Perú: Un estudio de la legislación social peruana, recopilada, comentada, anotada y concordada. Apéndice con las ejecutorias del fuero privativo del trabajo y de los tribunales de justicia* (Lima: Empresa Editorial "Rimac," 1937), pp. 440-41.

37. For continuing government actions, see: Oscar R. Benavides, *Mensaje que s.e. presidente de la república presenta al Congreso Ordinario de 1914* (Lima: Imprenta Americana, 1914), p. 13. An example of charges that the atrocities continued through the decade is: William H. Ramsey to Secretary of State, May 3, 1920, D.S. 823.5048/154.

THE BILLINGHURST INTERLUDE

The years 1912-15 were sterile for Indian legislation. In September, 1912, the brilliant but somewhat unstable Guillermo Billinghurst began his short tenure in the presidency. He embarked upon a program designed to alleviate many of the social ills that existed within the country, but his methods and language frightened many of the old Civilistas and other conservative factions. Although he concentrated on the urban proletariat, Billinghurst did in one instance address himself to rural Indian conditions.

During the first years of the century, the military head of the region around Chucuito, Teodomiro Gutiérrez Cuevas, had taken the part of the Indians in the disturbances, earning for himself the hatred of the landed class. He was transferred, and in 1912, while he was head of the military district around Canas in the department of Cuzco, he went to Lima with a book that he had written containing various complaints from the Indians and accounts of abuses committed against them. He secured an interview with President Billinghurst, who appointed him to head an investigative commission to study Indian problems around Puno. In 1913, several deputies, particularly Bernardino Arias Echenique from Puno, protested that the commission had rejected the position of the *hacendados* out of hand and was inciting rebellion among the Indians. They accused Gutiérrez Cuevas of provoking new race wars in the area and demanded that he be stopped. Billinghurst responded by charging that the *hacendados* and the deputies who represented them were guilty of concealing the facts of Indian oppression and were fighting to maintain their peons in a feudal state.[38]

Nevertheless, Billinghurst did not introduce one single piece of legislation for the Indians, and there was a notable lack of even executive and ministerial orders. The political problems facing the Billinghurst regime may have precluded any positive action on the Indian problem, and perhaps his entrance into this area would have brought his downfall even sooner. At any rate, it is evident that he did not regard helping the Indians as one of his more pressing duties. Meanwhile, in the Congress during his administration, the *indigenistas,* led by Capelo and Bezada, continued their attacks against the economic and social condition of the Indians. Capelo introduced several legislative proposals but none was enacted.

38. For accounts of this mission, see: Jorge Basadre, "Un fragmento de la historia peruana en el siglo xx," in *Visión del Perú en el siglo xx,* ed. Pareja Paz-Soldán, 1:401-2; and Mayer de Zulen, *El indígena peruano a los cien años,* pp. 56-57.

The overthrow of Billinghurst in February, 1914, brought Colonel Oscar R. Benavides to power for a first brief time. Benavides sought to cool the fires fanned by Billinghurst and he moved quite circumspectly. In Indian affairs he tried to ameliorate the manifestations of repression rather than to attack the causes. No new Indian legislation was introduced. Alejandrino Maguiña was appointed to head another commission to investigate an Indian uprising on the hacienda Urcón in the department of Ancash,[39] a move acceptable to the *indigenistas* but which appeared to hold no immediate threat to the landed interests. In dealing with Indian revolts in the departments of Junín, Loreto, and Cuzco, the cessation of hostilities and the maintenance of tranquillity were Benavides's ultimate aims.[40] He succeeded in accomplishing this, but the mere suppression of the manifestations of deep inequities was to result in explosions of violence at a later date, leaving his successor, José Pardo, an extremely dangerous and bitter legacy.

PARDO'S SECOND TERM

Pardo ran unopposed in 1915 and was elected to this, his second term, without incident. With the semblance of unity that such an election provided, Pardo immediately undertook a vast program of social and economic reform in which the Indian was to share. He had hardly taken office when, in October, 1915, the commission headed by Maguiña reported its findings. The uprising at Urcón had been the direct result of the attempts of the hacienda owner to charge the Indians for grazing livestock on their own lands as well as on the lands of the hacienda. The Indians refused to pay and even filed suit challenging the ownership of the lands claimed by the *hacendado*. There were several armed clashes and a number of Indians were charged with criminal acts. Maguiña's report was extremely thorough. It included all the claims and counterclaims, descriptions of the various incidents, and suggestions for the settlement of the affair. He charged that local authorities had aided the *hacendado* or at best refused to take action on Indian complaints.[41]

39. Oscar R. Benavides, *Mensaje que s.e. el presidente de la república excmo. señor General Oscar R. Benavides presenta al Congreso Ordinario de 1915* (Lima: Imprenta Americana, 1915), p. 11.

40. Benavides, *Mensaje de 1914*, pp. 16-17.

41. Basadre, *Historia de la república*, 8:3910-11. I was unable to locate the original Maguiña report on the situation at Urcón, although it did exist, as seen by references to it in the Ministerio de Relaciones Exteriores under Legación Italiana, Anaquel 15, Sección "D," Año 1912-1916, volumen 349.

Scarcely had this report been issued when the Pardo administration was faced with a serious incident. In late 1915, Teodomiro Gutiérrez Cuevas, taking the Quechua name of Rumí-Maqui (hand of steel), led an Indian uprising in Huancané and Azángaro in the historically troublesome department of Puno, organizing bands of Indians to attack various estates. His ultimate goal was the return of vast tracts of land to those he considered to be the rightful owners.[42]

Gutiérrez Cuevas was captured and sent to prison for treason. The charge of treason was based on a letter he had sent to the newspapers in Arequipa in which he stated: "It is necessary to destroy the *gamonales* and ally ourselves with Bolivia in order to form the most powerful, richest, noblest, and most Christian alliance in America."[43] The charge of treason was questioned by one deputy who asserted in October, 1916, that Gutiérrez Cuevas's only crime was to try to better the horrible condition of the Indians around Puno and that accusations against him of seeking to restore the old Inca Empire and of proposing the cession of land to Bolivia were contrived by powerful landowners to hide the realities of their crimes and to gain the sympathy of the authorities.[44]

As a result of this revolt and of the report by Maguiña, Pardo asked Congress for the power to name special traveling judges to deal with land disputes between the Indian *comunidades* and the haciendas and to hear Indian complaints of all kinds.[45] In the Congress itself there were calls for a coordinated body of Indian legislation to treat all facets of the problem, including land tenure and title, facilities for inscribing small parcels of land in the local register, protection of Indian personal property, and a fixed system for dealing with the legal problems arising from land ownership. Most of the proposals were defeated in Congress. The opposition utilized a myriad of arguments, but the most common was that the legislation was unconstitutional because it treated the Indian as a special person in the eyes of the law. Another contention was that the proposed laws would in reality harm the Indians more than they helped them.[46]

42. Basadre, *Historia de la república,* 8:3909-10.
43. PDD, Ordinario de 1923, Senadores, August 24, 1923, p. 218.
44. Quoted in Basadre, *Historia de la república,* 8:3910.
45. José Pardo, *Mensaje presentado al Congreso Ordinario de 1916 por el presidente de la república* (Lima: Imprenta del Estado, 1916), p. xiv.
46. For one such proposal by Severiano Bezada and the opposition to it, see: PDD, Ordinario de 1916, Senadores, September 9, 1916, pp. 333-41.

One proposal which was not defeated became Law No. 2285, signed October 13, 1916. It had originally been introduced in 1910 by Capelo, who took advantage of the liberal climate produced by the Billinghurst administration to reintroduce it in August, 1913. The proposal provided that no Indian could be forced to work in any agricultural or industrial capacity if his wages were not paid in money. The minimum amount was set at ten centavos per day, over and above any use of lands for grazing stock or growing crops. The Indians and their families would be able to move with all their stock and personal belongings anytime they so desired unless there was a contract, and contracts would be limited to one year. In the event of legal complaint against Indians by a landowner, the Indian was to be regarded as a minor and therefore entitled to legal aid from state authorities.

Under the proposal, all lands that had been taken from individual Indians or from Indian *comunidades* were to be subject to expropriation by the state and would be returned to the Indians that resided on them. This process was obligatory even if the original transfer had been accomplished through legal means. The Indians were to pay for the lands over a period of fifty years, but at no time could they lose them for debt. A special state bank was to be established to fund the expropriation and distribution of the lands.

A lengthy debate ensued. The Agriculture Committee of the Senate had reported favorably on the bill, but moved to exclude those provisions regarding the expropriation of lands and the creation of the special bank. The committee argued that those provisions would probably be impossible to enforce, but if they were enforceable they would upset the entire economic balance of the country.[47]

Several senators attacked the proposed law. Senator José Otero from Junín held that in a democratic country no one group could be treated preferentially under the law, so the measure was unconstitutional. He contended that the most important sections of the bill were those dealing with the expropriation of lands and the creation of the special bank, which should be made the nucleus of the law and applicable to all persons in the nation regardless of race.

47. For the text of the proposed law and the committee recommendations, see: PDD, Ordinario de 1913, Senadores, August 7, 1913, pp. 40-41.

Others argued that all labor was already paid, payment in kind being just as acceptable as payment in money. The section providing that the *fiscal* (district attorney) represent all Indians in suits was attacked on grounds that most Indians were already guaranteed protection under the poverty law which provided legal counsel for the indigent. The bill also met opposition on the grounds that it attempted to treat a problem which was more regional than national. Senator Leoncio Samanez from Apurímac held that since in his department all persons were paid in currency and not in kind, the proposed law applied only to certain areas.[48]

At the suggestion of a number of senators, the proposal was returned to several committees for further study. Although this procedure had often resulted in the death of a bill, it was finally reported back to the Senate in 1916. In the debate which followed on August 10, many senators used the same arguments they had used in 1913, but by now there were more who felt that special Indian legislation was needed as well as strong administrative support from José Pardo, and the law passed with a few minor alterations.[49]

In its final form, the law provided that each worker was to receive a minimum daily wage of twenty centavos apart from any concessions of land for crops or grazing. If food or other items were distributed by the owner, their total value could not exceed the total weekly earnings of the laborer, a provision which was an attempt to prevent further cases of debt peonage. Employees who worked on an hacienda that did not pay wages on a daily basis could leave at any time with their animals and personal belongings.

In cases where there existed a formal contract, it was valid for one year only, at the end of which the Indian could leave. In cases of debt, the landowner could not seize the animals or personal belongings of the Indian or force him to work off the debt. The Indians could never be forced to work in any agricultural or industrial enterprise against their will. In the event that a landowner filed suit against an Indian, the *fiscal* was required to aid the Indian.[50]

48. For the text of these debates, see: ibid., pp. 45-57.
49. PDD, Ordinario de 1916, Senadores, August 4, 1916, pp. 51-52, and August 10, 1916, pp. 85-91. See also: Pike, *Modern History of Peru,* pp. 210-11.
50. For text of the law, see: PDD, Ordinario de 1916, Senadores, October 10, 1916, p. 565. Reprinted in PMTAI, *Legislación,* pp. 132-34.

The law was one of the most important pieces of Indian legislation in the twentieth century. With it Congress made an attempt to guarantee the Indians proper payment for their labor and to end the practice of paying wages with useless and overpriced items instead of cash. It also sought to outlaw debt peonage on haciendas and to assure the Indians proper legal protection. Those sections dealing with monetary wages and with the prohibition against employing Indians against their will were lifted almost verbatim from Simón Bolívar's first decree of July 4, 1825. Almost one hundred years had passed, but the government was still trying to enforce basic legislation by reenacting it. No better evidence of government negligence and corruption exists.

Some attacked the law as being too little too late, asserting that twenty centavos could hardly be considered a living wage anywhere in the country,[51] but the fact remains that it was a good law, one which could have had far-reaching implications for the economic and social life of the Indians had it ever been enforced. But the landowners and the local government officials refused to obey it, and the executive branch of the government had neither the desire nor the power to make the law a reality.[52]

Exactly one year later, Congress approved Law No. 2472, which created near Puno a model agricultural and dairy farm for the study of improved crop production and betterment of dairy and stock breeding. The new law funded the school by imposing a tax of fifty centavos on every one hundred kilos of wool exported from the department. It made no mention of Indians, nor was the school specifically designed to aid Indians. Nevertheless, the mere approval of such a program represented a small victory for the *indigenistas*, as it was understood that the principal beneficiaries of this legislation would be Indians.[53]

Congress in this period also moved to assume a larger role in research and planning in regard to the Indian question. In 1913, Deputy Augusto Bedoya from Junín introduced legislation which authorized the appointment of regional commissions to study the economic, social, political, and legal condition of the Indian population. The commissioners were to be familiar with Indian culture and problems and conversant with the Indian language of their

51. Chira C., *Observaciones*, pp. 44-45.
52. See: Cornejo, *Visión objectiva*, pp. 88-89; and de la Barra, *El indio peruano*, pp. 153-54.
53. PMTAI, *Legislación*, p. 215.

region. After completing their studies, they were to report directly to the president and to the Congress regarding the true state of the Indians, offering suggestions for remedial legislation.[54] The proposal was reintroduced in August, 1918. The Chamber of Deputies approved the bill over the objections of a deputy who held there was no provision for payment of these commissions. The following day the law was amended to provide fifty thousand *soles* to defray the costs.[55] Although this did not represent a giant step forward, it did demonstrate a realization that something had to be done for the Indians in a systematic and orderly manner.

In December, 1918, the Congress approved Law No. 3019, which obliged all industries and haciendas with more than fifty employees located farther than one kilometer from the nearest town to construct houses for the employees and their families, schools for their children, and a first aid station. A resident doctor was required for businesses that employed over three hundred persons or were more than ten kilometers from the nearest town.[56] Although the Indians were not specifically mentioned in the law, it would have had a tremendous impact on their living conditions had it been enforced. Once again, however, such laws rarely if ever affected any of the large estates in the sierra where the majority of the Indians lived and worked. The enforcement procedures were too weak, if they existed at all.

While there had been considerable activity in Congress concerning the Indians during the first decade and a half of the century, executive support or concern had been notably absent. The second term of José Pardo proved to be different. Not only did he actively promote legislative proposals, but he himself moved into the realm of such social legislation in a positive manner. One of the most important administrative decisions since the Independence period came in December, 1917. From the days of Bolívar and San Martín, Peruvian law and Peruvian governments had treated the Indian *comunidad* as a loosely defined group of individuals rather than a legal entity. All the legislation in the nineteenth and early twentieth centuries dealt with individual Indians. As noted in an earlier chapter, this approach had provided the basis for land ag-

---

54. PDD, Ordinario de 1918, Diputados, August 16, 1918, pp. 146-47.

55. PDD, Ordinario de 1913, Diputados, September 17, 1913, p. 345.

56. See: Rodríguez Pastor, "Derecho peruano," p. 373; and Roberto Mac-Lean Estenós, *Sociología del Perú* (Mexico, D.F.: Universidad Nacional Autónoma de México, Instituto de Investigaciones Sociales, 1959), pp. 285-86.

grandizements on the part of the *hacendados.* Pardo did not reverse this process of land acquisition at the expense of the Indians, but he did provide the basis for subsequent legislation that would indeed overturn past practices.

The occasion was a land dispute between the *comunidad* of Tusi in the department of Huánuco and the Huánuco Department of Public Welfare. The Supreme Court held that the Indian *comunidades* ought to be represented in all suits by their own agents and that the municipality lacked the authority to appoint agents or lawyers for them. One justice's opinion asserted that the old Inca and Spanish customs and laws regarding legal recognition of the *comunidad* could not be considered to have expired simply because they had not been enforced. Thus, the Indian *comunidad* was reestablished as a legal entity that had the power to appoint its own representatives.[57]

Published simultaneously with the Supreme Court decision was a supreme resolution which assumed the same legal posture. Pardo followed it on May 10, 1918, with a circular ordering prefects to lend all assistance necessary to the Indian *comunidades* to guarantee them the justice to which they were entitled. He noted that riots and uprisings had resulted from oppression of the Indians and their continued state of vassalage on the haciendas.[58] These events laid the groundwork for the definition of the juridical status of the *comunidad* in more precise terms in the Constitution of 1920.

In further administrative action, Pardo issued a supreme decree on January 15, 1919, establishing the eight-hour day for all state-owned factories and agricultural estates. The decree also provided that all privately owned businesses had to reach agreement on the workday through consultation with their employees. In the event that such agreement could not be attainted, Congress was authorized to fix it at eight hours.[59] This decree formed a part of Pardo's overall social reform program and there was no mention of Indians, but it would have constituted a gain for the Indians had the arm of national law reached into the sierra. Nevertheless, the law was on the books, and it would be enforced at a later date.

57. See: Ejecutoria Suprema, 6 dic. 1917, in *Anales Judiciales,* (enero-marzo, 1918), p. 19. Reprinted in Varallanos, *Legislación indiana,* p. 5. See also: Bustamante Cisneros, *Condición jurídica de las comunidades,* pp. 78-81.

58. Bustamante Cisneros, *Condición jurídica de las comunidades,* pp. 102-5.

59. PMTAI, *Legislación,* pp. 136-37.

Though the first twenty years of the century included the concerned work of such elected officials as Capelo, Bezada, and, to a lesser degree, Pardo, the general attitude toward the Indians remained one of disinterest and even hostility. The outburst of social legislation in the second decade focused but little on the Indians. The basic premises and programs and attitudes of the nineteenth century remained to plague the twentieth. There were some beginnings in serious academic studies on the Indians, but on the whole intellectuals concerned themselves with other problems.[60] The Pro-Indian Association was an important institution in the development of a national Indian policy, but its effect on the total society was minimal. The great push for integration of the Indians would have to await the second administration of Augusto B. Leguía.

60. For example of the scholarly attention, see: Bustamante Cisneros, *Condición jurídica de las comunidades;* Félix Cossio, *La propiedad colectiva del ayllu* (Cuzco: Imprenta "El Trabajo," 1915); José Antonio Encinas, *Causas de la criminalidad indígena en el Perú: Ensayo de psicología experimental* (Lima: E. E. Villarán, 1919); and idem, *Contribución a una legislación tutelar indígena* (Lima: C. F. Southwell, 1918).

4

The Oncenio *of Augusto B. Leguía*

The second inauguration of Augusto B. Leguía was a major turning point in Peruvian history. Throughout his eleven-year rule (the *oncenio*), Leguía sought to revolutionize Peruvian society, albeit to enhance his own political power, and he enjoyed considerable superficial success in so doing.

From the 1870s to the 1920s, Peru had had a system of political parties. To be sure, they were not as easily categorized as the parties of other nations, but they were, nevertheless, political parties which continued in existence from one president to another. These parties —the Civilista, the Liberal, and the Constitutionalist—still existed in 1919. The old Democratic party of Nicolás de Piérola was badly splintered, but it too still functioned as a political entity.

Leguía had been a Civilista and had been elected on the Civilista ticket in 1908. He was never comfortable in Civilista ranks, however, and in 1918 he eschewed their support and sought instead to develop a new political base. During the *oncenio,* he sought to destroy politically the old socioeconomic class that had ruled Peru for forty years. He systematically suppressed the old political parties, particularly the Civilistas, while seeking the support of the rising middle class in rural and urban regions.

One study of Leguía demonstrates that he represented and reflected the aspirations of the middle class which had been kept small and powerless by the Civilista policy of inhibiting bureaucratic expansion and giving low priority to public works projects and to education. The economic progress of the 1920s, while not resulting in the complete displacement of the old oligarchy eco-

nomically, did provide for the expansion of the bureaucratic structure. As banks, insurance companies, and other businesses multi-
plied, unfamiliar names appeared on boards of directors and a new
monied class arose which, through its exercise of bureaucratic functions, began to gain economic and political power.[1]

Since middle sectors are heterogeneous groups,[2] much of Leguía's
administration was devoted to broadening his base of support
among the new groups while at the same time avoiding an open
rebellion among the old political forces. He also sought to counter
the appeal of the socialists and communists by calling for a sweeping social reform program.

Leguía was an astute politician who used issues and events to
further his own political career, and this was nowhere more evident than in his treatment of Indian integration, a key demand of
socialists, communists, liberals, and other reformers in the society.
Upon taking office, Leguía launched the most extensive program
of Indian legislation ever attempted in Peru. The term 1919-24
produced a volume of laws, decrees, and resolutions which ex-
ceeded that of the preceding one hundred years.

Leguía was elected president in 1919, but before the legal transfer
of power could occur, he led a coup which displaced President
Pardo. Leguía and his supporters asserted that Pardo was plotting
to reverse the popular mandate, but his real objective was to dis-
solve the newly elected Congress and with new elections ensure
the installation of a friendly body which would bend to executive
pressure.[3]

THE FIRST TERM, 1919-24

The new president's first important act was to call the election
of a National Assembly empowered to draft a new constitution.
The document that emerged in 1920 contained many important
provisions, and two of the most important dealt with Indians and
Indian *comunidades*. It represented a major departure from the
post-Independence legal philosophy which had denied the Indian

---

1. Howard L. Karno, "Augusto B. Leguía: The Oligarchy and the Modernization
of Peru, 1870-1930" (Ph.D. diss., University of California at Los Angeles, 1970), pp.
216, 258.

2. For one analysis of middle sectors, see: John J. Johnson, *Political Change in
Latin America: The Emergence of the Middle Sectors* (Stanford, Calif.: Stanford University Press, 1958).

3. Pike, *Modern History of Peru,* pp. 214-15.

comunidad recognition as a legal entity and prevented the enactment of protective legislation applicable only to the Indian race.
Article 41 stated that the lands of the state, of public institutions,
and of Indian *comunidades* were imprescriptible and could only
be transferred by means established by law. Article 58 read, "The
state will protect the Indian race and will dictate special laws for
its development and culture in keeping with its needs. The nation
recognizes the legal existence of the Indian *comunidades* and the
law will decide the rights that pertain to them."[4]

Surprisingly, there was very little debate on these articles. Members of the Assembly supported them to a man. The president of
the Constitutional Commission, eminent sociologist Javier Prado,
whose earlier opinions concerning racial inferiority made him anything but an *indigenista,* pointed to centuries of abuse to justify
the obligation of the state to protect and aid the Indians. He felt
that legal recognition of the *comunidades* would protect them against
land theft. He also called for schools to educate the Indians and
for a series of laws which would assist and protect the race. Prado
saw as the goal of the new legislation the rehabilitation of the Indians and their elevation to the high position they had held in pre-
Columbian Peru.[5]

Several delegates contended that these two articles were the most
important in the constitution; others noted that they merely provided constitutional recognition for an actuality already accepted
by the Supreme Court. But they all hoped the articles would provide a solid base for future Indian laws. Aníbal Maúrtua from
Huánuco felt Article 58 was so important that he demanded its
approval by acclamation.[6] Mariano H. Cornejo, president of the
Assembly, praised the articles concerning the Indians, but cautioned
against the development of a stifling bureaucracy in their implementation and called for aid to Indians rather than control of Indians. Leguía made special reference to these articles when he
signed the new constitution.[7]

4. PMTAI, *Legislación,* p. 40.
5. Sivirichi, *Derecho indígena,* pp. 103-4.
6. For discussions of the debates, see: ibid., pp. 103-5; Pareja Paz-Soldán, ed., *Las constituciones del Peru,* pp. 282-90, and José Pareja Paz-Soldán, *Derecho constitucional peruano,* 4th ed., enlarged (Lima: Ediciones Librería Studium, 1966), pp. 152-57.
7. República del Perú, *Asamblea Nacional de 1919: Discursos oficiales pronunciados en las sesiones de instalación y juramento, por el presidente de la república sr. d. Augusto*

Most intellectuals in the first years of the twentieth century had demonstrated little concern for the Indians, being more concerned with urban labor and industrial reforms. Now scholars attacked the problem with vigor. Articles and pamphlets appeared regularly and increased attention was devoted to Indian legislation. Entire civil and criminal codes were written and presented to various official bodies. In 1919, José Luis Abarca Arias presented a thesis to the Universidad del Gran Padre San Agustín de Arequipa in which he proposed a series of laws in 13 sections and 134 articles encompassing every aspect of Indian life. Deputy José Antonio Encinas from Puno, who prepared a comprehensive Indian code, argued that the abysmal state of the Indian was due to the lack of proper legislation.[8]

Three additional codes were proposed in 1920. Manuel A. Quiroga, deputy from Chucuito, offered a series of civil laws for the Indians; José M. Araníbar won a Bar Association contest with a code that dealt with both civil and criminal aspects of Indian law; and Manuel Yarlequé published a work which explored ways to protect the Indians and favor their advancement. The most extensive and comprehensive proposal for a code was put forth in 1921 by Atilio Sivirichi. It comprised 1,743 articles covering all facets of the Indian relationship with the state, containing sections on civil, criminal, economic, educational, and administrative legislation.[9]

Another section of the 1920 constitution, Article 140, attempted to counteract the extreme centralism which had characterized Peruvian politics by creating three regional congresses in the South, the center, and the North. They were to meet one month per year and were to send their resolutions to the executive branch for imple-

B. Leguía y por el presidente de la Asamblea Dr. D. Mariano H. Cornejo (Lima: Imprenta Torres Aguirre, 1919), pp. 16, 94.

8. José Luis Abarca Arias, *Proyecto de ley tutelar de la raza indígena* (Arequipa: n.p., 1919); and Encinas, *Contribución a una legislación*.

9. Manuel A. Quiroga, *Proyecto de legislación indígena, presentado por el diputado por la provincia de Chucuito, al Congreso Regional del Sur, 1920* (Arequipa: n.p., 1920); José M. Araníbar, "Ley tutelar del indígena," *La crónica de Lima*, August 28, 1920; Manuel Yarlequé, *La raza indígena: Artículos y documentos interesantes. Las comunidades indígenas implorando el amparo y protección de Wilson* (Lima: Sanmarti y Cía Impresores, 1920); and Sivirichi, *Derecho indígena*, pp. 171-550. For further treatment of the new intellectual attitude, see: Cesáreo Vidalón Menéndez, *El problema indígena: Breve estudio histórico-sociológico-legal de la materia* (Lima: Imprenta Peruana de E. Z. Casanova, 1920), pp. 6, 21-24.

mentation.[10] The attempt to divide the country along east-west lines was artificial and the congresses quickly became ineffective bureaucratic centers. Indeed, centralism increased during the Leguía period.[11] Nevertheless, the congresses did pass several Indian laws which were incorporated into the national legal structure.

In 1921, Leguía signed a law passed by the Central Regional Congress abolishing the office of *alcalde de vara,* or *comunidad* mayor. This was the nonpaying position for the direction of certain fiestas, the holder of which had to defray all costs incurred during the fiesta, thereby impoverishing himself and his family for years. In October, 1922, Leguía signed a law from the Southern Regional Congress prohibiting the use of free Indian labor by civil, military, or ecclesiastical authorities. These two laws represented a genuine advance by outlawing practices abusive of Indian rights, but the Leguía administration was remiss in not using the opportunity to extend the prohibitions to all of Peru, since the practices were not limited to the regions covered by the laws.[12]

Another regional law, No. 27 of February 7, 1920, established an experimental agricultural school in the Department of Cuzco to foster improved agricultural practices and production. Indians were not mentioned in the law, but they might have benefited from classes in stock breeding and crop production. However, when the school was organized, the Indians neither attended nor benefited from it.[13]

Soon after the Congress completed its constitutional work, it began regular deliberations. In the first months of 1920 José Antonio Encinas introduced a law in the Chamber of Deputies to establish a Bureau of Indian Protection in the Ministry of Justice, Religion, and Education, but it did not pass. He also called for the creation

10. For the text of the article and of Law 4504 creating operating procedures, see: Guillermo U. Olaechea, *La constitución del Perú dada por la Asamblea Nacional de 1919: Comentada, anotada y concordada con las leyes plebiscitarlas y decretos que tienen fuerza de ley. Leyes orgánicas, decretos, reglamentos y resoluciones referentes a ellas hasta 1922* (Lima: Imprenta Americana, 1922), pp. cxi, 589-94.

11. See: Basadre, *Perú, problema y posibilidad,* p. 216; and Richard N. Adams, *A Community in the Andes: Problems and Progress in Muquiyauyo* (Seattle: University of Washington Press, 1959), p. 43.

12. Varallanos, *Legislación indiana,* pp. 76-77; Mariano N. Echegaray and Ramón Silva S., *Legislación del trabajo y previsión social: Leyes, decretos y resoluciones concernientes al capital y el trabajo. Disposiciones que favorecen al obrero, la mujer, y el niño. Ley del empleado. Disposiciones que favorecen a los indígenas* (Lima: Imprenta Torres Aguirre, 1925), pp. 222-23; and Chira C., *Observaciones,* pp. 45-46.

13. For the text of the law, see: PMTAI, *Legislación,* p. 216.

of special commissions to study the Indian problem and to formulate an Indian code.[14]

For purely political reasons, Leguía accepted the latter suggestion, hoping that thereby he could retain liberal support without alienating large landowners. By supreme decree of June 19, 1920, he named a commission composed of Encinas; Erasmo Roca, an official in the Ministry of Development and a leading *indigenista;* Enrique Rubín, a former president of the Superior Court of the district of Ancash; and Humberto Luna, a Cuzco lawyer and professor. The commission was asked to investigate Indian complaints in the South, particularly in the department of Puno, and to prepare a report suggesting possible remedies.[15]

Leguía said that he expected the commission to propose "efficient methods for arriving at the desired goal in the shortest time possible."[16] However, when many Indians presented complaints and the great landowners became alarmed, the president bowed to *hacendado* pressure and recalled the commission. Without executive support the commission's report and proposed law received no attention in the Congress.[17]

In September, 1922, Deputy Maúrtua, feeling that the executive had shirked its duty, called for another commission, to be named and controlled by Congress, to study conditions in the South and suggest new legislation.[18] The proposal touched off a lengthy debate. Two of the most influential *indigenistas,* Deputies Manuél S. Frisancho from Cuzco and Encinas, argued that further investigative commissions with no power to act would only provoke false hopes among the Indians and called instead for a comprehensive Indian code. On the other hand, some deputies used racist arguments and scare tactics to oppose the measure. One asserted that various pro-Indian committees and commissions were inciting the Indians to riot and served no useful purpose because there was no

14. PDD, Ordinario de 1919, Diputados, March 2, 1920, p. 509, and March 18, 1920, pp. 756-57.

15. Mayer de Zulen, *El indígena peruano a los cien años,* pp. 57-58; and Pike, *Modern History of Peru,* p. 222.

16. *La evolución del Perú en el quinquenio, 1919-1924* (Lima: Talleres Tipográficos de La Prensa, 1924), p. 141.

17. Basadre, *Historia de la república,* 9:4189. For an example of *hacendado* pressure, see: Liga de Hacendados, Arequipa, *Memorial relativo a la cuestión indígena que la Liga de Hacendados eleva al supremo gobierno, aprobado por su comité ejecutivo en sesión de 15 de mayo de 1922 y sancionado por la asamblea general de 10 de junio del mismo año* (Arequipa: Tip. S. Quiroz, 1922).

18. PDD, Ordinario de 1922, Diputados, September 27, 1922, p. 331.

racial distinction in Peru. Deputy Dámaso Vidalón from Huancavelica stated that past Indian commissions had been purveyors of violence, and he charged that Indians were rejecting humility and demanding the same economic and social advantages enjoyed by other classes. Others were more subtle. Deputy Segundo Salcedo from Puno held that unethical lawyers exploited commissioners by presenting fabricated complaints in order to cheat Indians in subsequent court cases. He called for an end to all Indian commissions.[19]

Finally the opposition was successful. Deputy Frisancho moved to establish a permanent tribunal, composed of representatives from the three branches of government, to review all land titles in the southern departments, and Maúrtua withdrew his motion.[20] Supporting substitute measures was a favorite ploy of opponents of Indian legislation; the delays involved allowed them to rally additional opposition, and such was to be the case with Frisancho's motion.

The Frisancho plan proposed that Indian *comunidad* lands acquired since 1893 be returned to the *comunidad* or purchased by the *comunidad* at a just price. It provided for the creation of a tribunal, composed of two Supreme Court justices from Puno and Cuzco, one senator, one deputy, and a lawyer named by the executive, to treat all questions regarding *comunidad* lands and to resolve conflicts between owners and workers. They were to pay particular attention to conflicts over wages, hours, work location, and the Indians' freedom to market their own commodities. Although its offices were to be in Puno and Cuzco, the tribunal was to be mobile if the situation required. It was to maintain a register of all Indian *comunidades* and to send copies of complaints submitted to it to the Supreme Court, the Ministry of Justice, and the Congress. Deputy Miguel F. Gutiérrez from Apurímac proposed an amendment that the tribunal also deal with cases of forced labor, illegal fines, and free services required by landowners.[21]

Deputy Emilio Sayán Palacios from Lima attacked the measure on the grounds that it was local legislation, that the legislative branch was yielding power to the executive because of the composition of the tribunal, and that it would be impossible for the

19. Ibid., September 28, 1922, pp. 351-55; September 30, 1922, pp. 390-95; October 3, 1922, pp. 409-12; and October 4, 1922, pp. 427-29.

20. Ibid., October 5, 1922, pp. 441-46.

21. PDD, Extraordinario de 1922, Diputados, February 9, 1923, pp. 257-65.

tribunal to fulfill its overly complex duties. But the most devastating charges came from Deputy Luis F. Luna from Puno, who
argued that the law undermined the very foundation of the nation
by questioning the institution of private property. By undercutting
historic rights to property, the law would plunge Peru into economic and constitutional chaos. Moreover, it was retroactive and
provided special treatment for the Indians, both of which Luna
held to be unconstitutional. He accused the sponsors of the bill of
wanting to restore the Inca Empire and pointed to similar legislation in Mexico, Argentina, and Russia as examples of what could
happen in Peru. He also raised the old specter of racial war, one
of the more damaging legacies of the 1780 rebellion of Tupac Amaru
II. According to Luna, who called the Indians cannibals, the law
would lead to massive Indian revolts accompanied by massacres
of the white population. He demanded the measure be returned
to committee.

Frisancho countered that the law was constitutional because it
guaranteed justice to both Indians and landowners. Charging that
only persons guilty of land fraud were frightened of the law, he
held that Indian riots would occur only if the Congress refused to
act. Encinas argued that land has a social value and called Luna's
definition of property rights anachronistic. When he attacked Luna
personally, accusing him of being an old feudal landholder, the
debate dissolved into a shouting match.

This exchange is indicative of the tenor of the Leguía congresses.
The proposal was not brought to a final vote and the deputies
turned their attention to what they deemed more pressing matters.
Some vocal *indigenistas* were present, but they failed to muster the
necessary votes to pass this key legislation.[22] The lack of executive
interest in congressional action did not help; Leguía had again
adopted the delicate position of trying to maintain *indigenista* and
liberal support without incurring the wrath of conservative landowners by pushing too hard.

Meanwhile, the president did issue decrees affecting the Indians.
By supreme decree of March 4, 1920, the executive ordered all disputes between *yanaconas* and property owners submitted to bind-
ing arbitration. The decree attempted to provide the *yanaconas*
with written legal protection in their wage disputes, but it was unsuccessful because the *hacendados* could continue to charge high
prices for the goods bought by the *yanaconas* and to pay low prices

22. Ibid., February 15, 1923, pp. 280-91.

for the products they sold.[23] Criticism of the decree led to a supreme resolution on August 29 which regulated crop prices. The price paid by the *hacendado* was to be set at the beginning of the season by representatives of the two parties,[24] and in the event of conflict, the dispute was to be submitted to arbitration. The law was never enforced, however. At this time the government also issued a decree which regulated all labor disputes, but by failing to mention the Indians specifically, it failed to help them because the conditions of their employment demanded specific corrections.[25]

Leguía tried to appear as a leading *indigenista*. He even styled himself *Viracocha* after a white Inca god. In his 1921 message to Congress, he stated that special Indian legislation was indispensable, especially specific laws which would protect Indian property,[26] and on September 12, 1921, he issued a supreme decree creating a Bureau of Indian Affairs in the Ministry of Development. The bureau was to investigate and study the Indian situation, maintain vigilance of all Indian laws, attend to Indian complaints, and propose methods for relieving Indian oppression. It was to name special commissions to handle situations in diverse regions of the country and to provide liaison between local officials and the central government. All Indian complaints were to be presented directly to the bureau; matters falling within the jurisdiction of other ministries would be carried to the appropriate ministry by representatives of the bureau to ensure prompt settlement.[27]

The establishment of the Bureau of Indian Affairs was a response to a century-long need for a government agency that would confine itself to Indian problems. Indians who went to Lima had no idea of where to take their complaints. There existed no central clearinghouse and no ministry had sufficient staff or interest to tackle Indian problems. However, the bureau did not turn out to be an effective instrument for handling Indian problems. The Indians still had to travel to Lima, which imposed hardships of trav-

23. Chávez León, *Legislación social,* pp. 342-43. See also: Mac-Lean Estenós, *Indios de América,* pp. 309-11.

24. Chávez León, *Legislación social,* pp. 341-42; and Rodríguez Pastor, "Derecho peruano," p. 373.

25. For the text of the decree, see: PMTAI, *Legislación,* pp. 98-101. For a critique, see: Chira C., *Observaciones,* p. 54.

26. Augusto B. Leguía, *Mensaje presentado al Congreso Ordinario de 1921 por el presidente de la república sr. Augusto B. Leguía* (Lima: C. F. Southwell, 1921), p. 9.

27. PMTAI, *Legislación,* pp. 41-44; and Olaechea, *La constitución,* pp. 386-89.

el and costs of staying in the capital, and thus meant that many complaints went unheard. The proviso for the collection of data was never obeyed. Statistical information was spotty and local officials refused to cooperate in supplying it. Special commissions were never named and representatives were rarely sent to investigate Indian uprisings. Without files or commissions, the bureau also failed in its duty to enforce existing legislation. Its contact with Indians was limited to those who came to Lima; it had little concept of events or practices in the provinces.[28]

Indians were often forced to remain in Lima for months, and matters which fell within the jurisdiction of other ministries almost never passed out of the bureau. No records were kept of previous infractions and the bureau made no attempt to formulate new Indian legislation or write an Indian code. The bureau was understaffed and overburdened, it lacked the interest and energy necessary to fulfill its duties, and it received no support from either the Congress or the executive. Leguía often praised the agency, but he left it to its own devices, thereby destroying its chances for success.[29]

THE PATRONATO DE LA RAZA INDÍGENA

Leguía's flair for the spectacular led him to initiate many grandiose projects and establish agencies that accomplished very little. One such institution, introduced with great fanfare, was the Patronato de la Raza Indígena (Guardianship of the Indian Race). Created by supreme decree on May 29, 1922, the Patronato was supposed to provide protection for the Indians and to better their social, political, and economic state. There was a central Patronato, named by the president and headed by the archbishop of Lima, and departmental and provincial Patronatos named by the Ministry of Development.[30]

Accompanying the decree was a lengthy proposal defining the duties and organization of the Patronato. It was to investigate all Indian complaints, to study the causes of unrest and the system of Indian wages, and to enforce all existing Indian legislation, suggesting new laws where needed. In addition, it was to aid Indian education, to end Indian alcoholism, and to instill in the Indians a

---

28. Cornejo, *Visión objetiva*, p. 162.
29. For more about this agency, see: Chira C., *Observaciones*, pp. 46-50. See also: Augusto B. Leguía, *Mensaje presentado al Congreso Ordinario de 1924 por el presidente de la república* (Lima: Imprenta "Garcilaso," 1924), p. 67.
30. PMTAI, *Legislación*, pp. 44-45.

sense of duty and a spirit of hard work.[31] However, the Leguía administration never introduced the proposal in Congress, so the decree lacked the force of a congressional law.

Cuzco senator Miguel González moved to rectify the omission somewhat in October, 1922, by introducing a bill creating a departmental Patronato in Cuzco to deal with problems of Indian wages, the sale of Indian products, and land disputes. To be a member of the Patronato a man had to speak Quechua and could not be an *hacendado*. The agency's proceedings were to be conducted without lawyers to avoid lengthy and costly legalism. The minimum wage for Indians was to be set at between thirty and one-hundred centavos per seven-hour day, depending in part upon whether the worker was literate. Goods sold to or bought from the *hacendado* were to be priced within a certain percentage of the market price. The Legislative Committee of the Senate praised the bill, but suggested that it be expanded to include the entire nation to avoid charges of its being local legislation.[32]

Debate in the Senate began in August, 1923, and continued throughout the month. The proposal met early opposition, led by Senator José M. García from San Martín, who objected to the name *Patronato* because it suggested that a separate government agency was being established. This was contrary to Article 58 of the constitution, which granted Congress the authority to pass laws that aided the Indians but did not empower it to create new organizations. Senator Francisco Alvariño from Junín agreed and compared the Patronato to previous unsuccessful commissions, calling it more fanciful than realistic. Senator Pablo de Latorre from Cuzco maintained that the Patronato would serve no purpose because the proposal made no mention of education, that the Senate was wasting its time since what the nation needed was thousands of new schools.

Supporters of the measure, led by Senators Miguel Domingo González from Cuzco and Lauro A. Curletti from Huánuco, replied that the Patronato and education were distinct subjects and should not be confused. They further asserted that the creation of the Patronato did not conflict with the constitution and refused to alter the name. Opponents then shifted their attack to the provision that all members of the Patronato had to speak Quechua or

31. República Peruana, *Reglamento del patronato de la raza indígena* (Lima: Imprenta Americana, 1922), pp. 7-21.

32. PDD, Ordinario de 1923, Senadores, August 8, 1923, pp. 78-82.

Aymara. When several senators charged that this requirement was absurd, as many Indians in Peru, particularly in the jungle regions, spoke neither Quechua nor Aymara, the *indigenistas* changed the bill to read that local Patronato members must know the dialect of their region.

The bill was debated and approved article by article. However, in the debate on Article 6, Senator García charged that since the Patronato was designed to aid the Indians, it could never achieve impartiality. Senator Franco Echeandía from Piura then argued that Patronato commissions would conflict with the judicial process of the nation and with the efforts of the Ministry of Development. This seemed to be the opposition's most telling argument, and García immediately moved that the entire law be returned to committee for further study and revision. Senators Curletti and Eleodoro M. del Prado from Arequipa exploded, contending that the Senate could not return a partially approved law to a new commission. Angrily, del Prado removed his signature from the bill, and the Senate sent it to the Indian committee, from which it never emerged.[33]

Although the Patronato did not receive enabling legislation from the Congress, it still functioned under the supreme decree, and Leguía and his supporters pointed frequently to what they deemed its accomplishments. In 1922, Leguía predicted that the Patronato would educate the Indians and incorporate them into society. In 1928, the vice-president of the Chamber of Deputies, Manchego Muñoz from Huancavelica, praised the Indian work of Leguía and specifically mentioned the successes of the Patronato.[34] One government publication noted that the various Patronato groups "had yielded excellent results" and that they were effective auxiliaries to other government agencies in the effort to improve Indian conditions.[35]

On the other hand, Basadre was later to contend that the Patronato was not compatible with the regular exercise of political

33. Ibid., August 21, 1923, pp. 169-74, 185-94, and August 28, 1923, pp. 239-44.

34. Augusto B. Leguía, *Discursos, mensajes y programas,* vol. 3 (Lima: Editorial Garcilaso, 1926), p. 44; and *Patria nueva, 1919-4 de julio-1928* (Lima: n.p., n.d.), pp. 27-28.

35. Perú, Ministerio de Salud Pública, Trabajo y Previsión Social, Dirección de Asuntos Indígenas, *La política indigenista en el Perú* (Lima: Imprenta "Lux," 1940), pp. 13-14. See also: Reaño García, *Historia de leguiísmo,* pp. 97-98; and Francisco Alayza Paz-Soldán, *El problema del indio en el Perú: Su civilización e incorporación a la nacionalidad* (Lima: Editorial Imprenta Americana, 1928), p. 37.

and judicial authority and therefore failed.[36] Two other authorities have asserted that it lacked the power to force arbitration between the *hacendados* and Indians and thereby became a bureaucratic boondoggle issuing mountains of paper.[37] Some critics have been even less kind. Dora Mayer de Zulen, the indefatigable worker for Indian causes, believes that Leguía, influenced by "Saxon mercantilism," created the Patronato not to improve the general state of the Indians, but rather to improve their economic output, the fruits of which would accrue to the white and mestizo middle class which strongly supported Leguía. Still another *indigenista* writer has accused the Patronato of siding with *hacendados*, favoring powerful interests over those of the humble Indians.[38] Leguía's creation of the Patronato followed his pattern of using the Indian issue to build support among certain groups while still retaining the backing of the *hacendados*.

Leguía attempted to build his public image as a supporter of the Indians in other ways as well. On May 11, 1923, his administration took two apparently significant steps in the realm of Indian legislation. By supreme decree, it modified Law 2285 of October 13, 1916, which had set a minimum wage for Indians of twenty centavos per day. The decree stated that since the government was responsible for the well-being of the Indian race and since the current minimum wage was inadequate, the municipal councils in the Andean provinces were to fix the minimum Indian wage at the first session of each year. The wage was to be the average of those offered in the province and could never drop below the minimum set in 1916. In order to compute the average, the councils were to study local Patronato reports and figures of the district councils and municipal agencies, and the amount arrived at was to be reported to Lima. The municipal councils were required to report the names of local agricultural holdings and the wage they offered to the Bureau of Indian Affairs. Each employer within the province was required to pay the established wage and to maintain a detailed work record of each employee. The decree reiterated that

---

36. Basadre, *Historia de la república*, 9:4191-92.

37. Moisés Sáenz, *Sobre el indio peruano y su incorporación al medio nacional* (Mexico, D.F.: Secretaría de Educación Pública, 1933), pp. 208-9; and Poblete Troncoso, *Condiciones de vida*, pp. 160-61.

38. Mayer de Zulen, *Estudios sociológicos de actualidad*, pp. 103-5; and Chira C., *Observaciones*, p. 50.

advances of money, food, or clothing could not exceed the value of one week's wages.[39]

The decision to have a minimum wage set locally was not in the Indians' best interests. Although Peru needed decentralization of authority, it could not be expected to succeed in Indian affairs so long as local governments were composed of *hacendados* and represented only their interests. To allow them to set minimum wages was to ensure exploitation of the Indians. Moreover, the law was never properly enforced. The Indians continued to lose ground economically and oppression actually increased.[40]

The second administrative act of May 11 came from the Ministry of Development. By supreme resolution, it ordered the owners of the hacienda Lauramarca in the department of Cuzco to comply with Law 2285. The Indians on the hacienda complained that they were paid in grazing rights rather than money. They were now to receive twenty centavos for an eight-hour day, and only heads of families were to be required to work for the *hacendado*. They were to pay for grazing rights and to be allowed to sell their animals, wool, and crops to whomever they pleased.[41] This resolution was publicized and was a showpiece for the administration, but in reality it was an exception to normal procedures and not a very important one.

In July, 1923, the administration issued a circular to all prefects ordering them to obey the laws of the republic. Noting that continued oppression of the Indians resulted in uprisings, it called upon all officials to ensure justice to the Indians.[42] But many high officials held a low opinion of the Indians. In one memorandum from the Minister of Justice, Religion, Instruction, and Charity, they were pictured as being incapable of anything:

> Without undertaking an examination of those elements which constitute incapacity, whether physical, psychological or simply legal, I must state that Indians are in fact incompetent. I base this conclusion on the experience of personal observation. Whether it is because of the state of vassalage in which he has lived since the time of the Incas, continuing through the colonial period and existing today despite laws which affirm his freedom, or because of the atrophy of his facilities as the result of alcohol, or

39. Chávez León, *Legislación social,* pp. 361-62.

40. See: Castro Pozo, *Del ayllu al cooperativismo,* p. 213; and Chira C., *Observaciones,* p. 53.

41. Chávez León, *Legislación social,* pp. 363-64.

42. *La evolución del Perú,* p. 120.

finally because of his lack of basic necessities, the fact remains that the Indian has completely lost all character. Under these conditions there are no dynamisms which motivate him or ideals which captivate him or truths which allure him. Everything is the same for him. He satisfies his hunger with miserable food, adapts himself to the activity of gazing at the cattle for which he cares, and makes his home in a rickety hut which seems only to protect him from the elements. He passes his life as did the generations in the centuries and the epochs before him. His life style, inherited from his ancestors, has not altered at all; he vegetates as always in his miserable existence.[43]

A minister displaying such a bias could not improve or change the attitudes of local officials. His maintenance in office was, however, an indication of Leguía's lack of commitment to lasting Indian reform.

Conscripción Vial

Much of the value of legislation favorable to the Indians promulgated during the *oncenio* was nullified by Leguía's use of a program known as *conscripción vial* (road conscription). The idea for road construction had come from Carlos Oyague y Calderón, the head of the Bureau of Roads, Bridges, and Piers of the Corps of Civil Engineers, who had prepared a bill which required all able-bodied male citizens and foreigners between the ages of eighteen and sixty to work on roads in their area. Those between the ages of eighteen and twenty-one and those between fifty and sixty were to work six days· per year; those between twenty-one and fifty, twelve days per year. One could also meet the obligation either by paying a daily wage or by sending someone in his place. All men were to carry a passbook showing that they had either worked or paid the stipulated sum.[44]

Oyague y Calderón's intent was to improve the transportation network of the nation without straining the federal budget. He felt that it was just because it applied equally to all men, but he recognized that the bulk of the work would fall upon the Indians and he welcomed the fact. There was precedent for such required labor

---

43. Perú, Ministerio de Justicia, Culto, Instrucción y Beneficencia, *Memoria del Ministro de Justicia, Culto, Instrucción y Beneficencia* (Lima: n.p., 1924), p. 79. See also pages 80-84.

44. For the text of the proposal, see: Carlos Oyague y Calderón, *La conscripción vial ó servicio obligatorio de caminos: Ideas generales y argumentos que pueden servir de base para el estudio de una ley* (Lima: Imprento del Centro Editorial, 1915), pp. 29-33.

in the Inca past, and he argued that the Indian *comunidades* should be mobilized to meet the needs of the program; old Inca customs should be revived before they were lost forever.[45]

The Senate approved the bill in 1917, and the Chamber of Deputies began debate in 1918.[46] It was tabled then but reintroduced in April, 1920. Most members agreed that such a measure would be beneficial to Peru and there was little debate. Objections were limited to the fact that the law made no provision for workers' salaries. Deputy Javier Luna Iglesias from Cajamarca offered an amendment which would pay workers the minimum wage of their region. He argued that Article 22 of thè constitution prohibited free service and therefore the bill was unconstitutional. Deputy Maúrtua also favored payment of a daily wage in order to prevent exploitation of the Indians. Several deputies, including Eloy Castro from Piura, successfully opposed the amendment on grounds that it would defeat the purpose of the bill, which was to improve the road system without taxing the country's monetary resources. The law was signed by Leguía on May 1, 1920.[47]

Leguía considered the implementation of the *conscripción vial* to be one of his most important accomplishments. In 1922, he noted that it was functioning well in the central sierra and that soon the area would be connected with the eastern slopes of the Andes. Some years later, he listed the roads built during his tenure and praised the efficiency of the conscription, equating it in importance with military conscription because economic development deterred foreign aggression.[48]

The law, however, did not enjoy unanimous support. Even before it was put into use there were warnings of potential problems. In 1920, one author asserted that it would exploit the Indians and found as its only redeeming feature the fact that responsibility for enforcement lay with the provincial and district councils rather than with the more exploitive military conscription structure. On the other hand, *La crítica* of Lima, asserting that the law was a

45. See his proposal for utilization of the Indian population in ibid., pp. 10-15.
46. PDD, Ordinario de 1918, Diputados, September 9, 1918, pp. 372-75.
47. PDD, Ordinario de 1919, April 5, 1920, pp. 1002-6; and April 6, 1920, pp. 1016-21.
48. Augusto B. Leguía, *Mensaje presentado al Congreso Ordinario de 1922 por el presidente de la republica* (Lima: C. F. Southwell Imprenta, 1922), p. 13; and idem, *Mensaje presentado al Congreso Ordinario de 1929 por el presidente de la república* (Lima: Imprenta Torres Aguirre, 1929), pp. 92-93.

denial of liberty, justice, and democracy in Peru, predicted that *hacendados* in positions of authority would see to it that the benefits of Indian labor would accrue to themselves. The editorial charged that the law negated all previous Indian legislation and that its results would be far worse than those of the military draft, in which thousands of Indians had been exploited and killed. *El comercio,* another leading newspaper in Lima, likewise attacked the proposed law as an example of government oppression of the Indians.[49]

Criticism continued unabated throughout the *oncenio.* One leading *indigenista* asserted that the conscription affected only Indians; although it was called voluntary work, in practice it was forced labor under tyrannical officials. Another contended that the law represented further loss of freedom among the Indian population and demanded its immediate abolition.[50]

Similar criticisms were voiced in the Senate in 1923. In late 1922, Senator Miguel González had introduced a measure which would have modified *conscripción vial* by raising the minimum age to twenty-one years in conformity with military conscription. In addition, artisans, laborers, and agricultural workers who earned less than one thousand *soles* per month would be required to work only four days per year, while those earning more than that would have to work twelve days. González maintained that the Indians were being forced to work twenty-four days or more and that it was causing riots and uprisings. He claimed that persons who did not work often refused to pay the required sum.[51]

Opponents of *conscripción vial* used the debate to attack the entire law. Senator Roger Luján Ripoll from Ica said that although the concept of the law was admirable, the excesses in its operation should move the Senate to rescind it and halt the exploitation of the Indians. Senator Pablo de Latorre from Cuzco called it a miserable law which resembled the old *mita.* Indians were taken from their homes, worked from twenty days to three months, and were not even fed, let alone paid. Others objected to the law as being

49. Vidalón Menéndez, *El problema indígena,* p. 20; *La crítica,* April 20, 1920, reprinted in Mayer de Zulen, *El indígena peruano a los cien años,* pp. 112-14; and *El comercio,* April 29, 1920, reprinted in ibid., pp. 149-50.

50. Luis F. Aguilar, *Cuestiones indígenas* (Cuzco: Tipografía de El Comercio, 1922), p. 72; and Mayer de Zulen, *El indígena peruano a los cien años,* pp. 33-34, 84-88.

51. PDD, Ordinario de 1923, Senadores, August 13, 1923, pp. 111-18.

unconstitutional because it represented forced labor.[52]

The Senate approved González's bill, but it never became law and the abuses continued and increased. Pro-Leguía authors and officials refused to take cognizance of the oppression and injustice. Books and pamphlets published in the 1920s devoted long sections to the successes of Leguía's highway program, using statistics to prove that most of the country was now connected by a road network, and gave credit to Leguía and the *conscripción vial.* If these works mentioned the Indians at all, it was usually to say that as a result of the program the race had been improved, uplifted, and retaught old communal work customs.[53]

It is true that thousands of kilometers of roads were constructed or improved under Leguía and that thousands of small villages gained access to the outside world. This access helped to alter the life patterns and culture of some Indians and to speed their integration.[54] But such material gains were offset by the cost in Indian life and oppression. Badly dressed and poorly fed, Indians were forced to work in distant provinces. With diseases and injuries left untreated, they died by the thousands. What little benefit they derived from the new roads was lost in the destruction of their families and themselves. The development of Indian culture was retarded.[55]

With the fall of Leguía in 1930, the Indians' hatred of the law erupted into violence. In several parts of the country, Indians sacked government offices and burned the conscription files. Some government officials did the same, fearing possible investigations of their activities. Feelings ran so high that the military government of Luis Sánchez Cerro abolished *conscripción vial* by decree in August, 1930.[56]

52. Ibid., August 16, 1923, pp. 132-41.

53. For an example of this attitude, see: Oficina del Periodismo, ed., *La obra de Leguía no ha concluido* (Lima: Empresa Editorial Cervantes, 1926), pp. 58-60. See also: Reaño García, *Historia del leguiísmo,* pp. 102-3; and Abel Ulloa Cisneros, *Escombros (1919-1930)* (Lima: C.I.P., 1934), pp. 69-70.

54. Ford, *Man and Land,* p. 137; and Virgilio L. Roel Pineda, *La economía agraria peruana hacia la reforma de nuestro agro,* 2d ed., 2 vols. (Lima: Talleres de Grafcolor, 1961), 2:130.

55. See: Cornejo, *Visión objectiva,* pp. 59-61; Mariano Peña Prado, *El dominio del estado en el Perú* (Lima: "Editorial Minerva," 1934), pp. 49-52; Roel Pineda, *El sendero,* p. 118; and Fernando Belaúnde Terry, *Peru's Own Conquest* (Lima: American Studies Press, 1965), pp. 110-12.

56. See: Cornejo Bouroncle, *Tierras ajenas,* pp. 73-74; Miró Quesada Laos, *Pueblo en crisis,* pp. 163-64.

Apologists for Leguía later asserted that he was unaware of the excesses, but that is doubtful. Examples of abuse and repression were well publicized both in and out of Congress, and Leguía was certainly aware of some of them. Motivated as he was by a desire to modernize the country, he probably felt that his road program was more important than the well-being of the Indians.

However, Leguía seemed satisfied with the Indian accomplishments of his second term. In his annual message to Congress in 1922, he had claimed that he was completing the work of Ramón Castilla, "who only suppressed the tribute." During the 1924 presidential campaign, he called for further integration of the Indians through education and improved sanitation. He promised to rehabilitate the Indians now that their state of slavery had ended. Following his reelection, he repeated the promises of Indian integration and called upon all Peruvians to aid him in that endeavor in order to create a better nation.[57]

THE FINAL YEARS OF THE "ONCENIO"

Congressional measures relating to Indians were minimal in the years 1924-30. Some legislation was introduced which was never enacted into law;[58] and numerous Indian complaints were read on the floors of both chambers, but all were effectively disposed of without referral to the appropriate government ministries.[59] One explanation for this paucity of congressional action lay in the fact that Leguía had consolidated his power position by 1924-25 and no longer needed to make even a pretense of introducing or supporting *indigenista* measures in the Congress. Moreover, the tremendous body of legislation touching every facet of the Indian question, that had been issued in the first five years went unenforced and Leguía became increasingly vulnerable to charges that he was more interested in enhancing his public image than in truly aiding the Indians.

One subject did produce lengthy debate in the Senate. In 1923, José Antonio Encinas introduced a bill to return to the *comunidad* of Chancay in the department of Lima lands known as the hacienda

57. Leguía, *Mensaje de 1922*, p. 23; and idem, *Discursos, mensajes y programas*, 3:275-76, 339-43.

58. See: Carlos A. Ricketts, *Ensayos de legislación pro-indígena: Párrafos epilogales de Francisco Mostajo* (Arequipa: Tip. Cuadros, 1936), pp. 18-32.

59. See: PDD, Ordinario de 1925, September 10, 1925, pp. 400-401; September 17, 1925, p. 471; and November 13, 1925, pp. 1164-68.

Quepepampa. These had been expropriated by the government in 1875 and given to the district council, or governing board, of Chancay in 1903 on the condition that all profits be used by the council for education and sanitation. Encinas argued that the lands rightfully belonged to the Indians and should be returned to them.[60]

The issue was debated off and on for more than three years. Some senators contended that since the *comunidad* of Chancay no longer existed, the proposal was unacceptable because the government would be enriching private landowners. Others argued that the Congress did not have legal authority to require the transfer of land from one party to another. Each time the measure was placed in debate, opponents succeeded in returning it to committee. Finally, in November, 1926, the Senate approved a law which divided the hacienda into individual plots that were to be given to descendants of former *comunidad* members.[61]

The passage of this measure did not represent pro-Indian sentiment. Rather, it must be viewed as a conflict between the district council of Chancay and landholders in the valley. The correctness of returning stolen lands to Indians was not the point, and had it been so, it is doubtful that the Senate would have approved the law. Several senators who voted to divide the hacienda among private property owners would have rejected any attempt to give land to an Indian *comunidad.*

Early in 1927, Leguía sent a bill to the Senate requesting that the Congress suspend all legal proceedings against civilian, military, and police officials arising from Indian revolts in 1922-23 in the provinces of Ayacucho and La Mar in the department of Ayacucho and Tayacaja in the department of Huancavelica. Several senators attempted to extend the measure to other Indian uprisings but failed. Senators Miguel González from Cuzco, Alejandrino Maguiña from Junín, and Julio Ego-Aguirre from Loreto tried to include all arrested Indians under the same amnesty. The Senate, however, refused to accede to the *indigenista* proposals, and the Indians were excluded in the approved version of the bill.[62] Thus

60. PDD, Ordinario de 1923, Senadores, August 24, 1923, pp. 211-15.

61. For the debate in the Senate, see: PDD, Ordinario de 1924, Senadores, October 18, 1924, pp. 107-19; October 20, 1924, pp. 138-44; January 13, 1925, pp. 956-58; January 14, 1925, pp. 980-95; February 2, 1925, p. 1334; and February 6, 1925, pp. 1458-75. See also: PDD, Ordinario de 1926, Senadores, November 9, 1926, pp. 1084-86.

62. PDD, 1st Extraordinario de 1927, Senadores, January 3, 1928, pp. 315-16; January 5, 1928, pp. 358-60; and PDD, 2d Extraordinario de 1927, Senadores, February 15, 1928, pp. 259-61. See also: Basadre, *Historia de la república,* 9:4190-91.

the Senate displayed tolerance for the wrongdoings of officials but not those of Indians.

In August, 1927, Leguía again demonstrated his tendency to sacrifice Indian interests in the face of pressure from *hacendados*. He had called a congress of Indian *comunidades* in 1921 and out of that body emerged an organization called Pro-Derecho Indígena Tahuantinsuyo (Pro-Indian Law Tahuantinsuyo). The organization, which met annually until 1924, quickly became a forum for attacks on *hacendados,* corrupt officials, and *conscripción vial.* There were outcries from landed interests and, in October, 1922, Deputy Dámaso Vidalón from Huancavelica accused the new group of preaching hate and discord and of sacking and burning haciendas and killing the owners.[63]

In 1923, the organization adopted several radical resolutions, including ones which favored complete separation of church and state and the repeal of *conscripción vial.* At the same time, an anarcho-syndicalist Federación Obrera Regional Indígena was formed with the intention of uniting with the Pro-Derecho group. The Leguía administration smashed the Federación Obrera Regional Indígena by deporting its leaders and later acted against the Pro-Derecho Indígena Tahuantinsuyo.[64]

The supreme resolution of 1927 outlawing the group charged that it represented itself as a defender of the Indians when in fact it was guilty of exploitation and, moreover, that there was no need for it because the Patronato and the Bureau of Indian Affairs performed its ostensible function.[65] Of course, government organizations were ineffective in enforcing legislation and therefore constituted no threat to landowners.

Another act which aided *hacendados* was Law No. 6648 of December 14, 1929, which sought to rectify boundaries for those property owners who had deficient title documents or lacked them altogether. The purported aim was to prevent endless land disputes in the courts, but since the Indians were not aware of the law, very few *comunidades* took advantage of it. On the other hand, the law enabled many *hacendados* to get title to land for which they had

---

63. PDD, Ordinario de 1922, Diputados, October 3, 1922, p. 410.

64. Basadre, *Historia de la república,* 9:4192.

65. PMTAI, *Legislación,* pp. 164-65. See also: Basadre, *Historia de la república,* 9:4192.

hitherto lacked proper documentation because it was land stolen from Indians.[66]

Nevertheless, Leguía was not without interest in promoting the welfare of the Indians as long as it did not antagonize forces which might disrupt his tenure in office or interfere with his other programs. Thus he devoted much of the last half of the *oncenio* to two issues basic to Indian life: Indian education and formal recognition of Indian *comunidades*. However, as others had before him, he erred by viewing the Indian problem in middle-class terms; that is, he believed that if Indian children could simply be given a primary education with technical training, the Indians and the entire economy would benefit.

One of the most important steps in education was an administration bill establishing an experimental agricultural school for Indian children in Puno, approved without debate by the Congress in 1925. Students lived at the school, which began operating in 1925, and were provided with clothing, food, and medical attention. The five-year program included a primary education and instruction in methods of crop production and animal husbandry. The school enjoyed success for many years. Leguía frequently praised its work and used it as a model for the construction of other schools. He regarded these schools not only as vehicles for Indian education, but also as centers for improved stock breeding. He even expropriated several haciendas in the Cuzco-Puno area for school use.[67]

Leguía also created several mobile schools to work in rural regions and supported Church-related Indian schools on haciendas and in rural towns. He realized that the education of Indian children required specially trained teachers and special curricula, and he established a special Indian Bureau in the Ministry of Education to regulate the various Indian facilities. During his last few months in office, he created special Indian primary schools in the

---

66. For the text of the law, see: PMTAI, *Legislación,* pp. 167-69. For a critique, see: Chira C., *Observaciones,* p. 46.

67. PMTAI, *Legislación,* pp. 217-19; Augusto B. Leguía, *Mensaje presentado al Congreso Ordinario de 1925 por el presidente de la república don Augusto B. Leguía* (Lima: Imprenta "Garcilaso," 1925), pp. 22-23, 61-62; and idem, *Mensaje presentado al Congreso Ordinario de 1927 por el presidente de la república* (Lima: Imprenta "Garcilaso," 1927), p. 82. For a comment, see: Chira C., *Observaciones,* p. 54.

sierra and Indian normal schools to train Indian teachers.[68] The Leguía administration probably enjoyed more success in education than in any other area of its Indian program. While the schools did not solve the Indian problem or even alleviate it substantially, they did function and some Indian children received instruction.

Leguía viewed *comunidad* registration as one of the more important items in his Indian plan. He implemented Article 58 of the 1920 Constitution with a supreme decree of July, 1925, which ordered the Ministry of Development to send surveying commissions to Indian *comunidades* to establish boundaries and to inscribe the *comunidad* on official registration lists. The official register was drawn up in August and included data on population, animal holdings, principal industries of the *comunidad,* number of schools, and delineation of boundaries. In September and November of 1927, the government ordered the use of official boundary markers on *comunidades* and established detailed regulations for engineers and surveyors.[69]

The government recognized 59 *comunidades* in 1926, 54 in 1927, 97 in 1928, 81 in 1929, and 30 in 1930, for a total of 321. Leguía pointed with pride to the efficiency of the surveying commissions and noted several times that the register would enable government officials to determine the size and needs of the Indian population.[70] The success of the recognition procedure, however, was limited. Three hundred twenty-one *comunidades* out of a total of several thousand was not significant. The *comunidades* were not required to register and many did not. Moreover, the Bureau of Indian Affairs, which administered the program, was understaffed and could not function effectively.[71] Nevertheless, the registration was an important beginning.

68. PMTAI, *Legislación,* pp. 220-28; Augusto B. Leguía, *Leguía: Selecciones de discursos pronunciados por el presidente de la república, señor don Augusto B. Leguía durante el año 1927* (Lima: Editorial "Cahuide," 1928), p. 11; idem, *Mensaje de 1927,* pp. 32-33; and idem, *Mensaje presentado al Congreso Ordinario de 1928 por el presidente de la república don Augusto B. Leguía* (Lima: Imprenta "Garcilaso," 1928), pp. 32-33.

69. PMTAI, *Legislación,* pp. 111-13; and Varallanos, *Legislación indiana,* pp. 63-66.

70. Dobyns, *The Social Matrix,* p. 3; Augusto B. Leguía, *Mensaje presentado al Congreso Ordinario de 1926 por el presidente de la república, señor don Augusto B. Leguía* (Lima: Imprenta "Garcilaso," 1926), pp. 90-91; idem, *Mensaje de 1927,* pp. 60-61; idem, *Mensaje de 1928,* pp. 112-13; and idem, *Mensaje de 1929,* pp. 67-68.

71. Poblete Troncoso, *Condiciones de vida,* p. 161; and Chira C., *Observaciones,* pp. 53-54.

The president took several other steps to aid Indians. He issued a supreme decree which assured Indian *comunidades* their proper share of irrigation water without interference from *hacendados* or local authorities. He gave *comunidades* the right to administer their own finances without the intervention of district councils, and he abolished the practice of *alcanzadores,* lawyers who waited on the roads to intercept Indians and convince them they needed legal help in the towns. One of Leguía's final acts was to decree June 24 as the Day of the Indian (Día del Indio), for which teachers and professors were to prepare special lectures glorifying the Indian past.[72]

The *oncenio* was not indestructible, and the combination of old age and the world depression resulted in Leguía's downfall. Peru had undergone vast changes in the period, but the lack of good monographic studies of the 1920s impedes analysis of the regime. However, the results of the Indian program are not so difficult to assess. Leguía claimed he had liberated the Indians from slavery and had moved them closer to integration. He praised Indian culture and history and asserted that his goal had always been to uplift the Indians and renew the great spirit which had built the Inca Empire. In speeches he referred to the Indians as the hope of the country: "The Indians are all the past and all the future. They made the great past and now . . . are building, as if they were craftsmen of bronze in the volcanic bowels of the Andes, the glorious future of Peru."[73]

Pro-Leguía writers view their subject as the personification of excellence. One stated that Leguía was as much a liberator as Abraham Lincoln because he had freed the Indians. Another pointed to the efforts made in Indian education and noted that Leguía was the great benefactor of Indian children. Leguía's principal biographer asserted that he had tremendous sympathy for the Indians and sought to better their lives, and one of Peru's leading sociologists wrote that Leguía initiated the rehabilitation of the Indians and that any failures of his program were caused by

72. PMTAI, *Legislación,* pp. 161-66, 226-27; and Leguía, *Mensaje de 1926,* p. 82.

73. Augusto B. Leguía, *Leguía: Colección de discursos pronunciados por el presidente de la república, señor don Augusto B. Leguía durante el año 1928* (Lima: Editorial "Cahuide," 1929), pp. 24-26, 111. See also: José E. Bonilla, ed., *El siglo de Leguía, 1903-1928* (Lima: T. Scheuch, 1928), pp. 64-65; and Leguía, *Leguía: Selección de discursos,* pp. 60-63.

unethical judges and corrupt officials.[74]

Opponents of the *oncenio* deny that Lequía aided the Indians. Some, acknowledging the laws that were passed, contend that nothing substantive resulted and accuse Leguía of sentimental romanticism.[75] Others charge that by adopting the title of Viracocha and by creating the Patronato, Leguía used the Indians as a political tool, with no real thought for their welfare. Still others accuse him of actually perpetrating Indian massacres and of being responsible for the deaths of thousands of Indians.[76] One historian said, "The Leguía administration was interested more in appearance than substance."[77]

There is some truth in all these charges. He spoke eloquently about Indian reform and integration. He sponsored numerous laws, resolutions, and decrees, but he sought neither strict implementation nor enforcement. He claimed to be a champion of land reform, but he stopped short of actually returning lands to the Indians. *Conscripción vial* must stand as one of the most exploitive measures in Peruvian history, yet Leguía could call for Indian protection in one breath and praise his road program in another. He declared himself the enemy of landed interests, but he usually bowed to their will. One example was the Roca Commission in 1920 and another was the outlawing of the Pro-Derecho Indígena Tahuantinsuyo in 1927.

There is one final conclusion to be drawn which is difficult to document owing to a paucity of studies of Indian revolts, land transfers, and motivation for *comunidad* recognition in the 1920s. Simply stated, Leguía's *indigenismo* may have been a shield behind which he could aid small landowners and proadministration

---

74. Julio Oscar Yépez de la Torre, *Apoteosis de Leguía: Conferencia pronunciada por . . . en los teatros ideal y municipal, en las fiestas organizadas por el concejo provincial de Trujillo conmemorando las bodas de plata de la vida política del presidente de la república señor don Augusto B. Leguía y Salcedo, el 8 de setiembre de 1928* (Trujillo: Tipografía "Olaya," 1928), p. 15; Carlos E. Bustamante Robles, *Apellido símbolo Leguía y Salcedo* (Lima: Talleres Gráficos de "La Revista," 1928), p. 84; René Hooper López, *Leguía: Ensayo biográfico* (Lima: Ediciones Peruanas, 1964), p. 145; and Mac-Lean Estenós, *Sociología del Perú*, pp. 282-83. See also: Vicente Noriega del Aguila in Ulloa Cisneros, *Escombros*, pp. 96-97.

75. For example, see: de la Barra, *El indio peruano*, pp. 158-59; and Pareja Paz-Soldán, *Derecho constitucional*, p. 146.

76. Miró Quesada Laos, *Pueblo en crisis*, p. 87; and Abelardo Solís, *Once años* (Lima: Talleres Gráficos Sanmarti y Cía, 1934), pp. 8-9, 58.

77. Pike, *Modern History of Peru*, pp. 222-23.

hacendados at the expense of the traditional landed oligarchy. There is no doubt that Leguía used irrigation projects and sporadic enforcement of the water distribution code (so vital in desert regions) to favor up-and-coming groups in rural regions.[78] It is likewise probable that Leguía used *comunidad* recognition to reward or to punish *hacendados* and may have manipulated many Indian revolts to achieve the same end. Proof of these assertions requires detailed local studies, but it can be tentatively stated that Leguía viewed his primary goal as that of modernizing the country and regarded the Indian issue as one tool for use in achieveing this goal rather than as a problem to be solved in terms of increasing the well-being of the Indians themselves.

Thus, Leguía failed to help the Indians, whose conditions of life did not alter perceptibly in the eleven years of his rule. But the *indigenismo* which Leguía publicly promoted did develop and mature in politics, literature, music, and art. Men such as José Carlos Mariátegui and Hildebrando Castro Pozo in politics, Alejandro Peralta and Augusto Aguirre Morales in literature, Julio C. Tello in archeology, and José Sabogal in art initiated a movement which was to influence Peru in later years.[79]

The unofficial leader of this group was José Carlos Mariátegui, one of the most forceful proponents of *indigenismo* and one of the great intellectuals in Peruvian history. He was born in the slums of Huacho and contracted osteomyelitis early in life. His health was always poor — he died at the age of thirty-five — but he was one of the most influential men of the century. In 1918, Leguía awarded Mariátegui a scholarship to study in Europe and there he became converted to Marxism. Upon returning to Peru, he became active in political affairs and founded the magazine *Amauta,* which published works by the leading intellectuals of the day.[80]

78. Karno, "Augusto B. Leguía," pp. 239-46.
79. The best and most complete study of Mariátegui is Jesús Chavarría, "José Carlos Mariátegui, Revolutionary Nationalist: The Origins and Crisis of Modern Peruvian Nationalism, 1870-1930" (Ph.D. diss., University of California at Los Angeles, 1967). For analysis of Mariátegui's *indigenismo,* see chap. 6 and 7. See also: Basadre, *Historia de la república,* 10:4533-36; Chang-Rodríguez, *Prada, Mariátegui y Haya,* p. 288; and Pike, *Modern History of Peru,* pp. 233-36.
80. Alberto Tauro, *Amauta y su influencia (síntesis de los 32 números)* (Lima: Biblioteca Amauta, 1960). Although several authorities maintain that Mariátegui suffered from tuberculosis, Jesús Chavarría asserts that he in fact had osteomyelitis (letter of January 21, 1970).

In the broadest sense, Mariátequi's *indigenismo* was a continuation of the work of Manuel González Prada, one of his intellectual mentors. But González Prada had been a member of the bourgeoisie, while Mariátegui came out of the proletariat, which greatly influenced his philosophy.[81] He viewed the Indian problem in economic terms. He rejected Indian legal codes because they would be predicated on the old feudal landholding system and would not treat the socioeconomic problems facing the Indians. Furthermore, they would reflect the individualistic attitudes of their authors rather than Indian communal interests.[82]

Mariátegui not only rejected the idea of racial superiority, he denied the existence of a "racial" problem in Peru. He contended that attacks on the Indian race masked economic opportunism. Thus, he believed that the Indians could not be helped by idealistic groups, because for such groups their own economic considerations would ultimately prevail over moral obligations. He also excluded any hope for a religious solution, since the Catholic church had neither the power nor the influence to aid the Indians, and, moreover, most priests and bishops were controlled by *hacendados*.[83]

He did not think that Indian needs could be met by education. The *latifundistas* were enemies of education, because ignorant peons offered few complaints; and what is more, teachers were all imbued with feudal ideas. He viewed with alarm the demands for decentralization, believing that local governments were much more oppressive than the central government, and that any increase in their power would constitute a corresponding increase in the power of the *latifundistas* and other exploiters of the Indians.[84]

Mariátegui's remedy for the Indians was to cure the economic problems of the nation. He saw three distinct economic systems in Peru: the communism of the Indians, the feudal structure of the great haciendas, and the bourgeois capitalism of the coastal community. "The Indian question," he wrote,

> emanates from our economy. It has its roots in the land tenure system. While the feudalism of the *gamonales* still exists, any attempt to resolve

81. Basadre, *Perú, problema y posibilidad,* p. 170.

82. José Carlos Mariátegui, *Siete ensayos de interpretación de la realidad peruana,* 10th ed. (Lima: Biblioteca Amauta, 1965), pp. 34-36.

83. Ibid., pp. 36-39.

84. Ibid., pp. 39-40, 138-39, 174-76, 186-88.

it with administrative, police, or educational methods or with public road construction constitutes a superficial endeavor.[85]

Mariátegui's emphasis on Inca communism led him to regard the *comunidad* as the basis for the new order. He believed that despite centuries of attack, it had survived with a vitality which protected the Indians and their culture, that only by destroying the huge estates and returning the land to the Indians could Peru throw off the shackles of feudalism and truly progress. Thus, the uplifting of the Indian race depended solely on land reform: "The agrarian problem presents itself above all as the problem of liquidating feudalism in Peru."[86]

Although Mariátegui had no influence on the Leguía administration, he did influence an entire generation of intellectuals and politicians. Since Mariátegui's was not a fraudulent or politically inspired *indigenismo*, Jorge Guillermo Llosa could correctly aver that "he saw in *indigenismo* something more profound: the appearance of a new state of conscience in Peru, visceral and affectionate."[87]

Although he rejected Mariátegui's ideas, Leguía allowed him to sow the seeds of future political confrontation in the country. The roots of the movement which grew in the 1930s and 1940s with Haya de la Torre and others lie with Mariátegui. His ideas and writings were the most important product of the *oncenio.*[88]

85. Ibid., pp. 31-32.

86. Ibid., pp. 41-42. See also pp. 70-71, 85-89.

87. Jorge Guillermo Llosa P., *En busca del Perú* (Lima: Ediciones del Sol, 1962), p. 92.

88. Hundreds of books and articles have been written about Mariátegui and his philosophy, and almost every Peruvian writer devotes some attention to him. The best analyses are found in: María Jesús Wiesse de Sabogal, *José Carlos Mariátegui: Etapas de su vida y los ensayos de Benjamín Carrión, Jesualdo Sosa, Baldomero Sanín Cano, Medardo Vitier, Jorge Falcón, y Rubén Sardón* (Lima: Biblioteca Amauta, 1959); Chang-Rodríguez, Prada, *Mariátegui y Haya;* Llosa P., *En busca del Perú*, pp. 53-94; Guillermo Rouillon, *Bio-bibliografía de Jose Carlos Mariátegui* (Lima: Imprenta de la Universidad Nacional Mayor de San Marcos, 1963); Antonio San Cristóbal-Sebastián, *Economía, educación y marxismo en Mariátegui* (Lima: Ediciones Studium, 1960); Jorge del Prado, *Mariátegui y su obra* (Lima: Ediciones "Nuevo Horizonte," 1946); and Augusto Salazar Bondy, *Historia de las ideas en el Perú contemporáneo: El proceso del pensamiento filosófico*, 2 vols. (Lima: Francisco Moncloa Editores, 1965), 2:311-43.

5

The Chaotic Thirties

The fall of Augusto B. Leguía in August, 1930, left Peru in a near hopeless state of economic, political, and social chaos. Except for the Constituent Congress which wrote the Constitution of 1933 and remained in operation until 1936, when it was dissolved by President Oscar R. Benavides, constitutional government functioned very irregularly. The old political parties were dead and many of the old political leaders had been either silenced or driven into exile.

The new economic and political groups which Leguía had fostered and upon which he had based his regime never united into a cohesive political party (or parties), remaining divided and often mutually antagonistic. The myriad of splinter parties which formed following the 1930 coup d'état of Colonel Luis M. Sánchez Cerro further complicated the already confused political picture. They were small, powerless, and devoid of those charismatic leaders necessary to attract great masses of people.

The economic picture was likewise bleak. Leguía had retained much of his support by taking advantage of the "Dance of the Millions" in the 1920s. He vastly expanded the bureaucracy and embarked on ambitious public works projects. To finance these programs he borrowed heavily from Wall Street investors, and when the stock market crashed in 1929, Peru was one of the hardest hit of the Latin American republics. The resulting collapse of businesses and the increasing unemployment contributed to the disarray and increased the possibilities for violent social upheaval.

As with many Peruvian political figures of the twentieth century, it is difficult to find an objective analysis of the career of Sánchez Cerro. The available literature is almost completely polarized be-

96

tween those who portray him as a great statesman and those who consider him an ignorant criminal. His principal biographer wrote: "The figure of Sánchez Cerro embodies the characteristics of Peruvianism. One of the orators said at his burial: 'I have never seen a Peruvian so much a Peruvian, nor a man so much a man.' And that is certainly true."[1] One historian has described him as "a man of action, rather than reflection," adding that:

His forte was his intuitive ability to grasp a situation and to respond energetically to its exigencies. Because he could not or did not choose to articulate his understanding of a situation, he was often contemptuously dismissed by intellectuals as ignorant, uncultured and shallow. Still, by means of his shrewd understanding Sánchez Cerro had come to grasp conditions in Peru better than many intellectuals and had determined to play precisely the political role best suited to the times.[2]

Others were less impressed. In his memoirs, Aprista leader Luis Alberto Sánchez describes Sánchez Cerro's arrival in Lima:

The popular reception demonstration was impressive because of its size and fervor. Nevertheless, the *caudillo* paraded in a truck surrounded by troops with cannons pointing at the crowd. He was dressed in battle uniform. He was a small man of dark complexion which contrasted with a set of teeth like an orangoutang's. He smiled, or better yet, laughed, in a disagreeable manner from his vehicle, which bristled with machine guns. . . . Then the Commandant began to speak. He seemed very excited and he moved feverishly and his bright, square teeth stuck out. Among the things which he said, apart from the thousand insults against Leguía, his family, and his followers, was that he would not recognize the boundary treaties with Colombia and Chile because they reduced the territory of the republic; that he would jail all of his political enemies as "thieves"; and that he would be inflexible with Leguía. I listened stupified. I said then . . . "This is a catastrophe, the cure will be much worse than the disease."[3]

1. Carlos Miró Quesada Laos, *Sánchez Cerro y su tiempo* (Buenos Aires: Librería "El Ateneo" Editorial, 1947), pp. 283-84. Miró Quesada Laos was the son of the owner of *El comercio,* Lima's leading newspaper and the principal Civilista supporter of Sánchez Cerro.
2. Pike, *Modern History of Peru,* p. 251.
3. Luis Alberto Sánchez, *Testimonio personal: Memorias de un peruano del siglo XX,* 3 vols. (Lima: Ediciones Villasán, 1969), 1:326-27. Sánchez Cerro was an implacable enemy of the Apristas and most of their literature of the 1930s and 1940s contains attacks on him. For two particularly virulent works see: Alberto Hidalgo, *Sánchez Cerro o el excremento* (Buenos Aires: n.p., 1932); and Luis E. Heysen, *El comandante del Oropesa* (Cuzco: n.p., 1931).

Another contemporary political figure, who was anti-Aprista, wrote:

When I returned from Europe in December of 1930 after some years of exile, I took advantage of the stop the boat made in Callao to go to the National Palace and congratulate the military man who had overthrown Leguía. When I announced my visit, Sánchez Cerro received me affably. Conversing about the economic crisis which afflicted the world and which had had such deep repercussions in Peru, aggravated by the squandering of the *oncenio,* he told me: "The day I have two free hours I'll solve the economic situation of Peru which my Minister of Finance has been unable to do." ... When I referred to the necessity of his resigning from power, if he insisted on launching his candidacy for the presidency, to bolster public confidence in the honesty of the elections, he answered me: "I wouldn't give up power even if my naked mother asked me to." I didn't need to hear any more. I took my leave and returned to the ship, embittered by the physical, moral, and intellectual state of the man into whose hands we had fallen.[4]

Pedro Ugarteche, one of Peru's outstanding statesmen and politicians and former secretary to Sánchez Cerro, has published a multivolume collection of Sánchez Cerro's private papers, which help to illuminate his character.[5] In many ways, Sánchez Cerro was an old-style military *caudillo.* He had been active in revolts and attempted revolts since 1914, when he was wounded in the successful overthrow of Billinghurst. He had rebelled against Leguía in 1922, but was pardoned. His success in 1930 was due more to the internal collapse of Leguía's administration and to the weariness of the Peruvian people than it was to his own abilities. Initially, he enjoyed widespread support. He had freed the country from an eleven-year dictatorship, and he was a *cholo* (mestizo) who spoke the language of the common man as no other twentieth-century president had before him. He used these advantages, plus the existing political disorder, to establish himself in power.

He won approval from the anti-Leguía elements in the cities and

4. Manuel Bustamante de la Fuente to Luis Alberto Sánchez, May 23, 1970, private archive of Manuel Bustamante de la Fuente, Lima, Peru (hereafter cited as Bustamante Archive). In a letter to me of September 7, 1971, Bustamante de la Fuente expanded on his view of Sánchez Cerro: "Sánchez Cerro was an ignorant, abusive, and disloyal individual. ... He didn't have any ability at all as a statesman, lacking all culture and education, and he was manipulated by a group of Civilistas that helped him gain power."

5. Pedro Ugarteche, *Sánchez Cerro, papeles y recuerdos de un presidente del Perú,* 4 vols. (Lima: Editorial Universitaria, 1969-70).

drew support also from the Indians and mestizos of the sierra by attacking *conscripción vial* in his coup manifesto from Arequipa and then abolishing it on August 31, 1930. He charged that the Leguía government had been guilty of monstrous excesses and that criminals had despoiled the country of one hundred million *soles* since the program's inception.[6] He also promised to cure the Indian problem: "We will dignify and give homage to our Indian brothers. They will constitute the heart of our national program, and not in theory alone."[7]

Sánchez Cerro's popularity did not mean that he had the support of all factions, either in or out of the military junta that controlled the country. Suspect because of his skin color, rough manners, and lower-class family background, he was shunned by the upper classes in Lima. Many of his initial supporters soon deserted as they became involved in the nationwide struggle for power. He also encountered opposition from ambitious army officers, and in February, 1931, there were uprisings in several parts of the nation, including Callao, Arequipa, Piura, Cuzco, and Lambayeque. On March 1, Sánchez Cerro resigned and went to Europe, leaving the civilian leader David Samánez Ocampo, the man most acceptable to the Arequipa insurgents, as the titular head of government.[8]

Although preoccupied with matters requiring immediate attention, the new civilian-military junta did initiate some Indian legislation. By ministerial resolution of July 23, 1931, the government outlawed the practice of collecting tolls on public roads which passed through private property. This "fee" had been abolished by Ramón Castilla in 1856, but the large landowners had continued to collect the toll as well as grazing fees from Indians who used the roads to take their livestock to market. In addition to prohibiting tolls, the resolution ordered local officials to remove

6. Luis Alayza Paz-Soldán, et al., *Homenaje a Sánchez Cerro, 1933-1953* (Lima: Editorial Huascarán, 1953), p. 98. See also: Basadre, *Historia de la república,* 11:30-31. For an example of charges that *conscripción vial* survived Sánchez Cerro's decree, see the Aprista magazine, *APRA,* no. 4 (November 4, 1930), p. 9.

7. Alayza Paz-Soldán et al., *Homenaje a Sánchez Cerro,* p. 97. For an example of one *comunidad* which reacted to Sánchez Cerro's program, see: Adams, *Commuity in the Andes,* pp. 45-46.

8. The most complete description of this period is: Basadre, *Historia de la república,* 11:1-146. For a wealth of primary information and private documents of one of the key leaders of the Arequipa revolt, see the Bustamante Archive, which contains hundreds of letters and reports that are pertinent to the period August, 1930-October, 1931.

gates or fences that had been erected to halt the normal flow of traffic.[9]

In September, 1931, by supreme resolution, the junta ordered returned to the *comunidad* Rumuro in the department of La Libertad all lands which it had lost since 1884, including those taken by the Church.[10] Though an important decision, it remained an isolated case which did not affect the nation as a whole.

In the realm of Indian education, the junta tried to provide better organization with Decree Laws 7345 and 7346 of October 5, 1931. The first earmarked 25 percent of the beer tax in the department of Cuzco for an Indian normal school, and the second centralized in the Bureau of Indian Education the administration of all schools. It also called for the establishment of a general curriculum and for the cooperation of the Bureau of Agriculture in developing farming techniques.[11]

During the few months between the fall of Leguía and the exit of Sánchez Cerro, political parties began to function again. The strongest and most viable was the Alianza Popular Revolucionario Americana (APRA), founded in Mexico City in 1924 by Víctor Raúl Haya de la Torre and other like-minded intellectuals who had been exiled by the Leguía government. For years, scholars studying Latin America and Peru have been bombarded with hundreds of books, pamphlets, broadsides, and articles supporting, condemning, or "explaining" Apra. However, even a casual glance at the literature reveals that it is almost totally polarized between the fervent supporters of the party and its equally fervent detractors. Apra has been pictured by its admirers as a grass-roots lower- and middle-class reform movement designed to end foreign and oligarchical domination of the economy, to incorporate the Indian mass into national life, and to democratize the sociopolitical structure of the country. One United States scholar has written: "The Apristas have demonstrated the vigor of their ideas. Their slogan in 1966, just as it has been for over four decades, is 'Apra Si, Comunismo No.' They continue, as always, teaching, organizing, and working for the Peru of their ideal — free, just, and happy."[12]

9. PMTAI, *Legislación*, pp. 297-99. See also: Chira C., *Observaciones*, pp. 55-56.

10. Chira C., *Observaciones*, pp. 131-32.

11. PMTAI, *Législación*, p. 299. See also Sivirichi, *Derecho indígena*, p. 462.

12. Harry Kantor, *The Ideology and Program of the Peruvian Aprista Movement*, 2d ed. (Washington, D.C.: Savile Books, 1966), p. 143. For another laudatory and rather uncritical analysis of Aprismo, see: Robert J. Alexander, *Prophets of the Revolution: Profiles of Latin American Leaders* (New York: Macmillan, 1962). Much of the

Critics of Apra have long characterized the party as being composed of communistic terrorists who desired not the betterment of Peruvian society, but rather its total destruction. According to one historian, Apra sought "to tear down the whole Peruvian social, economic, and political structure so as to replace it with one based exclusively on their own esoteric theories, rather than on a consensus of national opinion. They were in Peru fully as subversive an element as is the Communist Party today in the United States."[13]

The most unfortunate result of this intensely partisan debate has been the tendency to view the issue in polemical terms of good and evil. Nowhere has this tendency been more evident than in the debate over the *indigenismo* of Apra and of Haya de la Torre, a debate which has produced an entire mythology asserting that Apra is the greatest defender of the Indian in Peruvian history. It is probably true, as one critical Peruvian journalist stated, that "in Peru all mass movements have been characterized by their love of the Indian,"[14] and Haya de la Torre and his followers have produced a body of *indigenista* literature which at least in volume surpasses that of any movement before or since. Despite this literature, however, Haya and Apra never mounted an effective *indigenista* campaign. Their Indian programs were lacking both in design and in execution.

Born in the northern costal city of Trujillo, Haya was supposedly influenced by the magnificent Chimu ruins of Chan-Chan outside the city, which caused him to write that "something unjust has happened in those arid lands, that some tremendous cruelty was responsible for those tombs, those dry wells, those desolate streets, those silent houses."[15] His germinal *indigenismo* bloomed

---

material on Apra has been drawn from my article: "The *Indigenismo* of the Peruvian Aprista Party: A Reinterpretation," *Hispanic American Historical Review* 51, no. 4 (November 1971): 626-45.

13. Fredrick B. Pike, "The Old and the New APRA in Peru: Myth and Reality," *Inter-American Economic Affairs* 18 (Autumn 1964): 10. See also his *Modern History of Peru*, particularly chaps. 8-10.

14. Federico Moré, *Una multitud contra un pueblo: Etiología diagnóstico terapéutica de un sicosis política* (Lima: Editorial Todo el Mundo, 1933), p. 23.

15. Alberto Baeza Flores, *Haya de la Torre y la revolución constructiva de las Américas* (Buenos Aires: Editorial Claridad, 1962), p. 48. See also: Felipe Cossío del Pomar, *Haya de la Torre, el indoamericano* (Lima: Editorial Nuevo Día, 1946), pp. 26-27. For Haya's personal recollection of Chan-Chan and its impact, see: Víctor Raúl Haya de la Torre, *Espacio-tiempo-histórico: Cinco ensayos y tres diálogos* (Lima: Ediciones La Tribuna, 1948), pp. vii-x.

during 1917 when he studied in Cuzco. Later as president of the Peruvian Student Federation, he traveled extensively in the southern sierra and wrote his father: "The suffering of the Indian pains me deeply. You cannot imagine what slavery is."[16]

While president of the student federation, Haya played an active role in the 1923 student-worker protest against the Leguía-sponsored convocation dedicating Peru to the Sacred Heart of Jesus, and was subsequently deported by the president. During the years abroad, he began to develop his *indigenista* campaign. In 1923, in Havana, he stated:

> I can't recall the Indian of Peru without saying a word of protest and accusation. Those who have seen our Andean solitudes will have seen those great masses of sad, ragged, and melancholy *campesinos* who carry the burdens of four hundred years of slavery on their shoulders.[17]

In 1925, he wrote:

> I am sure that in Peru no one will be able to achieve rehabilitation, renovation, or justice without fundamentally facing the economic problem of our Indian, the great base of our exploited class, who is the worker, the soldier, the producer, and the backbone of the nation. Because of that I consider the Indian problem of Peru basic and believe that our revolutionary action ought to orient itself toward it with seriousness and energy.[18]

Haya also invoked the philosophies of Manuel González Prada and José Carlos Mariátegui to lend further support to his *indigenista* pronouncements. He continually praised the writings of González Prada, adopted many of the old master's ideas, and named his student-organized popular universities for González Prada.[19] The neo-Marxist thought of Mariátegui also influenced Haya and

---

16. Quoted in Cossío del Pomar, *Haya de la Torre*, p. 77. See also Luis Alberto Sánchez, *Raúl Haya de la Torre o el político: Crónica de una vida sin trequa* (Santiago de Chile: Editorial Ercilla, 1934), pp. 56-58.

17. Víctor Raúl Haya de la Torre, *Por la emancipación de América Latina: Artículos, mensajes, discursos (1923-1927)* (Buenos Aires: M. Gleizer, Editor, 1927), p. 43.

18. Ibid., p. 124. For additional examples of his early *indigenismo*, see ibid., pp. 89-105; Víctor Raúl Haya de la Torre, *El antimperialismo y el Apra* (Santiago de Chile: Ediciones Ercilla, 1936), pp. 177-81; idem, *Construyendo el aprismo: Artículos y cartas desde el exilio (1924-1931)* (Buenos Aires: Editorial Claridad, 1933), pp. 9-11, 69-70, 98, 104-16; and Chang-Rodríguez, *Prada, Mariátegui y Haya*, pp. 288-94. For an account of Haya's early *indigenista* teachings, see Josefa Yarlequé de Marquina, *El maestro ó democracia en miniatura* (Lima: Librería e Imprenta J. Alvarez A., 1963), pp. 59-60.

19. Chang-Rodríguez, *Prada, Mariátegui y Haya*, pp. 123-25, 341. See also Luis Alberto Sánchez, *Don Manuel*, p. 203; Cossío del Pomar, *Haya de la Torre*, pp. 221-22; and Capuñay, *Leguía*, p. 184.

his followers. Although the two men broke over Haya's decision to convert his movement from an alliance into a political party, it is apparent that Haya borrowed many of Mariátegui's *indigenista* theories.[20]

The Apristas had supported Sánchez Cerro's takeover, but soon joined his opposition. The junta called elections for October, 1931, to select a president and a Constituent Congress, and Haya returned from exile and announced his candidacy for the presidency. Although the Apra was favored by the junta, Sánchez Cerro's supporters rallied to his cause and the *cholo* leader was also given the right to enter the campaign. Early in the campaign, Haya made the Indian problem an integral part of his political pronouncements. He wrote in 1931 in a letter to the Aprista organization in Cuzco: "For Apra the *campesino* is fundamentally and overwhelmingly Indian. Paraphrasing Lenin we can say: it is necessary to begin with the Indian."[21] In June, 1931, he wrote: "The state ought to abolish *latifundismo* gradually, protecting and giving a technical impulse to the *comunidades,* educating the Indian and securing Peru's rich production for the benefit of all."[22]

By the fall of 1931, however, he had softened his tone. In his speech in Lima's Acho bullring on August 23, Haya barely mentioned the Indian problem. He called for the creation of an agricultural credit bank to aid the small landowner and to initiate land reform and new agricultural techniques, and though he mentioned the Indian *comunidad* in this context, such a bank would undoubtedly have benefited the small, middle-class landowner rather than the Indians. Like countless politicians before him, Haya maintained that it was necessary to rescue millions of Indians from their state of ignorance and to educate them not only in liberal arts, but, more importantly, in trades and technical skills — a "practical education." Noting that the bulk of the army was composed of men from the middle and lower classes, he called upon the armed forces to aid in the education process and to join with engineers in constructing new roads and railroads to modernize the entire country.[23]

20. For an account of their disagreement, see Basadre, *Historia de la república,* 9:4209-12; and Roel Pineda, *El sendero,* pp. 120-21.

21. Partido Aprista Peruano, *El proceso Haya de la Torre* (Guayaquil: n.p., 1933), p. 13.

22. *Aprismo* (Lima: n.p., n.d.), p. 74.

23. For the complete text of this speech, see Víctor Raúl de la Torre, *El plan de acción,* vol. 4 of *Pensamiento político de Haya de la Torre* (Lima: Ediciones Pueblo,

In the Plan of Immediate Action which was published in 1931 as the official party platform and which still serves as the basic statement of Aprista principles, Haya devoted a short section to the Indians.[24] The principal proposals were: incorporation of the Indians into the national life; passage of legislation to conserve and to modernize the *comunidad;* promotion of small Indian industries and crafts; establishment of guidelines for revising work contracts between Indians and landowners; development of a general plan of education, taking into account the peculiarities of each region; establishment of rural Indian schools and use of Indian languages in conjunction with Spanish; introduction of agrarian cooperatives to help Indian farmers; and an energetic campaign against Indian consumption of alcohol and coca. Those sections of the plan dealing with agriculture called for a program of land redistribution geared to create a class of Indian yeoman farmers, a revival of the dream of Bolívar.[25] There was nothing in the plan which had not been proposed, and even enacted, under previous administrations. Moreover, it was vague to the point of being useless. Nevertheless, one Aprista writer concluded:

> Haya, and through Haya, Aprismo, treats the Indian problem in new terms. He ceases to consider it in abstract terms, as an ethnic and moral problem, thereby recognizing it concretely as a social, economic, and political problem. From this time on, one sees it illuminated and delineated for the first time.[26]

Although he traveled widely, called for Indian reform, and even gave some speeches in Quechua, in reality Haya and his party merely followed the Peruvian political tradition of nominal support for Indian integration. He voiced familiar campaign slogans but failed to formulate the details necessary for effective imple-

---

1961), pp. 19-67. French sociologist Francois Bourricaud acknowledges the paucity of *indigenismo* in the Acho speech, but asserts that the "Indian theme" was prevalent in subsequent Aprista literature *(Ideología y desarrollo: El caso del Partido Aprista Peruano* [Mexico: El Colegio de México, 1966], pp. 16-17).

24. The plan was reissued in 1963 as the party's program for the presidential elections of that year. A handbook containing all the party platforms is: S. Martínez G., *Para la consulta popular: Elecciones de 1963* (Lima: Ediciones Martínez, n.d.), p. 33.

25. For the complete text of the plan, see Víctor Raúl Haya de la Torre, *Política aprista,* 2d ed. (Lima: Editorial-Imprenta Amauta, 1967), pp. 9-30. The Indian section is on pp. 23-24.

26. Cossío del Pomar, *Haya de la Torre,* p. 231.

mentation. Moreover, Haya could not even claim a monopoly on *indigenismo* in the 1931 presidential campaign. Sánchez Cerro incorporated the Indian issue into his official Program of Government, echoing many Aprista points. He stated:

> We cannot resolve this basic national problem if the spiritual attitude of the whites and mestizos toward our Indian brothers does not change. As long as we do not consider ourselves all Peruvians with the same rights and duties, the true unity of the fatherland, which is its base for greatness, will not be realized. Peruvians, principally the leaders, must abandon that protective and superior attitude they adopt regarding the glorious race that created an admirable civilization.[27]

In regard to Indian agriculture, he called for the organization and registration of Indian *comunidad* lands, the restoration of lands usurped in the past, and the distribution of plots to landless Indians. He wanted to promote agricultural cooperatives by encouraging the *comunidades* to join with small property owners to pool technical knowledge and resources. He also called for the protection of small Indian industries in order to advance the economies of the Indians and the nation. Particular attention was to be devoted to Indian education by creating special industrial and agricultural schools as well as rural schools and mobile educational missions to reach the most isolated Indians. Sánchez Cerro asserted that in order to accomplish these goals, the government should abolish ineffective institutions such as the Patronato de la Raza Indígena and establish instead Indian bureaus in the Ministries of Education and Development, as well as a new Ministry of Labor and Indian Affairs. These actions were to be accomplished by administrative decentralization, improvement of the Indians' economic conditions, development of new lines of communication and transportation, and prevention of private or public exploitation of the Indians.[28]

An analysis of the political support the Apristas sought and received helps to explain the flaccid quality of Aprista *indigenismo.* That Haya drew 44 percent of his total vote in 1931 from the northern departments, 30 percent from Lima-Callao, and only 26 percent from the remainder of the country can be attributed to the

---

27. *Programa del gobierno del comandante Luis M. Sánchez Cerro, candidato a la presidencia de la república del Perú* (Lima: n.p., 1931), p. 35.

28. Ibid., pp. 35-36.

party's worker-middle-class orientation.[29] The Plan of Immediate Action was certainly not directed to the illiterate and culturally isolated Indians of the sierra, who had neither political influence nor the right to vote.[30] On the contrary, careful scrutiny of the document's salient economic points demonstrates that the focus was on the laboring class of urban centers and the large costal haciendas, on white-collar workers in rural and urban centers, on small landowners, and on the middle class in general. There were provisions for regulating wages, substituting direct income and inheritance taxes for the indirect taxes that weighed most heavily on the middle and lower classes, restricting the importation of luxury items and the exportation of capital, imposing government restrictions on commerce and industry, outlawing monopolies and trusts, developing production and credit cooperatives, and creating a national bank to serve particularly the interests of the small producer. In the area of agriculture, special attention was paid to the needs of the small landowner, including basic reforms in land tenure and expropriation, irrigation projects, rural labor, and the equal distribution of irrigation waters.[31]

The national Aprista program closely resembled the program for northern Peru published by the party some months earlier. In the northern departments of Lambayeque, La Libertad, and Cajamarca (the so-called Sólido Norte), the Apristas enjoyed and continue to enjoy their greatest popular support. The issues of the

29. Election figures for 1931 as well as an analysis of Aprista strength in the North are found in Peter F. Klarén, "Origins of the Peruvian Aprista Party: A Study of Social and Economic Change in the Department of La Libertad, 1870-1932" (Ph.D. diss., University of California at Los Angeles, 1969). See particularly pp. 191-92, 209-10. One former Aprista argued that Apra was never socialistic, but "was always an organization representative of the interests, dreams, and ambitions of the old middle class which was in danger of losing its bourgeois status" (Hernando Aguirre Gamio, *Liquidación histórica del Apra y del colonialismo neoliberal* [Lima: Ediciones Debate, 1962], pp. 197-99.

30. A total of 392,363 men were registered to vote in 1931, with a racial breakdown as follows: mestizos, 234,546; Indians, 97,940; whites, 56,135; and Negroes, 3,736. The great mass of Indians were illiterate and thus disqualified, as seen in the low number of registrations in the heavily Indian departments of the southern sierra. In Cuzco, there were 13,992 men registered to vote; in Puno, 10,341; and in Apurímac, 6,588, the great majority of whom, in all three departments, were mestizo. Moreover, those Indians voting tended to support Sánchez Cerro, who won easily in the rural regions of the country. For these and other electoral figures plus an analysis, see: Basadre, *Historia de la república,* 11:201-3.

31. Haya de la Torre, *Política aprista,* pp. 14-18.

1930s emanated from the fifty-year conflict between the large com- mercial sugar plantations on the one hand, and their workers and the middle class of the area on the other. The Apristas dealt ex- tensively with the plight of the sugar worker, demanding the aboli- tion of the piecework system, the prohibition of the contract-labor system *enganche,* the implementation of a minimum wage, the ac- ceptance of labor unions and collective bargaining, the abolition of salary disparities between foreign and national workers, and the establishment of health and education facilities for employees.[32] To help solve the problems of small landowners the party called for extensive new irrigation projects, a total revision of water al- lotment laws, and the creation of small agricultural banks designed to meet the credit needs of the small landowner. For merchants the Apra advocated the nationalization of railroads, the elimina- tion of special import privileges, and the abolition of company stores on the large haciendas.[33]

The party secured important financial aid from key northern businessmen such as Rafael Larco Herrera (he reportedly contrib- uted fifty-thousand *soles*), whose medium-sized sugar plantation, Chiclín, was in danger of being engulfed by the huge Gildemeister holdings at Casa Grande. Rafael's brother, Víctor Larco Herrera, had lost his hacienda, Roma, to the Gildemeisters in 1925.[34] Thus the Apristas enjoyed some northern upper-class support which in- fluenced the tenor of their party platform.

Another middle- and upper-class element in the Aprista ranks which militated against leftist extremism in general and radical

---

32. For a discussion of this program see: Klarén, "Origins of the Peruvian Aprista Party," pp. 179-81. The main thesis of Klarén's work is that there was an economic revolution in the Santa Catalina and Chicama valleys of La Libertad. The old families and the small landowners were displaced by foreign investors, who established huge sugar plantations operating as veritable economic entities. Plantation stores competed with local merchants. This economic dislocation produced a political dislocation, with the Aprista party being the principal beneficiary.

33. Ibid., pp. 179-81.

34. For the allegation that Larco Herrera contributed fifty thousand *soles* to the Aprista campaign, see Ambassador Fred Morris Dearing to Secretary of State, May 16, 1931, D.S. 810.43 APRA/83. Rafael Larco Herrera continued to support Aprista principles, and in 1933, through his Lima newspaper, *La crónica,* he declared himself in accord with various Aprista proposals. See Dearing to Secretary of State, Novem- ber 16, 1933, D.S. 823.00/1046. For an excellent analysis of the economic change in La Libertad and its effect on the Larco Herrera family, see Klarén, "Origins of the Peruvian Aprista Party," chaps. 1-3.

indigenismo in particular was the followers of former President Augusto B. Leguía. Since neither Leguía nor his followers had ever really been committed to alleviating Indian oppression, their views coincided with those of the northern coastal and urban supporters of Apra.

The overthrow of Leguía in 1930 had provided the Civilistas with a long-awaited opportunity to reestablish their former political and economic hegemony. However, owing in part to internal bickering, the Civilistas failed to agree on a single presidential candidate and turned instead to Sánchez Cerro.[35] On the other hand, the Leguiístas, who were also badly divided and bore the additional burden of blame for the political and economic excesses of the *oncenio,* were unable to run a candidate, much less win the election. Many of them drifted into Aprista ranks. The Civilistas and Sánchez-Cerristas attempted to discredit the Apristas with charges that Aprismo was merely an extension of Leguiísmo.

Although the Apristas strenuously denied any connection with the deposed president, Haya certainly accepted and even courted Leguiísta backing. During his return voyage to Peru in 1931, Haya passed through New York and reportedly spent some time with Alfredo Larrañaga, Leguía's son-in-law, and also with other high Leguiísta officials.[36] Jorge Basadre, the leading Peruvian historian of his generation, noted soon after the election of 1931 that "some

35. Apristas have long asserted that Sánchez Cerro was merely a tool of the Civilistas. Although this claim may be an exaggeration, there is no doubt that he received their political and financial backing. United States embassy officials in Peru reported as early as 1930 that "Colonel Sánchez Cerro is about to allow himself to be appropriated by the very reactionary old *Civilista* Party, representing the land owning aristocracy and vested interests, headed by Antonio Miró Quesada" (Dearing to Secretary of State, October 29, 1930, D.S. 823.00 Revolutions/75). Further examples of Civilista support for Sánchez Cerro and their attempts to regain power through him can be found in this same series of papers. For an anti-Aprista claim that Civilistas were the architects of Sánchez Cerro's reign of terror, see Federico More, *Zoocracía y canibalismo* (Lima: Editorial "Llamarada," 1933), pp. 36-37. For a comparable position, see: Jorge Basadre, "Letter from Peru: The Recent Election in Retrospect," a letter sent by Basadre to the Council on Foreign Relations in New York and filed as D.S. 823.00/851. See also a letter from Juan Pacheco Cateriano to Manuel Bustamante de le Fuente, October 12, 1931, Bustamante Archive.

36. Counselor of Embassy H. P. Starrett to Secretary of State, September 11, 1931, D.S. 823.00/743. Ambassador Dearing went so far as to state: "There seems to be no doubt that the old Leguiístas are throwing their fortunes in with Haya de Latorre" (Dearing to Secretary of State, September 16, 1931, D.S. 810.43 APRA/197).

people allied personally or for family reasons with Leguía's regime are now Apristas," and Miss Anna Graves, a long-time friend and financial supporter of Haya, wrote that much of the Civilista ferocity directed against Haya in 1931 was due to "the fact that Haya spoke to and seemed to be willing to receive as helpers some of the old Leguía men."[37] One anti-Apra and anti-Sánchez Cerro journalist asserted that former Leguiístas poured into the Aprista party, and that, in reality, the 1931 election was a battle between the pro- and anti-Leguía wings of the oligarchy rather than a contest between Sánchez Cerro and Haya.[38] This thesis is perhaps overdrawn, but former Leguiístas did provide the Apristas with political expertise, campaign funds, and a substantial number of votes.

Thus Haya derived much of his political backing in the early 1930s from middle- and upper-class elements who could hardly have been expected to support his radical pronouncements of the 1920s. Moreover, there are indications that the ideology which appealed to the intellectuals, the leftists, and the lower class was repudiated by Haya in private meetings with members of the upper class and the business community. Evidence of this is found in the reports of the United States ambassador to Peru, Fred Morris Dearing, a career foreign service officer.

At first Dearing was suspicious of Apra writing and noted in September, 1930, that Haya was returning to Peru "to exploit his communistic endeavors," and that "he is quite generally believed to be in the pay of the Soviets."[39] In January, 1931, he stated that Apra was

subversive in character and not entitled to the freedom of a normal and natural political party. Both Leguía's Government and the present Gov-

---

37. Basadre, "Letter from Peru"; memorandum by Miss Anna Graves to the United States ambassador in Peru; attached to Counselor of Embassy Louis G. Dreyfus, Jr., to Secretary of State, May 28, 1935, D.S. 810.43 APRA/205. Interestingly, Luis Eduardo Enríquez, the party's first secretary general in Peru, asserts that while in Europe in the late 1920s, Haya was secretly courting old Civilistas such as Francisco García Calderón, Mariano H. Cornejo, and Gonzalo Aramburu *(Haya de la Torre: La estafa política más grande de América* [Lima: Ediciones del Pacífico, 1951], pp. 73-74).

38. More, *Una multitud contra un pueblo,* pp. 22-26, 129-32. See also his *Zoocracia y canibalismo.*

39. Dearing to Secretary of State, September 23, 1930, D.S. 810.43 APRA/50.

ernment have found them enemies of public order and purely destructive in their aim and in spite of their denials, it is almost certain that they are still under the influence of Moscow. A story has been circulated that the Chief, Haya de la Torre, went to Moscow last year, became disgusted with what he saw and thereafter resolved to divorce his following from the Russians. There is reason to believe that this is a blind.[40]

By April, however, Dearing, commenting on the growing strength of the Apristas and the possibility that they might win, reported: "Somehow or other the prospect [of an Apra victory] does not seem to me to be particularly terrifying." The next month, the ambassador forwarded a copy of a *West Coast Leader* interview with Manuel Seoane (referred to in an earlier dispatch as "the reddest of the red and a very dangerous man") and observed: "I have noticed from some time past that in practically all of his public statements, Mr. Seoane has shown that he is a sensible and realistic man."[41]

Haya had sought out officials of important foreign companies in London and impressed upon them his desire to reform but not revolutionize Peruvian society. He also promised them that he would soften his antiforeign stance.[42] Haya and other party leaders also met with United States officials to try to convince them that Haya had considerably modified his views, particularly with reference to Yankee imperialism and extensive nationalization of railroads and industry.[43]

Haya himself requested a private meeting with Dearing, to be held on neutral ground so as to avoid charges that he was insincere in his attacks on foreign imperialism. Dearing's report of that meeting is most revealing:

40. Dearing to Secretary of State, January 19, 1931, D.S. 810.43 APRA/59.

41. Dearing to Secretary of State, April 22, 1931, D.S. 810.43 APRA/79; Dearing to Secretary of State, March 24, 1931, D.S. 810.43 APRA/82; Dearing to Secretary of State, May 11, 1931, D.S. 810.43 APRA/81.

42. Both Harold Kingsmill, general manager of the Cerro de Pasco Copper Corporation, and General Cooper, director of the Peruvian Corporation, met with Haya in London and were favorably impressed with his attitude. See: Dearing to Secretary of State, July 17, 1931, D.S. 810.43 APRA/89. Haya is said to have promised Kingsmill that he would reduce his antiforeign attacks, and apparently kept that promise by delivering a very mild campaign speech in Cerro de Pasco in September, 1931. See: Dearing to Secretary of State, September 16, 1931, D.S. 810.43 APRA/105.

43. For an account of one such meeting immediately after Haya's return to Peru in August, see Starrett to Secretary of State, August 18, 1931, D.S. 823.00/734.

Señor Haya de la Torre immediately impressed me by something warm and sympathetic in his character and by his apparent sincerity.... He scouted the idea that he was destructive or ultra-radical and he seemed to have a sincere regard for our country which he has visited several times.... Señor Haya de la Torre indicated clearly that if his party should ever be successful, he would expect as much understanding and helpfulness as possible from our Government and a real co-operation between our two countries; he merely wishes it to be careful, considerate and fair. ... At the moment the situation in the mining camps of the Northern Peru Mining and Smelting Company was active, and Señor Haya de la Torre told me, somewhat as an evidence of how he felt towards American interests, that he had that morning, through his various connections, counselled all of his people in and about the Trujillo district to prevent any violence of any kind and to throw their influence towards a peaceful settlement by a calm acceptance of the inevitable.... While talking to me, Haya de la Torre gave me the impression of relaxation, and while I was conconscious of his intensity of purpose and have the experience of the last few months to show that he is a man of ability and has the respect and adherence of many of his fellow-citizens, I am still uncertain as to whether I should say that he is a man of destiny or not. From what I know up to this point, however, I should think that if he should become president of Peru, we should have nothing to fear and on the contrary might expect an excellent and beneficient administration of strongly liberal tendencies in which justice in the main would be done, and a period of confidence and well being be initiated.[44]

That interview occurred on September 1, 1931, and was not an isolated incident. Haya met with embassy officials on several occasions and continued also to meet with leading members of important foreign business concerns.[45] A careful analysis of these interviews clearly demonstrates that Haya de la Torre was not sincere in his espousal of radical causes in general and extreme *indigenismo* in particular.

44. Dearing to Secretary of State, September 7, 1931, D.S. 810.43 APRA/102.

45. For examples of subsequent interviews with Haya, see: Starrett to Secretary of State, September 11, 1931, D.S. 823.00/743; and Dearing to Secretary of State, February 21, 1932, D.S. 823.00/843. For the view of one United States businessman, see: Norbert A. Bogdan to Edwin C. Wilson, Chief, Division of Latin American Affairs, Department of State, March 19, 1935, D.S. 835.00/695. Bogdan wrote: "I met De Latorre, the real leader of the whole movement and found him to be a very moderate and reasonable fellow, educated at Oxford, and wide awake to everything that goes on in the world today. I don't think that there is much danger that the mob may run away from their present leaders."

Although Apra maintained it was the victim of electoral fraud, and there did exist some irregularities on both sides, Sánchez Cerro won the election of October 11, 1931, with the combined support of the upper and lower classes.[46] Haya de la Torre refused to accept the results, and, in December, delivered an emotional plea to his followers in Trujillo to unite and continue the fight to free Peru from oppression, closing with the words "Only Aprismo will save Peru."[47] With that speech began a continuous civil war between Apra and the army. The bitterness between the two ran deep, exacerbated by massacres and assassinations on both sides. Throughout the 1930s, Haya de la Torre and the Apristas issued pronouncements similar to their 1931 program,[48] but they had little effect on the politics of either Sánchez Cerro or his successor, Oscar R. Benavides, except insomuch as they provoked negative reactions. The party was outlawed, its members persecuted, deported, and jailed, and its publications closed, forcing it to resort to the issuance of clandestine materials. Even all twenty-three Apristas in the Constituent Congress were arrested and deported in February of 1932.[49]

During this "underground" period (1932-45), the party renewed its verbal use of *indigenismo* and the volume of Aprista Indian propaganda increased.[50] The programs proposed did not differ in substance from those offered in 1931, and were still extremely

46. See: Basadre, *Historia de la república,* 11:201-3.

47. Haya de la Torre, *Construyendo el aprismo,* pp. 172-75.

48. For example, see: Partido Aprista Peruano, *40 preguntas y 40 respuestas sobre el Partido Aprista Peruano por el buró de redactores de "Cuaderno Aprista"* (Incahuasi: Editorial Indoamericana, 1941); Partido Aprista Peruano, *El proceso Haya*; and Haya de la Torre, *Política aprista.*

49. The best contemporary source is Luis Antonio Eguiguren, *En la selva política: Para la historia* (Lima: Sanmarti y Cía., Editores, 1933). See also: Basadre, *Historia de la república,* 11:213-39.

50. Although all Aprista publications of this period contained elements of *indigenismo,* the reader is directed particularly to the following works: Cossío del Pomar, *Haya de la Torre*; Carlos Manuel Cox, ed., *Cartas de Haya de la Torre a los prisioneros apristas* (Lima: Editorial Nuevo Día, 1946); Haya de la Torre, *Espacio-tiempo-histórico;* Víctor Raúl Haya de la Torre, *Y después de la guerra ¿qué?* (Lima: Editorial PTCM, 1946); Partido Aprista Peruano, *40 preguntas y 40 respuestas;* idem, *El proceso Haya;* Alfredo Saco, *Programa agrario del aprismo* (Lima: Ediciones Populares, 1946); Alfredo Saco, *Síntesis aprista (una exposición completa de la ideología del aprismo)* (Lima: Librería e Imprenta "San Cristobal," Editorial Atahualpa, 1934); and Sánchez, *Raúl Haya de la Torre.*

vague. For example, a communiqué released in 1933 by the Sindicato Aprista de Abogados called for the investigation of such themes as how to secure for the Indians the position they held during the Inca Empire, the social and legal posture of the nation toward the Indian *comunidad,* methods of providing financial aid to Indian *comunidades,* the conflict between *comunidades* and haciendas, how to convert *comunidades* into viable cooperatives, the relation of the *comunidad* to Peru's agricultural problems, and how to improve the Indians' technical abilities. The Apristas also called for renewed efforts in Indian education and proposed a massive national celebration of the four-hundredth anniversary of the death of Atahualpa.[51]

The brutal suppression of Apra by Sánchez Cerro and his successor, Oscar Benavides, had two results. First, it unified the party and intensified feelings of loyalty, and second, and perhaps more important, it enabled Haya to be all things to all men. Deprived of all elective or appointive offices and forced into hiding, Haya and his lieutenants were never required to deliver on their promises. They maintained a radical posture in their official publications while assuring rightist supporters that they had no intention of ever actually implementing such proposals. This opportunity for flexibility helps to explain the extremely low defection rate from Aprista ranks in the period 1933-45.

Despite the civil unrest accompanying the suppression of Apra, government activities continued. In August, 1931, the Samánez Ocampo administration had named a commission, headed by Manuel Vicente Villarán, to draft a new constitution. It was made public on December 5, and there were two articles concerning Indians. In the first the state would have gone on record as favoring the preservation of existing small and medium-sized properties and an increase in this kind of landholding. It called for legislation authorizing the expropriation of private lands that were not being utilized and their redistribution, with preference to be given to those Indian *comunidades* which lacked sufficient lands to support their populations. The second article recognized the legal existence of the *comunidades* and other Indian economic institutions and promised that laws would be enacted to aid the Indians in the

---

51. *La crónica* (Lima), August 23, 1933, included in Dearing to Secretary of State, August 28, 1933, D.S. 810.43 APRA/191.

acculturation process.[52] The two articles would have greatly benefited the Indians. Not only did they recognize the *comunidad,* but
they provided for an extensive land-reform program. For the Indians, it was a stronger document than that ultimately produced
by the Congress.

The Constituent Congress, elected with Sánchez Cerro, was
charged with drafting a new constitution. Very early in its deliberations an extremely important document pertaining to Indian legislation was prepared and presented to the Congress by the head
of the Bureau of Indian Affairs, Magdaleno Chira C., which traced
the history of the Indian problems, criticized past legislation, and
proposed needed changes. Chira C. called for immediate restitution
of usurped Indian lands, increased taxes on uncultivated property,
expropriation of the larger estates with distribution of land to the
Indians, regulation of all Indian wage agreements and work contracts, registration of all *comunidades,* creation of extensive educational facilities, and defense of the Indians by the Ministry of
Justice instead of by private lawyers in all civil and criminal suits.[53]

The Congress first dealt with the Indian problem in December,
1931, when a motion was presented requesting its Commission on
Indian Affairs to draft a comprehensive Indian code, incorporating
the guarantees, institutions, and programs necessary to achieve
Indian integration. The Socialist and Decentralist parties supported the motion, but two Aprista representatives, Pedro Muñíz
from Lima and Luis E. Heysen from Lambayeque, opposed it,
asserting that the Indians needed an economic revolution, not new
legislation. Representing Sánchez Cerro's Revolutionary Union
party (Unión Revolucionaria), Abelardo Solís from Junín argued
that the Indian problem was not racial in nature, but one of education, culture, hygiene, and economics, and this should concern
the representatives, not an Indian code. The motion passed, but
the commission never actually drafted a code.[54]

In August, 1932, the Indian Commission introduced for inclu-
sion in the constitution a *comunidad* proposal which provided the
following: the state would recognize the legal existence of the Indian *comunidades;* the departmental councils would inscribe them
in the official registry; the state would guarantee the territorial

52. Pareja Paz-Soldán, ed., *Las constituciones del Perú,* pp. 319-20, 998-1000, 1064.
53. Chira C., *Observaciones,* pp. 21-26.
54. Sivirichi, *Derecho indígena,* pp. 158-62.

integrity of the *comunidades* in conformity with their titles, or by the concept of continuous possession when titles were lacking; *comunidad* lands would be imprescriptible, inalienable, and not attachable; the *comunidad* Indians were to be collective owners of the lands and could form neither individual nor collective contracts that would compromise or limit their property; only the executive could, upon recommendation of the Supreme Court, order *comunidad* land divided and only when the land would remain inalienable, to be transmitted from father to son.

The measure also provided that the hereditary transfer of lands and private transfers of lands between members would be regulated by each *comunidad;* the state would aportion land to those *comunidades* which had insufficient holdings, expropriating private property when necessary; Indian property would be legally distinct from municipal property and neither the municipal councils nor any other corporation or authority could intervene in the collection or administration of the profits of a *comunidad;* the state would protect the Indians and dictate special laws to favor their development and culture; in each *comunidad* there would be a boarding school; and the state would recognize the authority of the mayor and other *comunidad* officials.[55]

This proposal was more comprehensive than the earlier Villarán draft. Led by Socialists Hildebrando Castro Pozo from Piura, Saturino Vara Cadillo from Huánuco, and Alberto Arca Parró from Ayacucho, the *indigenistas* delivered long, impassioned speeches in the Congress on the necessity for adopting the proposal. Castro Pozo and Arca Parró called for the socialization of the land and the institution of a cooperative organization for the *comunidades.* Opponents of the project held that the constitution should be a declaration of principles rather than a compendium of detail. Several asserted that the *comunidad* itself was an anachronism and should be abolished, while others argued that the proposal did not account for regional differences. At this juncture, many representatives who had originally supported the proposal withdrew their signatures and offered a substitute motion to the Indian Commission.[56]

The commission presented the revised proposal to the Congress on September 2, 1932. Under the new articles the state would

---

55. For a complete text of the proposal, see: Sivirichi, *Derecho indígena,* pp. 105-6.
56. Ibid, pp. 106-9.

recognize the legal existence of the *comunidades;* the departmental councils would inscribe the *comunidades* in the official register; the state would guarantee the territorial integrity of the *comunidades* and would institute a title registry; *comunidad* property would be imprescriptible, inalienable, and not attachable except in cases of expropriation for public utility; and the state would issue civil, economic, educational, and administrative laws according to Indian needs.[57]

The ensuing debate was spirited, with the Socialists calling for outright socialization of the land, the *indigenistas* demanding that the Congress protect the Indians by approving the proposal, and representatives of the landed oligarchy asserting that the *comunidad* should be abolished because it had been the ruin of the Indians. The moderates, men like Víctor Andrés Belaúnde from Arequipa, Ricardo Feijóo Reyno from Amazonas, and Manuel Jesús Gamarra and Luis Velazco Aragón from Cuzco, asserted that the Indians required legal protection, as did the *comunidad,* and that the proposals were not too detailed, given the complexity of the Indian problem. Arguing that special legislation did not imply inferiority, they predicted that without constitutional protection the *comunidad* would fall prey to greedy landowners.

Of all the speeches, Belaúnde's was the most thoughtful and reasonable. Agreeing that a constitution should not contain excessive detail, he urged the representatives to make an exception in the Indian section because of the need to incorporate the Indians into the society and to protect the *comunidad* lands. He offered two additions to the commission's draft. The first was that the state provide lands to those *comunidades* which lacked sufficient plots for their populations, expropriating private property when necessary, a proposal which he asserted was not a concession to the radical left as represented by the followers of Mariátegui, but one actually put forth by a Catholic archbishop in 1798. The second was that the constitution recognize the authority of Indian officials elected by the *comunidades.*[58]

On September 5, the Congress approved without alteration all the commission's articles. Immediately following the vote, several

57. Perú, Congreso Constituyente de 1931, *Diario de los debates del Congreso Constituyente de 1931,* September 2, 1932, 7:3287-88 (hereafter cited as Congreso Constituyente, followed by the date, volume number, and page number).

58. The text of this two-day debate is in: Congreso Constituyente, September 2, 1932, 7:3286-3304, and September 5, 1932, 7:3348-70.

amendments were formally presented, including several Socialist proposals which would have required a review of all hacienda land titles, the return of all stolen lands to the Indian, and gradual socialization of the sierra. Others tried to limit the size of agricultural holdings. Belaúnde argued for the adoption of his proposals to expropriate land for *comunidades,* to recognize Indian officials, and to prohibit municipal officials from intervening in the administration of *comunidad* affairs.

On October 20, 1932, the Indian Commission reported its decisions. It rejected all the proposed amendments except those of Belaúnde regarding the expropriation of property and the intervention of municipal authorities. The final draft of Title XI, which was incorporated into the constitution, reads as follows:

ART. 207. The Indian communities have a legal existence and juridical personality.

ART. 208. The State guarantees the integrity of the property of the communities. The law shall organize the corresponding register of real property.

ART. 209. The property of the communities is imprescriptible and inalienable, except in the case of expropriation on account of public utility, on payment of compensation. It is, moreover, not attachable.

ART. 210. Neither the Municipal Councils nor any corporation or authority shall intervene in the collection or administration of the income and property of the communities.

ART. 211. The State shall endeavor to provide by preference lands for Indian communities which do not possess them in sufficient quantity for their needs, and may expropriate lands in private ownership for this purpose, on payment of compensation.

ART. 212. The State shall enact the civil, penal, economic, education and administrative legislation which the peculiar conditions of the Indians demand.

Article 205 also pertained to Indians: "Indian communities shall have a representative, designated by them in the manner which the law specifies, in each district Municipal Council and in those created by a decision of the Departmental Council."[59]

The Constitution of 1933 represented an attempt to complete and to expand the *comunidad* provisions of the 1920 document. The various articles provided the legal structure upon which all

59. Pan American Union, *Constitution of the Republic of Peru,* 1933 (Washington, D.C., 1965), p. 23.

succeeding legislation was based. The Indians were guaranteed protection of their lands, recognition of the *comunidades,* and representation in local government; they were promised a comprehensive legal code. While the political orientation of the Congress had shifted to the right following the purge of 1931-32, this conservatism did not affect the Indian section, which was one of the most liberal and forward-looking parts of the constitution. However, as with past legislation, the enactment of laws favorable to the Indians was not necessarily followed by enforcement.

Article 208, which provided for the registration of *comunidades,* was implemented slowly. The Peruvian census of 1940 showed more than 5,000 Indian *comunidades,* but by the end of that year, only 794 had been inscribed, including the 321 from the Leguía period.[60] Article 212, which called for an Indian code, was considered by many *indigenistas* and legal experts to be the most important provision, but the code was never written, thus leaving the Indians in their traditional state of oppression.[61] The remaining articles were enforced only sporadically, and the hopes of the liberals and moderates in the Congress came to naught.

In a rather ironic move, the Congress also approved a law on October 29, 1932, commemorating the four hundredth anniversary of the execution of the Inca Atahualpa. In introducing the measure, Representative Alfredo Herrera from Lima stated that the day had special significance for all Peruvians because the divisions exemplified in the execution had now disappeared and Peru was a union of two races, a new nationality.[62] A different event would seem to have been more appropriate to commemorate.

During the constitutional deliberations, the Ministry of Development issued several decrees and resolutions affecting Indians. Because engineers and surveyors charged excessive fees for surveying *comunidades,* the ministry issued a resolution on November 19, 1931, fixing the maximum rate at two centavos per meter and establishing guidelines for transportation costs and other expenses. To guarantee payment of the surveying commissions, the *comunidades* were required to deposit 50 percent of the estimated

60. Dobyns, *The Social Matrix,* p. 3. See also: Vega, *La emancipación,* pp. 26-29.

61. On the importance of the code, see: Pareja Paz-Soldán, *Derecho constitutional peruano,* p. 421. On its failure of enactment, see: Sivirichi, *Derecho indígena,* pp. 140-41.

62. See: Chira C., *Observaciones,* pp. 168-70; and Basadre, *Historia de la república,* 11:392.

expenses in a special account before the commission began work. Two centavos, however, was a very high rate and placed a burden on most *comunidades* that they could not afford. The government would have promoted increased *comunidad* registration had it paid the surveying expenses.[63]

Some months later, the ministry settled the long-standing dispute between the *comunidad* of Acoria and the Huánuco Department of Public Welfare over title to the hacienda Cachimayo. Although the government had awarded Cachimayo to the department in 1898, the Indians of Acoria continued to work it until 1923, when department officals reclaimed it in a violent clash. The Ministry of Development awarded the hacienda to the *comunidad,* basing its decision on the principle of continual occupation. The department appealed, and in September, 1932, the ministry reaffirmed its decision and ordered the Department of Public Welfare to vacate the lands immediately.[64]

Throughout Sánchez Cerro's term, the Bureau of Indian Affairs investigated many *comunidad* claims and adjudicated several. In cases where the *comunidad* lacked proper documentation, the bureau dispatched special delegations composed of the head of the bureau, Magdaleno Chira C., and several engineers.[65] The effectiveness of the bureau was limited, however, in that the *comunidades* were required to pay all the expenses of the delegations and very few had sufficient resources to do so. Moreover, many of the isolated *comunidades* were unaware of the bureau and its services, and local officials undoubtedly discouraged Indians from taking their case to Lima. Those cases actually heard by the bureau represented a mere fraction of the existing disputes.

Decisions by the Supreme Court also affected Indian rights. On June 1, 1932, it held that a *comunidad* had to be inscribed in the official register of *comunidades* in the Ministry of Development in order to enjoy the protection of the government in legal suits or land disputes. On September 28, 1932, the court decided that all crimes committed by "semicivilized Indians" were to be handled with greater prudence, the sentence taking into account Indian culture.[66]

63. For the text of the resolution, see: PMTAI; *Legislación,* pp. 114-17. See also: Chira C., *Observaciones,* p. 56.

64. Chira C., *Observaciones,* pp. 133-37.

65. For several examples, see: ibid., pp. 79-83, 137-41, 187-89.

66. See: Fajardo, *Legislación indígena,* pp. 168-69; and Varallanos, *Legislación indiana,* p. 6.

President Sánchez Cerro remained silent toward the Indians. He issued no decrees pertaining to them and apparently had little concern for them despite his preelection pronouncements. Forced Indian labor, outlawed on numerous occasions, was still common in the central and southern sierra; the government made no effort to check it. On many haciendas, the Indians lived in a state of vassalage.[67]

Crimes and oppression by government officials also went unpunished. In August, 1931, the subprefect of Cuzco sent a circular to Lima describing how officials in the town of Paucartambo in the department of Cuzco had forced the Indians from several *comunidades* to man the government launch on the Paucartambo River. The lawyer hired by the Indians tricked them into assigning title to their lands to him. He also forced them to work on his hacienda in payment of legal fees and lent them to a priest, who also used them on his hacienda. The Indians sought legal recourse; when that failed, the subprefect requested action from Lima. Though the report went to the Ministry of Development and to President Sánchez Cerro himself, no action was forthcoming.[68]

Another example of government oppression occurred in Cuzco in 1932. The Guardia Civil (the national police force) arrested several members of the *comunidad* Molocahua for cattle theft. Several days later, two policemen returned to the *comunidad* to arrest additional Indians, attacked them, and were killed. More police were sent, and when the guilty Indians fled, they simply arrested all those who remained, including women and children, and imprisoned them in Cuzco. Unable to afford lawyers, the Indians languished in prison until they were finally released months later.[69]

These were but two of countless incidents to which the government in Lima remained deaf. Sánchez Cerro was occupied with political riots and uprisings such as that led by Apristas in Trujillo in 1932, but there is no indication that he ever intended to deal with the Indian problem. It is impossible to know, however, because he was assassinated on April 30, 1933, by an Aprista fanatic, Abelardo Mendoza Leiva.

The Congress "elected" General Oscar R. Benavides to complete Sánchez Cerro's six-year term. Benavides, who had served

---

67. Chira C., *Observaciones,* pp. 27-28.
68. For an account of the incident, see: Cornejo Bouroncle, *Tierras ajenas,* pp. 182-86.
69. Ibid., pp. 75, 79-82.

briefly as president in 1914, came from an upper-class background and sought above all to maintain peace in the country, imposing a tight dictatorship in the process. Upon taking power, he released all political prisoners, including Apristas, and allowed political exiles to return. However, when Apra requested new congressional elections, Benavides refused and again suppressed the party.[70] The Constituent Congress was instructed by Benavides to continue, which it did until December, 1936.

Confronted as he was with problems of taking office and of suppressing internal political turmoil, Benavides avoided issues, including the Indian problem, which might intensify the strife. In 1933, for example, the Constituent Congress approved a new *yanacona* law written by Manuel Bustamante de la Fuente of Arequipa. It provided that no *yanacona* could be dismissed except for failure to pay his rent or for willful destruction of crops or irrigation canals, and if so dismissed, he was still entitled to his portion of the crops. Upon completion of a contract, which could be oral, a *yanacona* had preference over all others in the competition for a new contract. Furthermore, the *yanacona* was not required to sell his crops or livestock to the owner, nor obligated to provide free labor services or to pay more than 14 percent interest on his debts.[71] Fearing disorders in the sierra, Benavides simply refused to issue the law, thereby vetoing it.[72]

Benavides continued to avoid the Indian issue for over two years. In the early period of his term he did press for construction of more roads to improve the economic infrastructure of the nation. He later pointed to his road program as being of

> incalculable benefit to the nation. The highways assimilate in a natural, organic, and progressive manner the numerous Indian peoples that live for the most part isolated in our economic world. A system of roads seems to be the most positive method of converting the Indian into a true citizen.[73]

70. The best account of the assassination and transfer of power is: Basadre, *Historia de la república* 11:457-93. See also: Pike, *Modern History of Peru,* pp. 267-70.

71. Congreso Constituyente, September 30, 1933, 13:3684-86. See also the Bustamante Archive. Fearing that the law might be issued later or reintroduced in Congress, the National Agrarian Society pressured Bustamante de la Fuente to introduce their own, conservative *yanacona* law. For a copy of this proposal, see: Gerardo Klinge to Manuel Bustamante de la Fuente, September 5, 1934, Bustamante Archive.

72. Letter from Bustamante de la Fuente, September 7, 1971, to me.

73. Oscar R. Benavides, *El General Benavides a la nación: Mensaje del 25 de marzo de 1939* (Lima: Imprenta C.V.L., 1939), p. 24. Pike *(Modern History of Peru,* p. 271) also praises Benavides's highway construction program, noting that thirty thousand men were employed by 1936.

Not only is Benavides's expansive assessment of the value of a highway network in alleviating the unjust conditions of Indian life open to question, his road-building program itself resulted in severe new infringements upon Indian life.

In 1936, Representative Saturnino Vara Cadillo published a book on the abuses committed in the construction of the Huánuco-Pucalpa highway. He charged the chairman of the Congressional Highway Commission with sending a circular in 1933 to local officials in the department of Huánuco ordering them to force all men between the ages of sixteen and sixty to work on road construction. They were to work in rotations of fifteen days with one month off and were paid a daily wage of one *sol.* Vara Cadillo asserted that the wage usually was not paid and that police and construction chiefs had been guilty of violence in recruiting men. Ill-clothed, ill-fed, and worked long hours, many Indians tried to escape, but were captured and forced to return to the construction camps.[74]

Some local officials objected to this exploitation and attempted to secure aid from Lima, but they were unsuccessful. The Socialists denounced the oppression in Congress, but their pleas for alleviation of it also fell on deaf ears. In 1936, the prefect of Huánuco denied the charges of oppression in a letter to the minister of government, enclosing a denial from the local commanding officer of the Guardia Civil.[75] Despite denials, abuses had been committed; local officials had in effect reinstituted the outlawed *conscripción vial.*

If highway construction practices were reminiscent of those of the *oncenio,* so was Benavides's first major Indian law. By supreme decree of July 8, 1935, he created the Superior Council of Indian Affairs (Consejo Superior de Asuntos Indígenas), composed of the minister of development, the public prosecutor of the Supreme Court, the deputy minister of development, the deputy minister of agriculture and livestock, the judicial adviser of the Ministry of Development, and the head of the Bureau of Indian Affairs as permanent members. Nonpermanent delegates from the Ministry of Justice and Instruction, the Bar Association of Lima, and the En-

---

74. N. Saturnino Vara Cadillo, *La trata de indios en la construcción de la carretera Huánuco-Pucalpa: Documentos parlamentarios* (Lima: Partido Socialista del Perú, 1936), pp. 8-16.
75. Ibid., pp. 31-32.

gineering Society of Peru were to be named by the president. The council was to hear and study all Indian complaints; to make recommendations for improvement of the Indians' economic, social, and educational state; to request reports from government officials; to compile all Indian legislation; and to propose Indian laws for consideration by Congress.[76]

There was little difference between Benavides's council and Augusto B. Leguía's Patronato de la Raza. Both were extragovernmental agencies created to aid the Indians, and both failed. Established for political reasons, both agencies lacked the power and support necessary to function effectively. Little was heard of the council after its creation, and it is doubtful that it made any contributions to Indian integration.

In August, 1935, Benavides sent an administration bill to Congress which would have empowered the president and the minister of development to divide state lands and sell the lots to Indians and mestizos on long-term credit.[77] The proposed law was never enacted, but another administration bill received more favorable treatment. Law 8120 of September 16, 1935, created arbitration tribunals in the Ministry of Development for adjudicating Indian labor and land disputes, particularly conflicts over cultivation and pasture privileges on haciendas, wage conflicts, and boundary disputes between *comunidades* and neighboring estates.[78] Benavides asserted that the tribunals would be able to settle all disputes and complaints, thereby pacifying the interior; they failed to do so. *Hacendados* appealed unfavorable decisions in an attempt to delay or kill the suits. The president sought to prohibit the practice in 1939, but the tribunals never functioned as planned.[79]

76. PMTAI, *Legislación*, pp. 46-47. See also the bylaws of the council in ibid., pp. 48-52.

77. Republica Peruana, Ministerio de Fomento, Dirección General del Ramo, Sección de Asuntos Indígenas, *Recopilación de leyes, decretos y resoluciones que se relacionan con la raza indígena, y recomendaciones para la organización de expendientes de reconocimiento e inscripción oficial y de levantamiento de planos de conjunto de las tierras de las comunidades de indígenas* (Lima: Imprenta y Librería del Gabiente Militar, 1935), pp. 12-14.

78. PMTAI, *Legislación*, pp. 97-98. See also a speech by General Armando Artola del Pozo, reprinted in Congreso Indigenista Interamericano, II, Cuzco, 1949, *Anales* (Lima: Editorial Lumen, 1949), p. 70.

79. Oscar R. Benavides, *Mensaje presentado al Congreso del Perú por el señor General de División don Oscar R. Benavides presidente constitucional de la república* (Lima: Talleres Gráficos "Carlos Vásquez L.," 1939), p. 169; and PMTAI, *Legislación*, p. 106.

On March 23, 1936, the president issued a series of four supreme decrees pertaining to Indians. The first detailed the proper procedures for the Bureau of Indian Affairs in the event of labor disputes between Indians and their employers; arbitration was to be obligatory in the event that efforts at conciliation failed.[80] The second required all employers to maintain complete wage records of their employees so that minimum wage and hour laws might be enforced;[81] the third was composed of specific regulations for the defense and protection of the Indians in accordance with the constitution and other legislation; the fourth established more complete guidelines for the recognition and registration of *comunidades*.[82] None of the decrees constituted a departure from previous legislation; rather, they were designed to explain and to expand established laws.

The executive also promulgated a new Código Civil (Civil Code) in 1936 which devoted five articles (70-74) to the Indian *comunidad*. The legal existence of the *comunidades* was recognized and they were ordered to register and provide boundary maps for official files. Elected representatives were given the authority to speak for the *comunidades* and were prohibited from ceding any *comunidad* land to neighboring estates. The code provided for the passage of a special Indian code, but none was ever enacted despite continuing interest and support from the *indigenistas*.[83]

The only substantive difference between the code and the Constitution of 1933 was the provision requiring *comunidad* registration; the implication was that the *comunidad* was neither protected nor qualified to receive government assistance without formal recognition. This was consistent with the Supreme Court position of June, 1932.

During the first portion of his rule, Benavides signed two international treaties which dealt with Indians. In June, 1934, Peru and Colombia signed a treaty which included two sections on protec-

---

80. Carlos, M. Alvarez Beltrán, *Estatuto de comunidades de indígenas del Perú (concordado y comentado)* (Trujillo: Editorial Escolar "Cabrera," 1964), pp. 84-88.

81. PMTAI, *Legislación,* pp. 137-38.

82. Chávez León, *Legislación social,* pp. 45-48, 98-104.

83. PMTAI, *Legislación,* p. 110. For an example of a proposed Indian code, see: Pedro Erasmo Roca Sánchez, *Por la clase indígena: Exposición y proyectos para una solución del aspecto legal del problema indígena, presentado a la Constituyente por el autor en su calidad de representante por el departamento de Ancash* (Lima: Pedro Barrantes Castro, Editor, 1935).

tion of jungle Indians. Wages, hours of work, education, health, and conditions of employment were regulated without regard to whether the Indian was working in Peru or Colombia. In September, 1936, Peru and Bolivia signed a convention under which each agreed to inform the other of all of its Indian legislation, labor legislation, special Indian studies, and programs to limit the consumption of alcohol or coca. In addition, both governments were to facilitate international travel for technical commissions dealing with Indian affairs.[84]

Sánchez Cerro's constitutional term expired in 1936, and Benavides, who had been grooming Jorge Prado for the presidency, allowed elections to be held on October 11. At that time, there were approximately eighteen political parties in Peru, but most of them combined to form fronts for the election. Jorge Prado was the candidate of the center-right Frente Nacional (National Front), Luis A. Eguiguren ran as the candidate of the center-left Frente Demócrata (Democratic Front), Manuel Vicente Villarán headed the rightest coalition Partido Nacional (National party), while Luis N. Flores ran as the candidate of Sánchez Cerro's old Unión Revolutionaria (Revolutionary Union). The Apristas supported Eguiguren, who won, but Benavides nullified the elections, announcing that he would serve a full six-year term from the time of his appointment.[85]

Many of the parties mentioned the Indian in their platforms and several actually attempted to write an Indian program. The Partido Liberal (Liberal party), headed by José Balta asserted that the problem was economic, not racial, and called for the protection of Indian lands, expropriation of private lands to augment *comunidad* holdings, and extension of the educational structure to provide schooling for all Indian children. It also called upon the state to provide machinery, seeds, and breeding stock to the Indians to better their agricultural production. The Partido Constitucional Renovador (Renovating Constitutional party), headed by Arturo Osores, advocated land reform, establishment of rural Indian schools, and economic development of the *comunidades*

84. PMTAI, *Legislación*, pp. 55-59. For an example of an apparent lack of cooperation between Peru and Bolivia, see: Ambassador Laurence A. Steinhardt to Secretary of State, December 20, 1937, D.S. 823.00/1296.

85. For a complete listing of political parties, see: Ambassador Fred M. Dearing to Secretary of State, March 16, 1936, D.S. 823.00/1190; and Louis G. Dreyfus, Jr., to Secretary of State, May 13, 1939, D.S. 823.00/1361.

through a combination of agrarian cooperatives and family-owned plots. The Partido Social Nacionalista (Nationalist Social party), headed by Elías Lozada Benavente, also demanded land reform, agricultural cooperatives within the *comunidades,* additional Indian educational facilities, and special treatment of Indian delinquents. The party declared that swift government action to destroy *latifundio* and feudalism was required if the Indians were to be integrated.[86] None of the parties included any original proposals in their pronouncements. They drew upon the platitudes of the past, and none seemed genuinely committed to implementing a comprehensive Indian reform program.

Immediately after annulling the 1936 elections, Benavides forced the Constituent Congress to approve a law extending his term to December, 1939.[87] Following the passage of this law, Benavides declared that the Congress had completed its work and dissolved it. All subsequent legislation took the form of executive laws and decrees. On June 11, 1937, he issued Law 8547 transferring the Bureau of Indian Affairs from the Ministry of Development to the Ministry of Public Health, Labor, and Social Security. The duties of the new bureau were identical to those of the previous one, the only difference being that it was under a different ministry.[88] Although one author charged that by this action the president was attempting to bolster his sagging popularity by stealing Aprista political issues, there are no grounds for the assertion. It was simply an administrative change. Benavides did feel that the

86. José Balta, *Exposición doctrinaria y programa del Partido Liberal del Perú* (Lima: Empresa Editora "Perú," 1934), pp. 11-12, 18-19, 22-23, 27, 59-61. See also: Partido Liberal del Perú, *Proyecto del programa de reformas políticas, sociales y económicas, sancionado por el comité central directivo reorganizador en sesión del 4 de marzo de 1931* (Lima: Imprenta Americana, 1933), p. 21; and Emilio C. Maldonado, *Apuntes acerca del liberalismo del Partido Liberal en el Perú: Opúsculo no. 1 instrucción especial para el pueblo* (Ica: Imprenta de la Regeneración, 1904), pp. 12-14; Partido Constitucional Renovador del Perú, *Programa del Partido Constitucional Renovador del Perú* (Lima: n.p., 1935), pp. 6, 19-20; Partido Social Nacionalista, *Nuestro partido* (Lima: Empresa Editora Peruana, 1944), pp. 68-71, 83, 89. See also: Partido Social Nacionalista del Perú, *Partido Social Nacionalista del Perú* (Lima: Imprenta "Minerva," 1935), pp. 65-66.

87. The proposal touched off a storm of protest from over forty representatives who signed a petition declaring the law unconstitutional. Though they succeeded in delaying the proceedings for a few hours, Benavides prevailed. For the original petition, see the Bustamante Archive. See also: Manuel Bustamante de la Fuente to Luis Alberto Sánchez, May 23, 1970, Bustamante Archive.

88. PMTAI, *Legislación,* pp. 79-82.

bureau was a necessity and praised its work.[89]

Benavides sought to regulate the use of child servants. It was and is common in Peru for a poor family in the sierra to sell or give their children to coastal families to be raised as household servants. Noting that the practice was widespread and had resulted in oppression and juvenile delinquency, the president prohibited parents giving up children below the age of sixteen without the express permission of a special board of judges. All public transportation facilities were required to report the relationship between adults and children using them, and children were to be registered with the proper authorities at their destination. Any person who failed to fulfill his obligations was subject to fines and imprisonment,[90] but the decree was never enforced and the practice continues today.

Benavides often pointed to his accomplishments in the recognition of *comunidades* and in the improvement of their crop and livestock production. He claimed credit for the recognition of over 700 *comunidades*, although only 311 were recognized in his six years, which amounts to a yearly average below that achieved during the Leguía regime.[91] Moreover, the president praised his administration's work in distributing land to the Indians and in providing them with free breeding stock, a program which came to naught. He issued new *comunidad* registration regulations which clarified existing procedures, but he also altered the traditional *comunidad* election pattern by instructing the Ministry of Public Health, Labor, and Social Security to name the ruling junta of the *comunidad*.[92] One *indigenista* noted that this gave the central government unprecedented control within the *comunidad* and warned that it would result in cultural disintegration of the Indians like that which had occurred in the United States.[93]

In the area of Indian education, Benavides took several important steps late in his rule. In July, 1938, he issued a law establish-

---

89. Benavides, *El General Benavides a la nación — 1939*, pp. 36-37; and Chang-Rodríguez, *Prada, Mariátegui y Haya*, p. 297.

90. PMTAI, *Legislación*, pp. 139-40.

91. Benavides, *El General Benavides a la nación — 1939*, pp. 25, 36-37; and Dobyns, *The Social Matrix*, p. 3.

92. Benavides, *El General Benavides a la nación — 1939*, pp. 25, 28-29; Dreyfus to Secretary of State, July 9, 1938, D.S. 823.002/304; and PMTAI, *Legislación*, pp. 117-24.

93. Dora Mayer de Zulen, *El indígena y los congresos panamericanos*, 3 vols. (Lima: Imprenta "Lux," 1938), 3:10-11.

ing an experimental school for Indian girls on a state-owned hacienda near Puno, stating that it was a necessary complement to male education. The experimental agricultural school in Puno was expanded and its laboratory facilities improved. Benavides also sought to train Indian teachers and to improve agricultural methods, thereby reducing internal migration.[94] By supreme decree of March, 1939, he ordered a more technical curriculum for rural schools to prepare students for a useful vocation in their region. Finally, to attack the problem of adult illiteracy, he created Brigadas de Culturización Indígena (Indian Acculturation Brigades) designed to instruct adults in their own language.[95]

Benavides's own evaluation of his record in Indian affairs was that although he had not solved the Indian problem, he had at least won the Indians' confidence, which was the most important part of the battle.[96] However, while it is true that Benavides made some gains in education and *comunidad* recognition, much of his program was meaningless. He effected many administrative changes and published many decrees and laws, but there was little of substance in the administrative changes, and almost none of the laws and decrees were ever enforced. The condition of the Indians did not improve measurably under Benavides. His most important contribution to Indians was in stepping down as president and allowing new elections.

Any overall assessment of Indian legislation and integration in the 1930s would provoke little optimism. The process of rebuilding the nation from the ashes of the *oncenio* made the decade one of political and economic turmoil and even all-out civil war. The running battle between Apra and the national government, the dearth of competent political leaders, and the deepening economic depression, which was not alleviated until World War II, precluded effective executive and congressional action in the realm of Indian affairs. But perhaps that says something about Peruvian national priorities, not only in the 1930s, but before and after. While integration of 50 percent of the population should have commanded full government attention, most leaders emphasized other issues and relegated the Indians to last place.

94. PMTAI, *Legislación*, p. 236; and Benavides, *El General Benavides a la nación—1939*, pp. 36-38.
95. Fajardo, *Legislación indígena*, pp. 153-54; Benavides, *Mensaje al Congreso (1939)*, pp. 56, 169-70; and PMTAI, *Legislación*, pp. 237-38.
96. Benavides, *El General Benavides a la nación—1939*, p. 37.

6

Prado, Bustamante, and the Return of Apra

Whereas the 1930s had been a decade of chaos and civil strife characterized by a limited commitment to social legislation and Indian integration, the 1940s witnessed a cooling of political tempers and the return to civilian government. Two successive presidents were freely elected, and both executive and congressional leaders turned again to pressing social issues of the day, including the Indians, who benefited from a new round of Indian laws and government programs aimed at integration. There were several reasons for this change in direction, but one of the most important was the decrease in violent political hatreds.

By 1939 Benavides's suppression and control of Apra had proved sufficiently effective that he could schedule new elections secure in the knowledge that his own candidate would win handily. Furthermore, Haya de la Torre and the Apristas had dropped their reliance on violence and armed revolution to achieve power, thereby ensuring a peaceful transfer of power. Benavides's choice was Manuel Prado y Ugarteche, brother of the 1936 candidate, Jorge Prado. The only opposition was the relatively weak candidacy of José Quesada, nominee of the Frente Patriótica (Patriotic Front), which contained the remnants of Sánchez Cerro's Revolutionary Union party.

Concerned with other issues, Quesada made scant mention of the Indians in either the campaign or his party platform. He did call for the uplifting of all Peruvians physically, racially, and culturally and for increased educational facilities, with special attention to Indian vocational schools as a means of better integrating the rural *campesino* into modern life.[1]

Prado called for immediate Indian integration. Early in the campaign, he stated that the Indian was the forgotten man of the nation and had lived in a state of feudalism since the days of the conquest, a condition which had to be altered if Peru was to progress. Improved communications, cultural development, and the conversion of the *comunidades* into modern cooperatives were the solutions he advocated. Later in the campaign, in a speech in Lima's Acho bullring, Prado reiterated his position on communications and on the creation of cooperatives and added that any definitive integration program would have to begin with a restructuring of the educational system, with emphasis on quality and technical skills rather than abstract knowledge.[2]

THE PRESIDENCY OF MANUEL PRADO

Prado won the October 22 elections, but his commitment to the Indians did not end with the campaign. Throughout his term, he was to press for Indian integration. In this effort he was aided by the reestablishment of internal peace and by the tremendous economic boom brought on by wartime demands for Peruvian products. Prado was a scion of one of Peru's leading commercial and banking families, and his background led to the recognition that Peru could never realize her full economic potential until the great mass of Indians had been educated and integrated into the society. In addition to a purely economic motivation, Prado's commitment to the Allied ideology reflected, in this period of world reaction against the racism of Nazi Germany and racism in general, his wish to alter Peru's world image by mounting a pro-Indian campaign.

On a speaking tour through the southern sierra in the fall of 1940, he reminded the Indians that the government had not forgotten them and promised to dedicate the remainder of his term to promoting the advancement of the Indians.[3] Prado's words presaged action. In February, 1940, he issued a supreme decree calling

1. *La prensa,* September 8, 1939. See also: Dreyfus to Secretary of State, September 13, 1939, D.S. 823.00/1390 and Dreyfus to Secretary of State, October 26, 1939, D.S. 823.00/1406.

2. Manuel Prado, *Un año de gobierno: Discursos de Manuel Prado, 1939 — 8 de diciembre de 1940* (Lima: El Universal, 1941), pp. 22, 51-52, 55.

3. For texts of his Indian remarks in Sicuani, Cuzco, Abancay, Puno, and Lima, see: ibid., pp. 347, 349-51, 393-94, 403-4, 413-14, 531-33, 540-41.

for the establishment of six rural normal schools for the training of Indian teachers in the departments of Apurímac, Ayacucho, Cajamarca, Cuzco, Junín, and Puno, each with an Indian primary school attached.[4] He envisioned the training of thousands of teachers, and hoped that they would lift the cultural level of the Indians, enabling them to produce more and thereby reducing their isolation. To coordinate his rural education program, the president appointed a commission to study local needs and to propose new curricula and more pedagogically advanced methods. Moreover, in 1940, he submitted an educational budget of more than one billion *soles,* the highest in Peru's history.[5]

Prado pushed rural education and special Indian schools throughout his term. Adopting the phrase "to govern is to educate" as his official motto, he devoted lengthy sections of his annual messages to educational problems. He noted that there had been only one rural normal school in 1939 but that there were ten by 1942 with almost six hundred teacher trainees and that additional construction was planned for both the sierra and the jungle.[6] By 1944 there were nineteen, each with its own Indian school. Most of the prospective teachers received scholarships and grants from the government, and many lived at the schools. Instruction was oriented toward agricultural techniques. The budget of the normal schools increased from 120,000 *soles* in 1940 to almost 900,000 in 1945.[7]

Prado believed adult education especially important and used Benavides's Brigadas de Culturización Indígena to promote it. Each brigade was to be composed of two normal school teachers (one woman and one man), one agriculture and stock-raising instructor, and a nurse, all of whom had to have degrees. In addition, an auto mechanic was to accompany each brigade. Prado sent brigades to Cuzco, Puno, Ayacucho, Junín, and Cajamarca to teach adult Indians Peruvian history, Spanish, and improved agricultural methods. The brigades also offered classes in hygiene, food preparation,

4. PMTAI, *Legislación,* pp. 238-39.

5. Manuel Prado, *Mensaje presentado al Congreso por el señor doctor don Manuel Prado presidente constitucional de la república* (Lima: n.p., 1940), pp. 53-55, 58-59.

6. Manuel Prado, *Mensaje presentado al Congreso por el señor doctor don Manuel Prado presidente constitucional de la república* (Lima: n.p., 1942), pp. 77-78.

7. Manuel Prado, *Mensaje presentado al Congreso por el señor doctor don Manuel Prado presidente constitucional de la república* (Lima: n.p., 1944), pp. 68-70; and idem, *Mensaje presentado al Congreso por el señor doctor don Manuel Prado presidente constitucional de la república* (Lima: n.p., 1945), p. 75.

rudimentary law, and prevention of alcoholism and overuse of coca.[8] All brigade members were expected to be fluent in the local native languages, to observe and to study the terrain and the habits and customs of the people, and to report to the government.[9]

Satisfied with the initial results, Prado ordered the brigade program expanded and convened a general brigade conference in March, 1941. The delegates presented their own experiences and results and proposed revisions and additions to the program.[10] The president continued to improve the program through reorganizations and changes in emphasis; he attempted to use the brigades to impress upon Indian parents the need to send their children to school regularly. He created a Bureau of Indian Acculturation in the Ministry of Education and ordered the brigades to cooperate with all branches of the educational structure.[11]

In April, 1941, Prado promulgated a new educational law, some sections of which dealt extensively with Indian needs. The law provided for the construction of new schools, expansion of the Indian Acculturation Brigades, development of vocational education in the sierra, and research into biological psychology in the Andean departments. Primary education was to be free and attendance mandatory. The rural schools were to concentrate on developing agricultural and livestock-breeding techniques best suited to the area. *Comunidad* schools were to incorporate other agricultural programs to provide the direct participation of Indian children. Traveling rural schools were to operate in those regions where scarce or scattered populations precluded the founding of a centralized school system. Teachers were to be conversant with the native language and to use it in conjunction with Spanish in order to encourage bilingualism among the population. Normal schools were to train teachers for Indian regions by instructing them in Indian languages and in technical skills. However, the law enjoined the creation of a special Indian school system designed to segregate the Indian population permanently; instead, it was to incor-

8. Prado, *Mensaje al Congreso* (1940), pp. 225-27; and Fajardo, *Legislación indígena,* pp. 152-53.

9. For the texts of five reports, see: Perú, Ministerio de Salud Pública, Trabajo y Previsión Social, Dirección de Asuntos Indígenas, *Boletín de la Dirección de Asuntos Indígenas* (Lima: Imprenta Americana, 1940), pp. 515-70.

10. Ibid., pp. 513-14.

11. For the texts of several decrees and resolutions, see: PMTAI, *Legislación,* pp. 240-43. See also: Prado, *Mensaje al Congreso* (1942), pp. 72-73.

porate the Indians into the national system as quickly as their culture and facility in language permitted.

The new law represented a comprehensive attempt to wipe out illiteracy. It created the post of education inspector, whose duties were to oversee curricula and to direct literacy campaigns, particularly those affecting Indians. Adult education classes, emphasizing vocational and literacy instruction, were to be held in the evenings. Prado implemented the law in October, 1941, by a supreme decree which at the same time created a special subbureau of Indian Education within the Ministry of Education.[12]

Congressional reaction to this program was favorable. In August, 1943, Deputy J. Ricardo Paniagua y Rojas from Puno praised its success and admitted that his early skepticism regarding the acculturation brigades had been unfounded. He asserted that in Puno alone hundreds of adult Indians had been taught to read and write and to maintain minimum standards of hygiene; he introduced a motion calling for an intensified campaign against illiteracy and for the construction of new and better-equipped facilities.[13]

Deputy Humberto Eduardo de Amat from Chucuito credited the acculturation brigades with reducing disease in his area through health education. He requested not only an increase in the number of brigades but also an expansion of their functions to include instruction in agricultural techniques and distribution of tools and seeds.[14] Other deputies demanded Indian schools and additional brigades for their areas.[15]

By supreme decree of March 4, 1944, Prado sought to coordinate literacy education efforts in a National Literacy Campaign (Compaña Nacional de Alfabetización) in which all regular teachers were to give instruction to adults in civics and health as well as reading and writing. These teachers, who were not to be paid for this extra duty, were to be honored for their services, notation of which was to be added to their personal files, and prizes were to be awarded to the best instructors.[16] The government also established an experimental school for Aymara-speaking children in Ojjerani,

---

12. PMTAI, *Legislación*, pp. 204-14, 239-40.

13. PDD, Ordinario de 1943, Diputados, August 18, 1943, 1:257-58, and August 19, 1943, 1:270-74.

14. Ibid., August 24, 1943, 1:312-13.

15. For one such request by Deputy Manuel T. Calle Escajadillo from Ayacucho, see: ibid., November 2, 1943, 3:1415-16.

16. PMTAI, *Legislación*, pp. 250-52.

department of Puno. Here various methods for teaching Spanish were to be tested and, if successful, applied throughout the republic.[17]

President Prado considered education one of his most successful programs. By 1945, he asserted that 7,196 literacy classes had begun and more than half a million students had matriculated. He claimed that of the 363,525 students who took classes in 1944, 140,000, or 40 percent, learned to read and write.[18] Prado's goal was the education of the more than two million illiterates, and he believed it could be accomplished rapidly.

One *indigenista* author attacked Prado's educational program as useless because it attempted to teach Indians arithmetic, reading, and writing, for which they would have little use. Instead, he believed that more practical subjects like sanitation, patriotism, racial equality, and pride in ancestry should be taught and that teachers ought to avoid all mention of national ills and concentrate on the great men and deeds of Peruvian history.[19] Such a parochial approach was representative of the feelings of many Peruvians. A more telling criticism was the inability of the government to provide well-trained teachers. There were gains in education under Prado, but the lack of facilities and instructors prevented any substantial progress; most of the Indians remained illiterate, without benefit of schools or teachers.[20]

Education did not, however, constitute the whole of Prado's Indian program. By supreme decree of November 14, 1941, he created a free legal office (Procuraduría de Indígenas) in the Bureau of Indian Affairs to serve both individual Indians and *comunidades,* even in the most remote areas of the country. At the same time, Prado attempted to halt the exploitation of the Indians by prohibiting the intervention of private lawyers in the proceedings of the bureau.[21] He extolled the work done by the Procuraduría and

17. For the text of the decree and the accompanying organization resolution, see: ibid., pp. 252-56.

18. Prado, *Mensaje al Congreso* (1945), pp. 65-67. For a favorable view of the program, see: "El Presidente de la República," in *Perú en cifras,* ed. Sainte Marie S., pp. 656-59.

19. Sivirichi, *Derecho indígena,* pp. 453, 462-63.

20. For figures on illiteracy in the department of Puno, see: de la Barra, *El indio peruano,* pp. 161-62.

21. PMTAI, *Legislación,* pp. 89-94. The original idea for creation of the office had been presented in Congress by Deputy M. Leopoldo García from Huancayo. See: PDD, Ordinario de 1941, Diputados, August 27, 1941, 1:371-72.

maintained that it had ended unethical legalism and prevented violence.[22] To aid the Procuraduría, regional inspectors were appointed to investigate land disputes on the spot and to make recommendations to Lima. The inspectors handled hundreds of complaints yearly and worked reasonably well with the Lima bureaucracy.[23]

Prado actively supported the *comunidades,* and during his term over four hundred were recognized and inscribed in the official register.[24] To facilitate registry, Prado required that the *comunidades* include adjoining lands on their application maps and stipulated that recognition of a *comunidad* did not constitute recognition of all the land claims. In addition, he sought to prevent manipulation by *comunidad personeros* (legal representatives) by limiting their terms to four years and by requiring them to reside in the *comunidad.*[25]

President Prado also fostered economic development of the *comunidad.* He expropriated a few small haciendas and parceled out several German and Japanese estates confiscated during the war; this was the first time land had ever been redistributed to the Indians. He supported the *comunidades'* efforts to purchase the private lands of its members;[26] and moreover, he alleviated *comunidad* tax burdens with two supreme resolutions. The first exonerated *comunidades* from paying all but property taxes on the grounds that they were sociopolitical aggregations rather than

22. Prado, *Mensaje al Congreso* (1942), pp. 247-48; Manuel Prado, *Mensaje presentado al Congreso por el señor doctor don Manuel Prado presidente constitucional de la república* (Lima: n.p., 1943), p. 58; idem, *Mensaje al Congreso* (1944), pp. 46-48; and idem, *Mensaje al Congreso* (1945), pp. 56-57.

23. For example, inspectors studied and reported on 308 different disputes in 1942-43. See: Prado, *Mensaje al Congreso* (1943), pp. 57-58. See also: Prado, *Mensaje al Congreso* (1942), pp. 246-47; idem, *Mensaje al Congreso* (1944), pp. 46-48; and idem, *Mensaje al Congreso* (1945), p. 57.

24. Dobyns, *The Social Matrix,* p. 3. See also: Manuel Prado, *Mensaje presentado al Congreso por el señor doctor don Manuel Prado presidente constitucional de la república* (Lima: n.p., 1941), p. 235; idem, *Mensaje al Congreso* (1942), p. 248; idem, *Mensaje al Congreso* (1943), pp. 57-58; and idem, *Mensaje al Congreso* (1945), pp. 56-57.

25. Fajardo, *Legislación indígena,* pp. 162, 168, 166-67; PMTAI, *Legislación,* pp. 124-25; and Prado, *Mensaje al Congreso* (1941), pp. 235-36.

26. For examples of *comunidad* purchases, see: PMTAI, *Legislación,* pp. 196-97; Prado, *Mensaje al Congreso* (1941), pp. 237-38; and idem, *Mensaje al Congreso* (1942), p. 247.

profit-making corporations. The second, issued a month later, lifted even the property tax.[27]

Further, the administration sought to promote and to expand nascent Indian industries and to improve agricultural techniques and production. Prado's policy aim was to provide every Indian with a job lucrative enough "to consolidate his private economic life and at the same time to facilitate the formation of small industrial centers."[28] In agriculture, Prado promoted the creation of *comunidad* cooperatives, hoping thereby to break traditional subsistence farming patterns by instilling the profit motive. Between twenty and thirty co-ops were actually begun, with excellent results,[29] but the program was too limited to affect the general Indian population.

Perhaps Prado's most innovative creation was the Indian collective colonies, which would later evolve into the Puno-Tambopata Program. By establishing colonies on the eastern slopes of the Andes, the administration hoped to relieve population pressure in the area around Lake Titicaca. In August, 1942, Prado ordered the Bureau of Indian Affairs to establish such colonies and to encourage in them the growth of small industries and the use of modern agricultural practices.[30] On the basis of the colonies' experiences a general economic development plan for all the *comunidades* was to be worked out. In December, 1942, the Congress approved funds to establish the Indian colonies, and in July, 1944, Prado created the Office of Puno Indian Migration in the Bureau of Indian Affairs. The new agency was to survey possible colonial sites and to aid in the relocation of Indians from Puno.[31]

Several colonies were established, but the one at Vilquechico, begun in April, 1945, enjoyed the greatest success. Designed to develop textile-making skills among the residents, it was expected

27. Varallanos, *Legislación indiana*, pp. 94-95; and PMTAI, *Legislación*, pp. 296-97.

28. Prado, *Mensaje al Congreso* (1942), pp. 248-49.

29. Prado, *Mensaje al Congreso* (1944), pp. 46-48; and idem, *Mensaje al Congreso* (1945), pp. 56-57. See also: Mac-Lean Estenós, *Sociologia del Perú*, p. 285; and Editorial Guillermo Kraft, *Perú: Obra de gobierno del presidente de la república dr. Manuel Prado, 1939-1945* (Buenos Aires: Editorial Guillermo Kraft, 1945), p. 111.

30. Archivo Vilquechico, Box I of Puno-Tambopata, Files Relating to Indian *Comunidades*, Instituto Indigenista Peruano, Ministerio de Trabajo y Comunidades, Lima, Peru (hereafter cited as Archivo Vilquechico, followed by box number).

31. Prado, *Mensaje al Congreso* (1941), p. 239; PMTAI, *Legislación*, pp. 142-43; and PDD, Ordinario de 1942, Diputados, November 19, 1942, pp. 1472-74.

to become a self-sufficient cooperative. The government provided a truck, and the production of alpaca and vicuña cloth was sufficient to enable members of the colony to pay their director almost two thousands *soles* per month.[32]

Ironically, the dramatic increase in concern by the executive in Indian welfare during the Prado administration was accompanied by a decline in congressional involvement. In one of its few actions concerning Indians in the years 1939-45, the legislature did deal with one of the more serious problems in both criminal and civil justice—the language barrier. Since most judges in the southern and central sierra spoke neither Quechua nor Aymara, the gulf between citizen and judge could only be bridged by an interpreter. In March, 1940, Senator Francisco Pastor from Puno had introduced a bill requiring judges to possess a working knowledge of the Indian dialects of their areas. Pastor asserted that if the judge was able to question the Indians directly, thus ascertaining their psychological motivations, he would be better able to decide guilt or innocence. The Committee on Legislation reported favorably on the bill, and it was placed in debate on August 18, 1942.[33]

Pastor tried to convince the Senate that improved communications would prevent the conviction of innocent Indians and in general improve the legal climate in those areas of heavy Indian population. He said his proposal was necessary because fraudulent interpreters accepted bribes from landowners and in other ways acted illegally against Indian interests. In response to criticism from other senators and some Supreme Court justices, he noted that the education code required teachers in rural areas to be familiar with Indian languages and argued that such a requirement was infinitely more important for judges. Finally, Pastor yielded to pressure and offered a substitute motion which stated that it was preferable that judges in Indian areas speak Indian dialects. After a short debate, the Senate approved the revised motion, and

---

32. Archivo Vilquechico, Boxes I-II. Problems arose after 1948 when control of Vilquechico was transferred from the Bureau of Indian Affairs to the Bureau of Industries. From that time the community declined. Aid was requested in the early 1950s, but the government of Manuel A. Odría sent only a broken-down truck, which failed to run. During the second Prado administration (1956-62), the community again failed in its efforts to secure government assistance. The importance of Vilquechico, however, was that it functioned well for several years, dying from a lack of government interest.

33. PDD, Ordinario de 1942, Senadores, August 18, 1942, 1:169-70.

on September 29, 1942, the Chamber of Deputies passed the bill without debate.[34]

Aside from this, Congress did virtually nothing for the Indians during the Prado administration. Several deputies and senators introduced bills to expropriate land and divide it among Indian residents, but none received approval.[35] Moreover, while in the past congressional debates had always been replete with the texts of formal complaints from *comunidades* regarding oppression or land disputes, in the period 1939-45 there were few such complaints and none were acted upon.[36] There seemed to be a total lack of interest in the Indians on the part of the legislators. No one introduced any far-reaching reform legislation, although there were several bills of questionable value, such as one by Deputy Francisco Ponce de León from Cuzco which would have taxed the Indian *comunidades* in order to secure funds to buy land for other *comunidades*.[37]

Congressional inactivity notwithstanding, the Indian record of the Prado administration was good. Substantial progress was made in the fields of education and economic development. The program to create Indian industrial and agricultural colonies in the *montaña* was admirable and, had it been expanded, might have altered the economic and demographic picture of the sierra. There was a sincerity of purpose under Prado that had been lacking during previous presidencies. This was reflected in the tone of the ministerial and executive documents as well as by concrete achievements. However, what little had been accomplished under Prado was destroyed by the political upheavals of 1945-48 and by the complete lack of interest of Manuel Odría (1948-56).

Prado had been a popular president, receiving credit for the military victory over Ecuador in the short-lived boundary war of

34. Ibid., 1:170-72, and August 28, 1942, 1:314-16; PDD, Ordinario de 1942, Diputados, September 29, 1942, 1:769-71. For the text of the law, see: PMTAI, *Legislación,* pp. 303-4.

35. PDD, 2d Extraordinario de 1940, Senadores, January 30, 1941, pp. 514-15, 582-83; and PDD, Extraordinario de 1943, Diputados, December 30, 1943, pp. 667-69.

36. See: PDD, Ordinario de 1942, Senadores, October 21, 1942, 3:1108, 1121-22; PDD, Ordinario de 1943, Diputados, September 30, 1943, 3:930-31, October 20, 1943, 3:1246-47, and November 23, 1943, 4:1869-71; PDD, Ordinario de 1943, Senadores, November 15, 1943, 3:1122-23; PDD, 1st Extraordinario de 1943, Senadores, December 15, 1943, 1:263; and PDD, Ordinario de 1944, Senadores, October 27, 1944, 3:1006-8.

37. PDD, Ordinario de 1943, Diputados, August 10, 1943, 1:115-17.

1941 and also for the economic prosperity engendered by World War II. There is no doubt that he entertained thoughts of standing for reelection, or perhaps of remaining in office without benefit of reelection. Benavides returned from his self-imposed exile in Europe and also considered running, but the ambitions of both men were thwarted by the emergence of a new political group, the Frente Democrática Nacional (National Democratic Front), which by reason of its popular following assured Peru of new elections. During the years 1939-45, Apra had remained underground, but the government suppression had lessened to such a degree that everyone knew where Haya de la Torre was "hiding." The Apristas were legalized at this time and immediately aligned themselves with the front, whose nominee was José Luis Bustamante y Rivero. Benavides and the outgoing administration supported the candidacy of General Eloy Ureta, the victorious commander of Peruvian forces in the war with Ecuador. With the support of the Apristas and those elements who were tired of the fifteen-year rule of the oligarchy, Bustamante won the June 30, 1945, elections with 305,590 votes to Ureta's 150,720. The Apristas, running openly for the first time since 1931, won 18 of 46 seats in the Senate and 48 of 101 in the Chamber of Deputies and sought to dominate the Congress.[38]

Publicly espousing their Indian proposals of the 1930s and promising they would now convert their ideas into legislation, the Apristas presented numerous Indian complaints and petitions on the floors of Congress in the three years 1945-48. They also introduced several pieces of Indian legislation and claimed credit for the passage of several laws.[39] Although the Apristas asserted they were adhering to a program of radical *indigenismo,* however, it was clear from the outset that they had in fact adopted a moderately conservative position on the issue.[40]

38. See: Pike, *Modern History of Peru,* pp. 279-81; and Kantor, *The Ideology and Program of the Peruvian Aprista Movement,* pp. 15-16.

39. Aprista speeches and bills are too numerous to be cited fully. The complete texts are to be found in PDD, Ordinarios y Extraordinarios, Senadores y Diputados, 1945-48. See also: Chang-Rodríguez, *Prada, Mariátegui y Haya,* p. 298; and Mario Peláez Bazán, *De la provincia al aprismo* (Lima: Talleres Gráficos EETSA, 1961), p. 82.

40. For a dissident Aprista view which asserts that Apra betrayed both land reform and the Indians, see Magda Portal, *¿Quiénes traicionaron al pueblo?* (Lima: Empresa Editora "Salas é Hijos," Cuadernos de Divulgación Popular "Flora Tristan," 1950), pp. 8-9. For comparable positions by other former Apristas, see: Enríquez,

One of the first Aprista bills called for the establishment of August 29 (the date of the execution of Atahualpa, the last of the Inca rulers) as the Day of Tahuantinsuyo in order to glorify the Indians and their history. Several senators and deputies opposed the measure, noting that June 24, which Leguía had earlier decreed to be the Day of the Indian, should be retained because it coincided with the Indian celebration of Inti Raymi (the Inca sun and harvest festival). Senator Luis Enrique Galván from Ayacucho argued that August 29 was a day of pain and national disgrace and that one should never celebrate the death of a great civilization. Nevertheless, the bill passed.[41]

On August 29, the Day of Tahuantinsuyo, which was declared a national holiday, all schools were to provide special lessons stressing the significance and grandeur of the Indian past and the promise of the Indian future.[42] Although the law referred to Indians, this Aprista victory was a rather useless one for the modern Indians of Peru. What the Indians needed, as several legislators noted, was either new protective legislation or enforcement of previously enacted laws.

A far more necessary and useful law was that dealing with ownership of the land left by the receding waters of Lake Titicaca. Since 1938, the level of the lake had been dropping sharply because of drought conditions, and in September, 1940, Benavides issued a supreme resolution declaring all newly exposed lands to be the

---

Haya de la Torre; Alberto Hidalgo, *Por que renuncié al Apra* (Buenos Aires: Imprenta "Leomir," 1954); and Víctor Villanueva, *La tragedia de un pueblo y un partido (páginas para la historia del Apra),* 2nd ed. (Lima: Talleres Gráficos "Victory," 1956). Villanueva recounts that on May 20, 1945, Haya delivered a speech in the Plaza de Armas in Lima and intentionally selected a balcony within earshot of the prestigious, oligarchical Club Nacional. He pardoned all past injustices of his opponents and stated that the party "does not desire to take riches from those that have them, but to create riches for those who do not." Villanueva notes that the speech was received coldly by party faithfuls, but "was very well received by the great landowners, the large industrialists, and the capitalists in general. The timorous were calmed. Those with their bags already packed suspended their travel plans. . . . They stayed. They waited. They did not wait in vain" *(La tragedia de un pueblo,* pp. 28-29).

41. For the debate in the Chamber of Deputies, see PDD, Ordinario de 1945, Diputados, August 29, 1945, 2:632-45. For the entire Senate debate, see PDD, Ordinario de 1945, Senadores, November 24, 1945, 5:2708-23. See particularly speeches by José Antonio Encinas from Puno (pp. 2711-12), Luis E. Heysen from Lambayeque (pp. 2712-13), Luis Enrique Galván from Ayacucho (pp. 2714-15), and the shouting match between Heysen and Galván (pp. 2715-19).

42. PMTAI, *Legislación,* p. 7.

property of the state. The Indians who owned lands contingent to the lake considered the new land a part of their *comunidades* and proceeded to take possession, but the Guardia Civil moved to deny them not only possession of it but even access to the lake itself. Deputy Pedro L. Repetto from Puno had introduced a measure in November, 1943, which would have forced the Guardia Civil to desist, but it was not acted upon.[43]

In January, 1946, the Aprista congressional caucus *(célula)* introduced legislation in the Chamber of Deputies which declared as Indian property all newly exposed lands both on the shore and on islands in the lake. The minister of development was to be responsible for surveying the lands and transferring free titles to both *comunidades* and individual Indians in lots not to exceed ten hectares. Furthermore, since the land was to be transferred to Indians, it was to be inalienable, imprescriptible, and not attachable. There was some discussion as to whether the law would apply to a government-owned island in the lake, but the deputies passed the bill with no opposition, and the Senate followed suit in May.[44] The Apristas, in August, 1946, tried to gain approval for a bill dismissing all charges against Indians arrested during the land dispute, but the measure failed.[45]

Since the 1920s Haya de la Torre and the Apristas had championed land reform as a solution to Peru's economic, agrarian, and Indian problems. It was only natural to expect, therefore, that upon achieving partial power in 1945 they would initiate agrarian reform legislation. They did not, however, introduce a comprehensive land reform law; rather, they treated each land dispute and each *comunidad* as a separate, isolated case, and their success was limited. For example, in December, 1945, the Aprista caucus introduced a bill calling for the expropriation of two haciendas (La Tina and Lalaquís) in the department of Piura. The expropriation was to include all buildings, machinery, and livestock, and the Indian residents of the two haciendas were to form cooperatives which would then reimburse the government. The Chamber of Deputies, acting on advice from its Finance Commission, ap-

43. PDD, Ordinario de 1943, Diputados, November 12, 1943, 4:1628-29.
44. PDD, 3d Extraordinario de 1945, Diputados, April 9, 1946, 2:867-72; PDD, 4th Extraordinario de 1945, Senadores, May 27, 1946, 1:309-10. See also: PMTAI, *Legislación*, pp. 174-75.
45. PDD, Ordinario de 1946, Diputados, August 29, 1946, pp. 154-56.

proved the proposal on April 10, 1946, but it was rejected by the Senate.[46]

On December 14 and 15, 1946, the Bureau of Indian Affairs convened a regional assembly in the city of Huancayo of *personeros* representing 750 *comunidades* from the departments of Huánuco, Pasco, Junín, and Huancavelica. The object of the meeting was the study of a prospective *comunidad* statute as well as the discussion of general Indian needs and problems. To the surprise of its sponsors, the assembly produced a document which demanded that the government solve the economic, cultural, and health problems of the Indians; dictate laws which would effectively guarantee Indian property; attend to Indian requests and complaints; organize a health and sanitation campaign and establish traveling medical commissions; establish agricultural schools in every *comunidad;* extend agricultural credit to the *comunidades* and pass legislation creating *comunidad* cooperatives to meet current economic needs; restore all lands usurped from *comunidades;* simplify the *comunidad* registration procedure and undertake a comprehensive census of all *comunidad* lands; approve legislation protecting *yanaconas* and other Indian laborers; and grant to the Bureau of Indian Affairs the legal right to intervene in *comunidad* land disputes, guaranteeing the security of the *comunidad* and redistributing *comunidad* lands to prevent any one Indian or group of Indians from gaining control of large tracts.[47]

The Apristas in both chambers called for the immediate implementation of the assembly's demands. Deputy Julio Garrido Malaver from Cajamarca stated that the Indians remained Peru's greatest problem and called for land reform and a comprehensive Indian code.[48] Senator Cirilo Cornejo from Huancavelica likewise demanded a comprehensive Indian code in order to protect and to reform the economic structure of the nation.[49]

The focus on the Indian problem provided by the Huancayo conference was intensified a month later by a bloody clash between the army and the Indians of several *comunidades* in the Huancayo Valley. The incident, unrelated to the conference, had its roots in the Benavides period when some Indians had filed a complaint with the Bureau of Indian Affairs charging that neigh-

46. PDD, 3d Extraordinario de 1945, Diputados, April 10, 1946, 2:989-91.
47. PDD, 1st Extraordinario de 1946, Diputados, December 24, 1946, 2:179-83.
48. Ibid., 2:180-82.
49. PDD, 1st Extraordinario de 1946, Senadores, January 3, 1947, 2:982-84.

boring haciendas had usurped large plots of their land. The government did nothing and there was a small clash in 1942 when the *hacendados* had several Indians arrested for trespassing. Finally, in December, 1946, several groups of Indians invaded one of the haciendas and constructed huts. The *hacendado*, not wanting violence, referred the matter to the Bureau of Indian Affairs, but the neighboring *hacendados* of Antapongo, Ancahuasi, and Laive, fearing for their own lands, called in the army. In the battle which followed, nine Indians were killed and eleven wounded, but the army suffered no casualties.

In January, 1947, Manuel Gutiérrez Aliaga from Junín, representing the National Democratic Front of Bustamante y Rivero, demanded a full investigation by the Ministries of Government and Justice. Communist deputy Sergio Caller Zavaleta from Cuzco called for the creation of a special investigative body representing all political parties that would go to Huancayo, restore the stolen Indian land, and initiate disciplinary action against those authorities responsible for the massacre. Deputy José Angel Escalante from Cuzco objected, arguing that since the Indians had invaded private property, the army had every right to eject them forcibly. He blamed the incident on unnamed outside agitators and called for congressional action to halt the activities of such men. The Chamber of Deputies rejected Caller Zavaleta's suggestion, but approved Gutiérrez Aliaga's plan for a government investigation.[50] In February, Deputies Guillermo Luna Cartland from Cajamarca and Alfredo A. Pérez Alcázar from Tacna introduced legislation to expropriate the hacienda Antapongo and divide it among the Indians, but the bill was defeated.[51]

In the Senate, Alberto Arca Parró from Ayacucho rose to condemn the army massacre and demanded a thorough investigation into the antecedents of the clash, and Senator José Antonio Encinas from Puno pointed to it as further proof that an Indian code, such as the one he had written, would be the only way of guaranteeing Indian rights. The constitution and the Civil Code had both failed to provide the protection necessary, he said, and the Huancayo incident would be repeated many times if the Congress did not act.[52]

50. PDD, 2d Extraordinario de 1946, Diputados, January 23, 1947, 1:98-108. The speeches of Gutiérrez Aliaga and Caller Zavaleta include the background of the original dispute.

51. PDD, 2d Extraordinario de 1946, Diputados, February 14, 1947, 2:258-62.

52. PDD, 2d Extraordinario de 1946, Senadores, January 24, 1947, 1:117-20.

Congress reacted to the continuing land crisis in the sierra, of which the Huancayo conference and the massacre were evidence, with a barrage of expropriation proposals, some of them completely untenable. One Communist proposal called for the expropriation of the hacienda Pata-Pata in the department of Cuzco. The hacienda, owned by the Convent of Santo Domingo, contained 150 Indian families who were granted two-thirds of the lands for their personal use in return for working the other one-third. Communist Deputies Sixto Coello Jara, Sergio Caller Zavaleta, and Juan J. Paiva, all from Cuzco, wanted to expropriate the lands and divide them among neighboring *comunidades.* The Apristas, led by Deputy Garrido Malaver, objected on the grounds that dividing the hacienda among the *comunidades* would in effect deprive the current residents of their land. The Communists held that there was more than enough land for all, but the proposal was rejected overwhelmingly.[53]

Caller Zavaleta introduced another expropriation bill on January 14 aimed at an *hacendado,* Santos Porras Cechuancho, who allegedly had stolen lands from the *comunidad* Pariahuança in the department of Junín. Caller Zavaleta's bill demanded not only the return of the usurped lands, but also the expropriation and division of the hacienda. Once again, the Apristas opposed the measure, substituting a bill by Deputies Gutiérrez Aliaga and Fernando León de Vivero from Ica calling upon the Bureau of Indian Affairs to conduct a nationwide investigation of all *comunidad* land titles to avoid future conflict.[54]

In November, 1945, Senator Felipe Alva y Alva from Cajamarca introduced a bill calling for the expropriation of the hacienda Santa Ursula owned by the Purísima Concepción Convent in Cajamarca. Earlier in the year, the Bureau of Indian Affairs had mediated a dispute between the convent and the Indians residing on the hacienda with an agreement that the Indians would purchase the hacienda for eighty-thousand *soles.* The Indians sold their livestock and crops and deposited the required sum in a special account in the Bank of Credit of Peru. At this juncture, the abbess

---

53. For the texts of the extensive debate, see: PDD, 1st Extraordinario de 1946, Diputados, January 9, 1947, 3:21-23, January 14, 1947, 3:150-68, and January 15, 1947, 3:207-10.

54. PDD, 1st Extraordinario de 1946, Diputados, January 14, 1946, 3:125-31.

changed her mind, proposed new conditions for the sale, and signed the Indians to a new ten-year labor contract.[55]

Senator Alva y Alva's bill ordered the government to expropriate the hacienda and divide it among the Indians, using the deposited funds and returning to the Indians any interest earned in the interim. The Legislative Commission approved the measure but substituted an article which would ensure that the land be divided among the original Indian families, not recent arrivals, and the Senate approved the bill.[56] The Commissions on Budget and Public Finance in the Chamber of Deputies revised the bill to read that no family could receive more than ten hectares nor less than five. Indians who had been residents before 1945 would be given preference and the money they had paid to the Credit Bank would be applied to the purchase price of their lands. Those who had arrived after the initiation of legal action would be given second choice and would be provided with long-term credit up to ten years. With Aprista support, the deputies approved the revised bill and, after consultation with the Senate, in 1947 enacted Law 10883 expropriating the hacienda Santa Ursula.[57]

The expropriation of one hacienda, however, should not be taken as an indication of effective congressional or Aprista concern over *comunidad* land disputes or land needs. There were many expropriation bills introduced in both houses, but the technique used to defeat them was to have them die in the various committees rather than to allow them to come to a vote on the floor of the chambers. Indian education and sanitation bills met an identical fate. Several senators and deputies attempted to expedite Indian bills and complained about the slow action of the committees, but to no avail.[58]

The only really important Indian legislation enacted by the Congress during the Bustamante y Rivero period was the new *yanacona* law that was passed in February, 1947. For decades the *indigenistas* had demanded reforms in the system or its outright abolishment. Beginning with the *oncenio* of Leguía, there were sev-

---

55. PDD, 3d Extraordinario de 1945, Senadores, April 10, 1946, 2:1094-96.

56. Ibid., 2:1096-1104.

57. PDD, 2d Extraordinario de 1946, Diputados, February 28, 1947, 4:206-12; and PMTAI, *Legislación,* p. 196.

58. For one example, see a speech by Sergio Caller Zavaleta, PDD, 2d Extraordinario de 1945, February 15, 1946, 2:751-54.

eral supreme decrees and resolutions issued to correct abuses in *yanaconaje,* but none proved effective. The issue arose in the 1940s when in August, 1943, Deputy Federico Urganda Elejalde from Ica called for a thorough investigation and proposed a bill to reform the practice. In September, 1944, Urganda Elejalde demanded to know what had happened to his bill, but once again nothing was done.[59]

In August, 1945, the Chamber of Deputies, acting on a motion proposed by the Aprista deputies, agreed to reconsider the *yanacona* law which had been passed by the Constituent Congress in 1933 and vetoed by President Benavides.[60] The matter was referred to the Agricultural Committee, which made its report on December 31, 1945. Noting that the 1933 law was outdated and deficient and that there existed a need to protect all small tenants and renters, the committee proposed a twenty-four-article law which included the following points: any form of sharecropping would fall under regulations for the *yanacona* contract, and that contract was to be a written one, with copies sent to the Ministry of Justice and Labor and the Ministry of Agriculture; the contract was to establish the amount of land provided the *yanaconas* (not to exceed fifteen hectares) and to include its exact boundaries, quality, and water rights, the limits on the use of the land, and the duration of the contract; the Ministry of Agriculture was to study each specific region where *yanaconaje* was practiced and set the wage to be paid the *yanaconas* — which could not be altered during the life of the contract — using the agricultural production figures of 1941-42; if the crop failed completely, the *yanaconas* were not to be held responsible for debts of any kind; the *yanaconas* could not be forced to sell to the owner their own portion of the harvest; the owner could not require special free services except for the clearing of irrigation ditches proportionally to the size of each plot; the *yanaconas* could never be forced to plant or to harvest crops or lands of the owner; the value of all seeds, tools, fertilizers, and plows provided to the *yanaconas* were to be computed in money, the interest for which could not exceed 12 percent per year, and each year the Ministry of Agriculture was to

59. PDD, Ordinario de 1943, Diputados, August 18, 1943, 1:243-46; PDD, Ordinario de 1944, Diputados, September 22, 1944, 2:841-43.

60. PDD, Ordinario de 1945, Diputados, August 9, 1945, 1:175-76. See also: Congreso Constituyente, September 30, 1933, 13:3684-86.

establish the regional price for such items; the minimum contract period was to be five years and the incumbent *yanaconas* were to have first preference on renewal; owners were allowed to evict a *yanacona* if he failed to pay his rent, if he abandoned the land or leased it to another party, or if the contract expired, but could not evict him for debt in the event of natural disaster; the owner was required to proportion irrigation water equally, including that for his own lands; a National Board of Yanaconas and Campesinos was to be created to aid the *yanaconas* and to protect their interests; the Agricultural Bank of Peru was to grant at least 25 percent of its loans to *yanaconas;* and all conflicts arising between owner and *yanacona* were to be arbitrated by the Ministry of Justice and Labor.[61]

Debate on the issue, which took place throughout the following year, was extremely lengthy and filled several volumes of congressional proceedings. Aprista deputy Alfredo Saco Miró Quesada from Lima, the president of the Agricultural Commission, delivered a long supporting speech in which he traced the history of *yanaconaje,* abuses committed in the practice during the republican period, and previous attempts to regulate it. In his article-by-article defense of the measure he held that the proposed law had socio-economic as well as political connotations and described the benefits which would accrue to the individual *yanaconas* and to the nation.[62]

All of the Aprista deputies who spoke on the proposal supported it enthusiastically and even the Communists came out in favor of it.[63] However, several deputies, led by Manuel Sánchez Palacios from Lima, feared that even under the new proposal the agrarian laborer would be exploited. Sánchez Palacios predicted that since the minimum contract was for five years, the *yanaconas* would lack mobility and thus remain under the control of the *hacendado.* Moreover, the proposed law still allowed the *hacendado* to fix the crop, the amount of rent, and his own percentage of the harvest, thereby providing all the machinery necessary for exploi-

61. For the preface and the text of the commission's proposed law, see: PDD, 1st Extraordinario de 1945, Diputados, December 31, 1945, 2:523-29.

62. Ibid., January 8, 1946, 2:693-701. See also his speech proposing a few minor modifications, PDD, 2d Extraordinario de 1945, Diputados, January 22, 1946, 1:45-47.

63. See speeches by Communists Juan Jacinto Paiva and Sergio Caller Zavaleta, both from Cuzco, in: PDD, 2d Extraordinario de 1945, Diputados, January 24, 1946, 1:105, and January 28, 1946, 1:150.

tation. Sánchez Palacios wanted *yanaconaje* completely abolished and replaced with a system of tenancy whereby the renter received at least half of the crop. Other deputies also suggested modifications to ensure better protection for the *yanaconas*.[64]

After days of debate, the Chamber of Deputies approved the measure with modifications.[65] The most important points of the bill which passed were as follows: the size of the plot was not to exceed fifteen hectares in irrigated regions or thirty hectares in the sierra; all contracts were to be written and were to include name, age, address, fingerprints, and marital state of both parties, a detailed description of the plot, a statement of whether the rent was to be paid in money or in kind, the exact portion of the crops that the *yanacona* owed, and an agreement regarding the use of irrigation water; *yanaconas* were not obligated to sell crops or livestock to the landowner, or to perform free services, or to work on land other than their own, or to buy food, clothing, or any other items from the hacienda store; the duration of the contract was to be fixed by both parties, but the minimum period was three years and the *yanacona* could not be evicted before the end of six years; the rent could not exceed 6 percent of the value of the land; the value of all seeds, tools, fertilizers, and machinery was to be figured in monetary terms, with 12 percent the maximum interest that could be charged; the landowner was required to provide living quarters for the *yanaconas* or was to pay construction costs; in the event of crop failure the rent was to be decreased accordingly and suspended in the event of total disaster; a special Bureau of Inspection of Yanaconaje was to be established in the Ministry of Justice and Labor; and provisions were made for the eviction of a *yanacona* in case he did not meet the terms of his contract.[66]

After extensive debate, the Senate passed the bill with only a few word changes, and the Chamber of Deputies approved the revisions on February 27, 1947.[67] Promulgated on March 15, 1947,

64. See speeches by Sánchez Palacios in: ibid., January 23, 1946, 1:75-83, and January 28, 1946, 1:142-50. See also the speeches by Deputy José Angel Escalante, ibid., January 24, 1940, 1:101-4, 110-13.

65. The complete debate is in: ibid., January 23, 1946, 1:73-83; January 24, 1946, 1:101-13; January 25, 1946, 1:126-31; January 28, 1946, 1:133-66; and January 29, 1946, 1:200-256.

66. PDD, 1st Extraordinario de 1946, Diputados, December 23, 1946, 2:161-65.

67. The Senate debate fills nearly two volumes, PDD, Ordinario de 1946, Senadores, vols. 4 and 5. PDD, 2d Extraordinario de 1946, Diputados, February 27, 1947, 3:488-91. See also: PDD, 1st Extraordinario de 1946, Diputados, 2:353-64. For the text of

the new law soon encountered difficulties. Most *yanacona* contracts had been oral in the past, and rather than submit to the new regulations, many *hacendados* simply evicted their *yanaconas*. Others, who had used written contracts previously, substituted oral ones to avoid the massive paperwork required by the law. The section which based the rent on the assessed value of the land was difficult to enforce, with the result that the courts were flooded with suits from both landowners and *yanaconas*.[68] Government efforts to clarify the law and to establish procedures for its implementation failed,[69] and the law was never enforced. The *hacendados* had won again; but the Apristas took credit for passage of the law, and even though they had defeated most attempts to simplify or improve it, in later years they referred to it as a major accomplishment.[70] Anti-Aprista Peruvians attacked the law and Apra's role in its passage, claiming that it had actually oppressed the *yanaconas* further and should be known as the Law of the Hacendado.[71] The condition of the *yanaconas* actually worsened,[72] and Aprista *indigenismo* lost much of its glitter.

Apra's failure to espouse measures for Indian integration, redistribution of land, and general economic reform — all of which had long been part of its fundamental program — cost the party in the 1940s and 1950s several of its outstanding leaders, among them Magda Portal, Luis Eduardo Enríquez, Alberto Hidalgo, and Víctor Villanueva. The political coalition with Manuel Prado (1956-62) was to produce additional defections and lead to the formation by leftist elements of Apra Rebelde in 1960. When, in 1963, Haya formed an alliance (La Coalición) with his former

the law, see: PMTAI, *Legislación,* pp. 144-51. For the text plus subsequent amendments and an explanation of each article, see: Leonor Breña Pacheco and Nelson Cáceres A., *Legislación de yanaconaje: Contiene todas las leyes, reglamentos y ejecutorias supremas hasta la fecha* (Lima: Editorial "Jolay," 1951), pp. 3-32.

68. See the speech by Deputy Albino Molina Sánchez from Ica in: PDD, Ordinario de 1947, Diputados, August 14, 1947, 1:25-26. See also: ibid., August 18, 1947, 1:55-57, and September 16, 1947, 1:187-88; and Ford, *Man and Land,* pp. 84-88.

69. See: Supreme Decrees of June 22, 1947, and July 10, 1948, and Supreme Resolution of April 7, 1948 in: PMTAI, *Legislación,* pp. 151-56, and Fajardo, *Legislación indígena,* pp. 108-9.

70. See: Peláez Bazán, *De la provincia al aprismo,* p. 82; and Alfredo Saco Miró Quesada, *Programa agrario del aprismo* (Lima: Ediciones Populares, 1946), pp. 24-25.

71. Alfredo Hernández Urbina, *Los partidos y la crisis del Apra* (Lima: Ediciones Raíz, 1956), pp. 74-75; and Portal, *¿Quiénes traicionaron al pueblo?,* p. 14.

72. Ford, *Man and Land,* p. 84.

rival, Manuel A. Odría, all but the most dedicated Apristas were convinced that the party had completely abandoned its reformist stance. Several Aprista writers and sympathizers have attempted to explain this ideological transformation by asserting that it was not Haya who had changed, but the world around him.[73] One scholar has suggested that Aprista radicalism had appealed to the middle class during the economic depression of the 1930s, but not after World War II. Hence Apra had altered its ideology to retain middle-class support.[74] Neither of these theories, however, explains the inconsistencies in Apra's *indigenista* program during both the 1931 campaign and the 1945-48 presidency of Bustamante y Rivero.[75]

The Indian record of the Bustamante Congress was mediocre and the role of the Apristas suspect, but the performance of the president himself was not much better. In all fairness, however, it should be noted that the years 1946-48 were ones of constant turmoil and tension brought on by the Apristas' attempts to dominate the Congress and compel the president to accede to their political demands. Nevertheless, only in the area of Indian education did the administration make any real progress. Throughout his term, Bustamante asserted that Peru's progress depended upon the mobilization of youth in a systematic program of national de-

73. An excellent example of this thesis is in Enrique Chirinos Soto, *Cuenta y balance de las elecciones de 1962* (Lima: Ediciones Perú, 1962), pp. 109-10. See also Pablo Silva Villacorta, *A dónde van las ideas de Haya de la Torre: Una nueva visión sobre las ideas que conforman la doctrina del Apra* (Lima: Talleres de la Imprenta E.R.V., 1966).

74. For a detailed treatment of this view, see Pike, "The Old and the New APRA."

75. On February 17, 1968, I interviewed Haya de la Torre in the party headquarters in Lima. By that time, Haya de la Torre had discarded all pretenses of the fiery *indigenismo* that characterized his early career. He no longer felt special Indian schools were needed because language barriers would be overcome by the Indian children's ability to learn Spanish rapidly. He stated that racial prejudice no longer existed in Peru and praised the great work of both the army and the Catholic Church in integration programs. There was no danger, he said, of Indian uprisings because the Indian was a passive being and not inclined to violence. His major concern had become the city slums, or *barriadas,* rather than the rural Indians. This same preoccupation was voiced by Deputy Luis Llanos de la Mar from Pasco, who was chairman of Apra's National Bureau for Campesinos and Barriadas. In an interview on February 14, 1968, his principal concerns were urban problems and cooperatives. He wanted to convert the *comunidades* into co-ops, but he emphasized large, capitalistic middle-class co-ops rather than small ones which would pertain to the Indians. Fervent *indigenismo* formed a basic part of stated Aprista doctrine in the 1930s and early 1940s, but it has long since disappeared.

velopment, and he viewed the education of the Indians and the *campesinos* as a key factor in this mobilization. In November, 1945, Luis A. Valcárcel, minister of education, and Jorge Calero Vásquez, his Bolivian counterpart, signed a convention calling for the exchange of studies regarding the Indians of the Lake Titicaca Basin; for the initiation in that area of an educational, sanitation, and agricultural campaign utilizing the government agencies of both countries; and for a revision of all reciprocal agreements relating to Indians and Indian education.[76]

One result of the agreement was a convention of Bolivian and Peruvian teachers held in Bolivia to discuss problems involved in teaching Indians.[77] A direct outcome of the discussion was Bustamante's creation of the Núcleos Escolares Campesinos (Nuclear Peasant Schools) in April, 1946. A supreme decree of April 22, 1947, provided the organization of the schools, giving as their goals: instilling in the Indians a desire for a better life; the integration of the Indians into modern society; improvement of agricultural practices; extension of education to both children and adults; betterment of Indian social organization; and teaching of Spanish. The system was composed of sixteen central schools in the departments of Pasco, Huánuco, Junín, Cuzco, and Puno, each with fifteen to twenty satellite schools grouped around it. The central school offered a complete primary education for children which began in the Indian language, with a gradual transition into Spanish. The dependent schools offered secondary education for young people and adult classes in Spanish, sanitation, agriculture, livestock, and development of small industries. Specialists operating out of the central schools provided the technical skills needed throughout the system.[78]

The government also increased the number of normal schools and developed special courses for teachers in hygiene, agriculture, livestock raising, and crafts; authorized the use of Quechua and Aymara in the classroom; and ordered the adoption of a new alphabet for the writing of Indian languages. In addition, the San

---

76. PMTAI, *Legislación*, pp. 73-75.

77. José Luis Bustamante y Rivero, *Mensaje presentado al Congreso Nacional al inaugurarse la Legislatura Ordinaria de 1947 por el señor presidente de la república doctor don José Luis Bustamante y Rivero* (Lima: Imprenta del Colegio Militar Leoncio Prado, 1947), pp. 173-74; and idem, *Tres años de lucha por la democracia en el Perú* (Buenos Aires: Artes Gráficas Bartolomé U. Chiesino, 1949), p. 403.

78. PMTAI, *Legislación*, pp. 270-88.

Jerónimo Institute of Educational Experimentation was established in Cuzco to coordinate the various activities and programs of the nuclear schools. It was to devote particular attention to the problems of teaching in Quechua or Aymara, to the drafting of new curricula and educational programs, and to organizing conferences and conventions to acquaint the public with the problems of Indian education and to provide opportunities for teachers to exchange ideas.[79] Bustamante also appointed special educational commissions to study the cultural and psychological aspects of successful Indian education.[80]

Although one *indigenista* criticized the Indian education program because it did not include instructing Indians in their legal rights,[81] there is no doubt that the nuclear schools did enjoy success. They not only confronted the problems of illiteracy among the Indian population, but also sought to improve the sanitation, agriculture, and arts and crafts industries of the southern sierra. In cooperation with the Peruvian-North American Educational Service, the schools continued operation throughout the 1950s and well into the 1960s, justifying Bustamante's pride in them.[82]

Outside of education, Bustamante accomplished little in terms of Indian integration. An act with long-range value was the establishment of the Peruvian Indian Institute (Instituto Indigenista Peruano) in May, 1946, as a dependency of the Ministry of Justice and Labor. Affiliated with the Interamerican Indian Institute in Mexico, the Peruvian organization was to study Indian problems and to coordinate Indian studies.[83] In 1946, it began publication of the scholarly journal, *Perú indígena,* which has continued to the present.

In June, 1946, Bustamante decreed the reorganization of the

---

79. See ministerial resolutions of April 25, 1946, October 16, 1946, and October 29, 1946, in ibid, pp. 272-79.

80. José Luis Bustamante y Rivero, *Mensaje presentado al Congreso por el doctor don J. L. Bustamante y Rivero presidente constitucional de la república* (Lima: Tipografía Peruana, 1946), pp. 91, 96-97; idem, *Mensaje al Congreso de 1947,* pp. 173-74; and idem, *Tres años de lucha,* p. 403.

81. Cornejo Bouroncle, *Tierras ajenas,* pp. 207-12.

82. For two analyses of the nuclear schools, see: Jorge Basadre, *Materiales para otra morada: Ensayos sobre temas de educación y cultura* (Lima: Librería "La Universidad" Editorial, 1960), pp. 93-95; and Antonio Pinilla Sánchez Concha, "Los núcleos escolares rurales en el Perú," *América indígena* 12, no. 3 (July, 1952): 225-26.

83. PMTAI, *Legislación,* pp. 72-73; and Bustamante y Rivero, *Mensaje al Congreso* (1946), pp. 81-82.

Bureau of Indian Affairs, which had passed to the Ministry of Justice and Labor in 1942. Without altering the duties or responsibilities of the bureau, he sought to increase its efficiency by creating within it the following departments: complaints, economic and social organization, technical affairs, legal affairs, Indian studies, regional inspectors, and public relations.[84] Despite the reorganization, however, the bureau did not improve its operations.

In other actions, Bustamante, through a series of supreme decrees in July and September of 1946, allowed the occupant of land in contention to retain possession until after completion of the bureau's investigation to reduce violence in land disputes; ordered the Bureau of Indian Affairs to maintain a complete registry of Indian children employed as domestics in urban regions to ensure their well-being; and founded in Lima a House of the Indian (Casa del Indio) to maintain a permanent Indian exhibition and also to provide temporary lodging for Indian delegations arriving in the capital.[85]

Bustamante was more circumspect in praising his own accomplishments in Indian affairs than his predecessors had been, but he did assert that he had planted the seeds of advancement, had recognized hundreds of Indian *comunidades,* and had begun the tedious process of obliterating illiteracy.[86] Although he enjoyed some success in education, he accomplished less in this area than Prado. As for the *comunidades,* during his regime only a few more than two hundred were inscribed and little was done to aid them economically, socially, or politically. His running battle with Apra precluded full attention to internal matters; and despite what he wrote later, Bustamante committed neither himself nor his administration to Indian reform.[87]

This ten-year interlude of civilian rule (1939-48) was ended in 1948 by a coup d'état led by General Manuel A. Odría, who ruled

84. PMTAI, *Legislación,* pp. 83-89; and Bustamante y Rivero, *Mensaje al Congreso* (1946), pp. 81-82.

85. PMTAI, *Legislación,* pp. 94-96, 140-41, 172-74.

86. Bustamante y Rivero, *Mensaje al Congreso de 1947,* pp. 17-18, 96, 107-8; and Bustamante y Rivero, *Tres años de lucha,* pp. 333, 407.

87. For an example of Bustamante y Rivero's later analysis of his regime as well as his philosophy on Indians, see: José Luis Bustamante y Rivero, *Mensaje al Perú, y "Peru, estructura social"* (Lima: Editorial Universitaria, 1960), pp. 30-31, 50-66, 109-13, 130-32, 163-68. See also his remarks in: Secretaria General del Episcopado del Perú, *Exigencias sociales del catolicismo en el Perú: Primera semana social del Perú, 1 al 9 de agosto de 1959* (Lima: Talleres Gráficos Mercagraph, 1959), pp. 187-88.

until 1956. An analysis of the period reveals both successes and failures, with the emphasis on the latter. Manuel Prado's successes were due in large part to factors not of his making. The internal political situation was calm in 1939 and throughout his term and there was even some clandestine cooperation between the government and Apra. The economic boom engendered by World War II lifted the depression in Peru and enabled Prado to focus on other matters. Finally, Prado enjoyed tremendous popular support from all segments of the society owing both to improving economic conditions and to Peru's victory in the short-lived war with Ecuador in 1941.

José Luis Bustamante y Rivero inherited a relatively peaceful and stable nation and hopes ran high for even greater progress in the future. That dream, however, quickly vanished when the economy disintegrated with the postwar decline in exports. The Apristas, thwarted in their attempts to dominate the government, turned again to obstructionist and even violent tactics.

Thus, it is understandable why Prado's Indian program achieved greater levels of success than that of Bustamante. It is also further proof of the thesis that attention is given to Indians during periods of relative economic prosperity and political tranquillity, but that attention decreases proportionately to the worsening of problems deemed more important.

7

Conclusion

A critical appraisal of the level of Indian integration in Peru by 1948 clearly demonstrates the failure of 120 years of Indian legislation and integration programs. At mid-twentieth century the Indians were still isolated economically, politically, socially, and culturally from the mainstream of Peruvian society. The years of effort chronicled above did not result in any meaningful Indian reform. Indeed, one might even argue that the general condition of the Indians had worsened during the republican period.

The tone of nineteenth-century Indian legislation was established by Independence leaders José de San Martín and Simón Bolívar. Both demanded Indian integration and attempted to abolish forced labor, Indian tribute, and other abuses. Bolívar, in particular, sought to break up the Indian *comunidad,* to redistribute land, and to convert the Indians into yeoman farmers. Both men failed to realize that the liberal precepts of the nineteenth century were not applicable to the realities of Indian life. Nevertheless, subsequent nineteenth-century legislation reinforced the errors of the Liberators and the Indians' condition continued to decline. The emphasis on private property and equality before the law, particularly in the realm of work contracts, favored the rise of a strong *latifundista* class at the expense of the Indians.

There was some emphasis on education as a vehicle for Indian integration and in 1840, Ramón Castilla, then finance minister, sought to improve and expand Indian education and educational facilities. Peru's first civilian president, Manuel Pardo, also concentrated on Indian education as the most feasible method of assimilating Indians into Peruvian society. He envisioned a national system of Indian trade schools to train a wide range of Indian artisans, but his programs were thwarted both by the Church and by the landed oligarchy.

The one bright spot in the nineteenth century was the rise of the neopositivists. Intellectuals such as Carlos Lissón, Mariano H. Cornejo, Joaquín Capelo, and Manuel Vicente Villarán argued forcefully for Indian education and integration. Manuel González Prada, whose ideas and writings occupy a unique position in Peruvian history, promoted a new brand of *indigenismo* which influenced several generations of Peruvian intellectuals. Despite his efforts, however, the end of the century found the Indians in worse condition than at the start of the republican period.

There was no change in official policy or ideology in the early years of the twentieth century and no president exhibited true concern for the Indians, but there was a gradual change in the tone of the proposals offered for Indian integration. Several *indigenistas* argued that the state had an obligation to intervene actively in socio-economic matters, including Indian affairs. This movement gained impetus through the efforts of Alejandrino Maguiña, Manuel Vicente Villarán, and Pedro S. Zulen, whose Pro-Indian Association enjoyed some influence in the Congress. Examples of the new tone were the passage in 1909 of Law 1183, which prohibited government authorities from requiring free services of Indians, and in 1916 of Law 2285, which required that Indian laborers be paid in currency. Neither law was enforced, in part because of a lack of coordination between the executive and legislative branches of government, but they were a beginning.

The election of Augusto B. Leguía in 1919 ushered in a new era in Indian legislation. With the adoption of the Constitution of 1920, the state not only recognized the legal existence of the *comunidad* for the first time, but also assumed responsibility for protecting the Indian population. This new attitude, in turn, awakened interest in Indian problems and led to the seeking of solutions for them. *Indigenista* congressmen proposed many new Indian laws and integration schemes during the Leguía years, but all failed owing to an almost total dearth of presidential support.

Leguía himself is often pictured as a great *indigenista* president who sought to alleviate Indian problems through a liberal and humane integration program. In reality, he was one of those false champions of Indian reform who often do more damage than the *gamonales*.[1] Leguía's creation of the Bureau of Indian Affairs and

---

1. Several authors have fiercely attacked the false champions, but one of the most cogent analyses is in Aguilar, *Cuestiones indígenas,* pp. 101-5.

the Patronato were empty gestures and could not compensate for the damage done by his continued support of *hacendado* interests and his implementation of *conscripción vial.* He refused to support Peru's *indigenistas,* both in and out of Congress, and his highly vaunted program produced no Indian relief. Leguía is a good example of those Peruvian politicians who have used *indigenismo* as a political rallying cry, but who, in the end, lacked the necessary sincerity and commitment to implement their ideas.

One important event of the 1920s was the emergence of José Carlos Mariátegui as one of Peru's most forceful *indigenista* spokesmen. By applying Marxian economic principles to the problems of land distribution and Indian integration, Mariátegui sought to formulate an indigenous brand of communism based on the ancient Inca *ayllu.* Through his devastating attacks on the government, the Church, and the landowners, he opened new directions in *indigenista* thought and emerged as one of Peru's most dedicated fighters for Indian justice, a reputation which history has not altered.

The decade of the 1930s was unproductive in the realm of Indian legislation. The civil war which erupted between the followers of the Apra party and the Civilista supporters of President Luis M. Sánchez Cerro diverted government attention from needed domestic reforms. Sánchez Cerro, for example, did not issue one piece of Indian legislation. His successor, Oscar R. Benavides, offered little that was substantive in the way of Indian reform, and, in fact, one of his programs (that of road construction) resulted in further exploitation of the Indians. The Constituent Congress which met irregularly from 1931 to 1936 likewise failed to provide leadership on the Indian question.

The Constitution of 1933 is the only example in the decade of continuing development of the 1920s concept that the state had a duty to protect the Indians and to provide for their welfare. It included one section devoted to Indians which incorporated such points as the legal recognition of Indian *comunidades* and the state's promise to protect Indian lands, to ensure administrative integrity of the *comunidad,* and to issue a comprehensive Indian legal code. As in the past, however, the lack of executive and legislative support frustrated the effective implementation of these articles.

Perhaps the most important event of the 1930s was the emergence of the Aprista party as a political force in Peru. Víctor Raúl Haya de la Torre and the Apristas have been the subjects of hundreds of articles and books, most of which are extremely polemical. Though influenced by the thought of both González Prada and

Mariátegui, Haya sought to construct a movement based on the desires of the middle class and of the former followers of Leguía, while at the same time offering hope for radical change to the lower classes through his writings and public speeches. In these early years, Haya and the Apristas did demand Indian integration and tried to present themselves as great *indigenista* leaders. Because of the government repression which forced him into hiding, Haya succeeded in masking his opportunism in the 1930s and early 1940s. During the years 1945-48, however, Apra was forced to choose between its middle-class supporters and its *indigenista* pronouncements, and by choosing the former and opposing both agrarian and Indian reform, the party irreparably damaged its *indigenista* reputation.

The election of Manuel Prado in 1939 marked an improvement in the Peruvian government's relations with the Indians. The target of many historians' disdain, Prado changed the direction of Indian programs and accomplished more for the Indians than any previous president. His efforts in Indian education, colonization, and legal protection were exemplary. Unfortunately, his mediocre Congress damaged his overall program both by refusing to initiate Indian legislation itself and by offering only minimal support for Prado's programs.

President José Luis Bustamante y Rivero's administration enjoyed neither the political stability nor the economic prosperity of his predecessor's. The collapse of the Peruvian economy together with the legislative and executive crisis caused by the legalization of the Apra party would have precluded the implementation of any reform program Bustamante might have proposed. However, it is clear that he lacked a true commitment to Indian integration and would not have provided the necessary executive leadership under any circumstances.

The 1948 overthrow of Bustamante by Manuel A. Odría did not produce any alteration in government attitudes toward the Indians. Like so many of his predecessors, Odría touted grandiose promises of new breakthroughs in Indian integration; he publicly committed his administration to full cooperation with such international programs as the Cornell University project at Vicos. Few if any of his promises were ever implemented, however, moving one historian to describe his social program as "at best . . . spotty. It was confined primarily to Lima and a few costal cities and virtually no attempt was made to improve the conditions of the truly destitute members of the population, the Indians of the sierra."[2]

The second administration of Manuel Prado (1956-1962), unlike the first, lacked even an apparent intent or desire to better the Indians' condition. While it is true that Prado announced a National Plan for the Integration of the Indian Population in 1959, that program was poorly implemented. Furthermore, Prado's proposed land reform program contained a section on Indian *comunidades* which reflected Simón Bolívar's belief that the *comunidad* was economically unproductive and should be abolished, an action which would undoubtedly have resulted in further usurpation of Indian lands.

President Fernando Belaúnde Terry (1963-68) spoke eloquently of the need for Indian integration and for the construction of a new Peru. His program of *cooperación popular* (popular cooperation) was intended to bring the Indians into the mainstream of Peruvian life. Belaúnde argued that if the government supplied the tools and materials to the Indian *comunidades,* the Indians would supply the labor necessary to build new roads, schools, sanitation facilities, and health centers. Though hundreds of projects were begun, few were completed because of bureaucratic inefficiency and strong opposition from the Congress, which cut off funds for the program in 1966. By the time of the military ouster of Belaúnde in 1968, it was evident that he had largely failed in his Indian programs.

The military junta which took power in 1968 has made land reform and Indian integration a cornerstone of its revolutionary program. The 1969 agrarian reform law includes an Indian *comunidad* section which promises to restore all lands alienated from the *comunidades* since 1920. Moreover, all lands contingent to *comunidades* which the state declares abandoned will be given to the *comunidad* and all lands taken by the state to facilitate irrigation projects will likewise be restored. If these provisions are actually implemented, the results could be startling, but the process is far from complete and final judgment must be reserved for the future.

Thus, aside from opportunistic proposals and demagoguery, the Indian integration record for the first century and a half of independence is poor. Though political parties incorporated Indian planks into their platforms and politicians climbed on the *indigenista* bandwagon, few of those in policy-making positions

2. Pike, *Modern History of Peru,* p. 292.

were sincere. Moreover, those leaders who did demonstrate some commitment to Indian reform were unable to effect lasting change, owing to several factors which hampered the implementation of Indian legislation.

Decrees issued and laws passed in the urban, coastal atmosphere of Lima did not intimidate rural *hacendados* in the sierra. Local implementation or enforcement of these acts, however, would have met fierce opposition, probably with unpleasant consequences for the political careers of local and national leaders. Another inhibiting factor which is less easily documented was the specter of widespread racial war. White and mestizo fear of bloody Indian revolts has been a part of the Peruvian psyche since the colonial period and many politicians not only exploited it, but sometimes succumbed to it themselves. In addition, there never existed a co-ordinated executive-legislative plan to effect profound change in Indian affairs. There is no instance of a president joining forces with congressional leaders to enforce or implement Indian legislation. Indeed, there are cases where the two branches cooperated to accomplish the exact reverse. Thus, it is doubtful that much could have been accomplished even without the fear of the *hacendados'* reaction and the cry of Indian revolution.

There is one final factor which contributed immensely to the failure of government Indian programs—the lack of proper conceptualization of the problem. Almost all of Peru's politicians and *indigenistas* were whites and mestizos from the coast with a culture which was almost exclusively Spanish and European. Few possessed a profound knowledge of either Indian culture or conditions in the sierra. In short, they viewed the Indian problem through Western European eyes and their solutions reflect this cultural bias.

Most political leaders and many *indigenista* writers felt that one or more reforms within the society would result in the immediate integration of the Indian population. Simón Bolívar's panacea was to transform the Indian into a yeoman farmer. Others such as Manuel Pardo, José Pardo, Oscar Benavides, and Manuel Prado viewed Indian education programs as the answer.[3] Augusto B. Leguía, Benavides, and Fernando Belaúnde Terry argued that im-

---

3. Several examples of *indigenista* emphasis on education are: Cornejo, *Visión objetiva*, pp. 49-50; de la Barra, *El indio peruano*, pp. 208-10, 223-25; and Mac-Lean Estenós, *Indios de América*, pp. 453-54.

proved transportation and communication systems would bring Indian integration, while still others held that military service would break down cultural barriers. Some reformers maintained that the solution lay in ending coca and alcohol addiction and generally improving health and sanitation facilities among the Indians. Implicit in all efforts to write special legal codes for the Indians and to pass new legislation was the assumption that Indian integration could best be achieved juridically or at least administratively through the creation of Indian bureaus and ministries.

Many liberals, socialists, and communists, led by Mariátegui, argued that the Indian problem could never be solved without first transforming the nation's economic structure and instituting a thoroughgoing land reform program. Mariátegui wrote that the problem of the Indian was in reality the problem of the land tenure system and that any successful attempt to incorporate the Indians had to begin with land reform.[4] One contemporary analyst has noted that "the present system of the hacienda with peonage is one of the principal determining factors in the continuance of the Indian problem and also in the economic, political, and social backwardness of the country."[5]

There can be no doubt that most of these socio-economic reform measures will be necessary if Peru is ever to achieve cultural and national unity, and most of their proponents have presented their cases well. Those who have adopted a multipronged approach to the problem certainly offer more credible solutions than those whose solutions are deterministic,[6] but the fact remains that a key ingredient is missing. No politician or government official has ever sought out the advice and counsel of the Indians themselves. Laws were passed and government agencies created without consultation with the Indians as to what they perceived to be their problems and the solutions.

Without even minimal Indian input, government officials and

4. This is the principal thesis of his book *Siete ensayos.* See particularly chaps. 1-3.

5. Vásquez, *Hacienda, peonaje y servidumbre,* p. 49. For other assertions that the solution to the Indian problem lies in economic development and land reform, see: Aguilar, *Cuestiones indígenas,* pp. 90-92; Valcárcel, *Ruta Cultural del Perú,* pp. 200-202; and de la Barra, *El indio peruano,* pp. 195-207.

6. For examples of this multipronged approach, see: Alfredo Hernández Urbina, *Compendio de sociología peruana* (Lima: Ediciones Raíz, 1963), pp. 98-102; A. Eduardo Beteta B., *Apuntes: Socio-económicos del Perú y Latino-América* (Lima: Offset La Confianza, n.d.), pp. 56-61; and Ford, *Man and Land,* pp. 116-17.

administrators could only propose Western European solutions to the problems of non-Western European peoples. The failure of the Indian affairs bureaucracy in the twentieth century, therefore, was due not only to *hacendado* and conservative opposition, but also to the general cultural ignorance of the administrators involved.

Perhaps the only solution to this particular problem is to request and encourage Indian participation. This did not happen in the past because of the Indians' lack of economic and political power, and future governments should undoubtedly concentrate part of their efforts in overcoming that obstacle. This is not to say, however, that all the past Indian laws and programs are worthless. On the contrary, they can and should serve as the basis for the legitimacy of the Indians' demands when they come to be made. Only when the Indians themselves demand their implementation and become sufficiently organized to back such demands with power will the laws enacted by earlier reform-minded Peruvians become reality.

Appendix: A List of Major Indian Legislation 1900-1948

The Indian legislation listed below represents the most complete compilation of laws that I was able to make for the period 1900-1948. Many of these laws appear in several sources, while others are extremely difficult to find. Although the list cannot be considered definitive, it should provide a solid working base for those researchers interested in pursuing some aspect of twentieth-century Indian affairs.

DECRETOS SUPREMOS

Jan. 15, 1919:   Maximum hours of work.
Mar. 4, 1920:   Arbitration between *hacendados* and *yanaconas*.
Mar. 6, 1920:   Peaceful solution of Indian land conflicts.
May 14, 1920:   Election of *comunidad personeros*.
Sept. 3, 1920:   Business representatives for *yanaconas*.
Sept. 12, 1921: Establishment of Bureau of Indian Affairs in the Ministry of Development.
Dec. 7, 1921:   Work standards in the Chicama and Santa Catalina valleys.
Sept. 12, 1921: Protection of Indians.
May 29, 1922:   Creation of the Patronato de la Raza Indígena.
May 11, 1923:   Minimum salary for Indians.
May 11, 1923:   Implementation of Law No. 2285.
July 24, 1925:   Recognition of Indian *comunidades*.
Jan. 8, 1926:   *Comunidad* irrigation rights.
Apr. 1, 1929:   Penalties against *Alcanzadores*.
Apr. 1, 1929:   Prohibition of the tribute *La Rama*.
Apr. 1, 1929:   Prohibition of *La Falla*.

June 22, 1929:	Establishment of the Bureau of Indian Education.
Apr. 26, 1930:	Indian normal schools.
May 24, 1930:	Establishment of the Día del Indio.
June 28, 1930:	Fiscal schools in Indian zones.
Feb. 24, 1932:	Rules for distribution of rural lands.
July 8, 1935:	Creation of the Consejo Superior de Asuntos Indígenas
Mar. 23, 1936:	Rules for adjustment of Indian labor conflicts.
Mar. 23, 1936:	Settlement of Indian *comunidad* claims.
Oct. 5, 1936:	Guarantee of lands to the neighbors of the hacienda Chongoyape.
July 2, 1937:	Protection of Indian children.
June 24, 1938:	Functions of the Bureau of Indian Affairs.
June 24, 1938:	Recognition and inscription of Indian *comunidades*.
July 18, 1938:	Election of Indian *comunidad* representatives.
Mar. 15, 1939:	Structure of rural schools.
May 9, 1939:	Creation of the Brigadas de Culturización Indígena.
June 14, 1939:	Effects of the arbitration tribunals.
June 24, 1939:	Surveying of *comunidad* lands.
Feb. 7, 1940:	Rural normal schools.
Jan. 13, 1941:	Term of *comunidad* representative to last four years.
Oct. 27, 1941:	Sub-Bureau of Indian Education.
Nov. 14, 1941:	Creation of the Procuraduría Gratuita de Indígenas.
Mar. 25, 1942:	Reorganization of the Brigadas de Culturización.
Nov. 14, 1942:	Attributes of the Procuraduría Gratuita.
Apr. 21, 1943:	Agricultural schools in Huancabamba.
Aug. 17, 1943:	Establishment of the Ministry of Education and Indian Acculturation.
Mar. 4, 1944:	The Campaña Nacional de Alfabetización.
Mar. 20, 1944:	Literacy school for Aymaras in Ojjerani.
July 17, 1944:	Indian Migration Office in Puno.
Oct. 18, 1944:	Spanish instruction for Indians.
July 17, 1945:	Recognition of *comunidades*.
Apr. 25, 1946:	Creation of nuclear rural schools in Puno.
May 15, 1946:	Regulations for rural normal schools.
June 10, 1946:	Reorganization of the Bureau of Indian Affairs.
July 18, 1946:	Registration of minor Indian domestics.
July 18, 1946:	Solutions for Indian land claims.
Sept. 13, 1946:	Creation of the Casa del Indio.
Apr. 22, 1947:	Regulations for rural education around Lake Titicaca.
June 22, 1947:	Regulations for the *yanaconaje* law.
Aug. 20, 1947:	Clarification of Article 9 of the *yanaconaje* law.
Aug. 20, 1947:	Expropriation of Tincocancha.
Dec., 1947:	Distribution of lands according to Law No. 10883.
July 10, 1948:	Relationship between *yanacona* and *yanaconizante*.
July 10, 1948:	Functions of the private courts.

EJECUTORIA ADMINISTRATIVA

June 4, 1946:	Restrictions on *comunidad* lands.
Aug. 22, 1946:	Indian property and the Bureau of Indian Affairs.
Aug. 26, 1946:	Regulations for renting of lands.
Sept. 27, 1946:	Resolution of *comunidad* land conflicts.

EJECUTORIA SUPREMA

Apr. 4, 1913:	Role of the *personero*.
Dec. 6, 1917:	Role of the *personero*.
Dec. 6, 1917:	*Comunidad* representation.
June 1, 1932:	*Comunidad* recognition.
Sept. 28, 1932:	Special treatment of Indian crime.
Sept. 4, 1935:	Penalties for Indian crimes.
Dec. 19, 1935:	Regulations for *comunidad* lawsuits.
Sept. 7, 1938:	*Comunidad* registration required for initiating lawsuits.
Sept. 25, 1939:	Bureau of Indian Affairs to arbitrate inter-*comunidad* disputes.
Sept. 25, 1939:	Regulations for *comunidad* pasture lands.
Oct. 31, 1939:	Indians are owners of the lands on which they reside.
Nov. 22, 1940:	Indian homicide.
Jan. 7, 1941:	Indian *comunidad* property.
Jan. 7, 1941:	Imprescriptibility of Indian lands.
Dec. 21, 1945:	Jurisdiction of Ministry of Labor and Indian Affairs.

LEYES, DECRETO LEYES, LEYES REGIONALES

Ley 4831, Oct. 11, 1893:	Indian payment of taxes.
Ley 1183, Nov. 23, 1909:	Authorities prohibited from contracting Indian services.
Ley 2285, Oct. 13, 1916:	Minimum salary for Indians.
Ley 2472, Oct. 11, 1917:	Creation of model experimental school in Puno.
Ley 4504, Mar. 20, 1922:	Functions of the regional congresses.
Ley 5257, Nov. 11, 1925:	Creation of experimental Indian boarding school.
Ley 6648, Dec. 14, 1929:	Rectification of rural boundaries.
Ley 7653, Oct. 21, 1932:	Ratification of various *Decreto Leyes*.
Ley 7654, Oct. 21, 1932:	Creation of rural Indian school in Tingua.
Ley 7658, Oct. 21, 1932:	Creation of an experimental school in Puno.

Ley 7652, Oct. 29, 1932:	Commemoration of Atahualpa.
Ley 8120, Mar. 14, 1935:	Establishment of Indian Arbitration Tribunes.
Ley 8547, June 11, 1936:	Establishment of the Bureau of Indian Affairs.
Ley 8698, July 7, 1938:	Appropriation of funds for Indian school in Puno.
Ley 8930, Aug. 3, 1939:	Arbitration Tribunes.
Ley 9359, Apr. 1, 1941:	Education code.
Ley 9679, Dec. 11, 1942:	Transfer of Bureau of Indian Affairs to Ministry of Labor and Justice.
Ley 9680, Dec. 11, 1942:	Credit facilities for Indian colonies.
Ley 10209, July 19, 1945:	School gardens in Chucuito.
Ley 10236, Sept. 16, 1945:	Judges should know Indian language.
Ley 10356, Dec. 31, 1945:	Creation of Día del Tahuantisuyo.
Ley 10842, May 31, 1946:	Award of new Lake Titicaca lands to Indians.
Ley 10841, Mar. 20, 1947:	Renting of rural property.
Ley 10883, Mar., 1947:	Expropriation of the hacienda Santa Ursula.
Ley 10885, Mar. 15, 1947:	*Yanacona* contracts.
Decreto Ley 7346, Oct. 5, 1931:	Bureau of Indian Education.
Decreto Ley, Mar. 23, 1936:	Reclamation and arbitration of land titles.
Decreto Ley 10922, Dec. 3, 1948:	Prohibition of *yanacona* eviction.
Ley Regional 27, Feb. 7, 1920:	Creation of experimental agricultural school in Cuzco.
Ley Regional 479, Aug. 22, 1921:	Prohibition of free labor.
Ley Regional 605, Oct. 6, 1922:	Prohibition of free labor in southern Peru.

Resoluciones Directorales

June 9, 1926:	Approbation of regulations for rural mobile schools.
Oct. 2, 1941:	Possession of Indian lands during litigation.
May 12, 1943:	Election of *personero*.
Feb. 17, 1944:	Recognition of *comunidades*.
Apr. 24, 1944:	Regulations of Indian school in Ojjerani.
June 3, 1944:	Bureau of Indian Affairs to arbitrate inter-*comunidad* conflicts.
Dec. 6, 1944:	Indian conflicts.
Dec. 19, 1944:	Indian *comunidad* property.
Jan. 22, 1945:	*Comunidad* lands.
Mar. 13, 1945:	Regional Indian inspectors.
Apr. 9, 1945:	Recognition of *comunidad* boundaries.
Apr. 24, 1945:	Election of the *comunidad junta*.

RESOLUCIONES MINISTERIALES

Feb. 16, 1922:	Civil engineer for the *comunidad* of Tauca.
Apr. 11, 1922:	Civil engineers for three *comunidades*.
Aug. 28, 1925:	Requirements for *comunidad* registration.
Sept. 7, 1925:	Creation of rural mobile schools.
Sept. 11, 1925:	Amplification of *RM* of Aug. 28, 1925.
Apr. 19, 1926:	Regulations for rural mobile schools.
May 12, 1926:	Mobile schools in Anta.
May 19, 1926:	Establishment of Indian boarding school in Pumamarca.
Aug. 19, 1927:	Protection of Indians against shyster lawyers.
Sept. 16, 1927:	Regulations for *comunidad* boundary markers.
July 23, 1931:	Prohibition of tolls on public roads.
Nov. 19, 1931:	Regulations for payment of engineers working for *comunidades*.
June 27, 1936:	Regulations for suits by *comunidades*.
Nov. 19, 1940:	Distribution of lands to Indians.
Sept. 27, 1941:	Residence of the *personero*.
Oct. 27, 1941:	Vacancy of the office of *personero*.
Feb. 9, 1942:	Regulations for office of *personero*.
Oct. 19, 1942:	Defense of Indian claims.
Aug. 25, 1943:	Rectification of *comunidad* boundaries.
Nov. 19, 1943:	Abrogation of taxes on *comunidad* industrial profits.
Dec. 1, 1943:	Regulations for office of *personero*.
Mar. 16, 1944:	Election of the *personero*.
Apr. 12, 1944:	Regulations for office of *personero*.
June 5, 1944:	Regulations for office of *personero*.
June 7, 1945:	Spanish instruction for Indians.
Aug. 10, 1945:	Organization of Indian agricultural cooperatives.
May 15, 1946:	Creation of the Instituto Indigenista Peruano.
May 20, 1946:	Revisions of *comunidad* accounts.
June 4, 1946:	*Comunidad* lands.
Oct. 16, 1946:	Teaching in Indian languages.
Oct. 29, 1946:	Official Quechua and Aymara alphabets.
Aug. 20, 1947:	Provision of funds for the Casa del Indio.

RESOLUCIONES SUPREMAS

Jan. 2, 1911:	Labor regulations for the *montaña*.
May 11, 1917:	Labor regulations for the *montaña*.
Dec. 6, 1917:	Litigation over the *comunidad* Tusi.
May 14, 1920:	*Comunidad* water rights.
Aug. 29, 1920:	*Yanacona* claims.
Dec. 15, 1922:	District councils for *comunidades*.
Mar. 23, 1923:	Housing regulations for laborers on rural farms.
May 11, 1923:	Payment for services of Indian *yanaconas*.
May 11, 1923:	Indians own hacienda Lauramarca.

Apr. 17, 1925:	Establishment of preschool nurseries on rural agricultural holdings.
July 11, 1925:	Creation of rural mobile schools.
Aug. 28, 1925:	Creation of official registry for *comunidades*.
Sept. 11, 1925:	Recognition of *comunidades*.
Mar. 12, 1926:	Possessions of the Indians of Villanueva.
Aug. 7, 1926:	Approval of regulations for rural mobile schools.
Nov. 5, 1926:	Establishment of *comunidades'* control over their profits.
Mar. 5, 1927:	Approval of regulations for vocational schools.
May 7, 1927:	Approval of regulations for Indian boarding schools.
July 2, 1927:	Appointment of new chief of rural education.
Aug. 19, 1927:	Abolishment of the Comité Central del Pro-Derecho Indígena Tahuantisuyo.
Sept. 16, 1927:	Official boundary markers for *comunidades*.
Nov. 18, 1927:	Regulations for engineers surveying *comunidades*.
July 23, 1931:	Prohibition of toll collecting on public roads.
Sept. 7, 1931:	Possessions of the Indians of Rumuro.
Nov. 19, 1931:	Regulations for engineers surveying *comunidades*.
Jan. 22, 1932:	Claims of the Indians of Acoria.
Sept. 6, 1932:	Request of the Sociedad de Beneficiencia Pública de Huancavelica.
Sept. 21, 1932:	Requests of haciendas Vicos and Vilcabamba.
Nov. 9, 1932:	Request of the *comunidad* of Huachos.
Nov. 9, 1932:	Request of the *comunidad* of Pachas.
Dec. 30, 1932:	Request of the hacienda Vicos.
Feb. 17, 1933:	Request of the Indians of Taquila.
Apr. 21, 1933:	Request of the *comunidad* of Chicla.
Apr. 9, 1934:	Regulations for the rural school at Chopitea.
Apr. 9, 1934:	Regulations for the vocational school at Tingua.
June 27, 1935:	Official recognition of *comunidades*.
Mar. 23, 1936:	Regulations for hacienda account books of wages and salaries.
May 20, 1936:	Modification of *RS* of March 23, 1936.
May 20, 1936:	Regulations of the Consejo Superior de Asuntos Indígenas.
June 27, 1936:	Modification of *RS* of Aug. 28, 1925.
Oct. 27, 1936:	Maximum work hours in the work centers.
Mar. 22, 1937:	Responsibility of Ministry of Education and municipal councils for school furniture.
Aug. 19, 1940:	*Comunidad* inscription.
Aug. 19, 1940:	Recognition of *comunidad* does not imply recognition of boundary.
Feb. 6, 1941:	Land expropriation for Indians.
Apr. 16, 1942:	Locations for the Brigadas de Culturización.
Oct. 19, 1942:	Regulations for Indian defenders.
Jan. 16, 1943:	Creation of a rural normal school in Apurímac.

July 7, 1943:   Indian lands in litigation.
Dec. 30, 1943:   Exclusion of *comunidades* from land taxes.
Jan. 24, 1944:   Recognition of *comunidades.*
Mar. 4, 1944:   Regulations for the *Campaña Nacional de Alfabetización.*
Jan. 2, 1945:   *Comunidad* recognition.
June 7, 1945:   Indian teachers required to know Indian languages.
July 17, 1945:   Recognition and inscription of *comunidades.*
Aug. 10, 1945:   Organization of Indian agricultural cooperatives.
Apr. 25, 1946:   Special requirements for nuclear school teachers.
Aug. 3, 1946:   Official school year for rural schools.
Apr. 22, 1947:   Nuclear school study plan for Cuzco and Puno.
Apr. 22, 1947:   Regulations for the *Instituto de San Jerónimo.*
Apr. 22, 1947:   Organization of the *Instituto Educacional del Puno.*
May 9, 1947:   Regulations for *campesino* nuclear schools.
June 22, 1947:   Term of *yanacona* contracts.
Apr. 7, 1948:   Application of LEY 10885 on *haciendas* and *yanaconas.*
Aug. 28, 1948:   School manual labor exhibition.

MISCELLANEOUS INDIAN LEGISLATION

Resolución Legislativa,
   Oct. 11, 1893:   Indian ownership of their own lands.
Resolución Legislativa 673 of the
   Congreso Regional del
   Centro, Jan. 2, 1926:   Establishment of experimental
                              agricultural school in Pampas.

Resolución del Consejo Superior
   de Contribuciones, Nov. 19, 1943:   Abolition of certain *comunidad* taxes.

Files Relating to Indian *Comunidades,* Instituto Indigenista Peruano, Ministerio de Trabajo y Comunidades. Lima, Peru.

Records of Indian *Comunidades.* Ministerio de Trabajo y Comunidades. Lima, Peru.

OFFICIAL PUBLICATIONS

Perú. Biblioteca Nacional. *Anuario bibliográfico peruano.* 13 vols. Lima: Various publishers, 1945-69.

Perú. Congreso. Cámaras de Diputados,*Compilation de la legislación peruana concordada.* 4 vols. Lima: n.p., 1950.

Perú. Congreso. Cámaras de Senadores y Diputados, 1900-1947. *Diario de los Debates.* Lima: Various publishers, 1900-1948.

Perú. Congreso Constituyente de 1931. *Diario de los debates del Congreso Constituyente de 1931.* 23 vols. Lima: Various publishers, 1932-36.

Perú. Ministerio de Gobierno y Policía.*Memoria que el Ministro de Gobierno y Policía sr. Leónidas Cárdenas presenta al Congreso Ordinario de 1902.* Lima: Imprenta del Estado, 1902.

Perú. Ministerio de Justica, Culto, Instrucción y Beneficencia. *Memoria del Ministro de Justicia, Culto, Instrucción y Beneficenia.* Lima: n.p., 1924.

Perú. Ministerio de Salud Pública, Trabajo y Previsión Social. Dirección de Asuntos Indígenas. *Boletín de la Dirección de Asuntos Indígenas.* Lima: Imprenta y Librería del Gabinete Militar, 1938.

————. *Boletín de la Dirección de Asuntos Indígenas.* Lima: Imprenta Americana, 1940.

————. *La política indigenista en el Perú.* Lima: Imprenta "Lux," 1940.

Perú. Ministerio de Trabajo y Asuntos Indígenas. *Atlas comunal.* 2 vols. Lima: Ministerio de Trabajo y Asuntos Indígenas, 1964.

Perú. Ministerio de Trabajo y Asuntos Indígenas. Dirección General de Asuntos Indígenas. *Legislación indigenista del Perú.* Lima: Talleres Gráficos de la Penitenciaría Central, 1948.

República del Perú. *Asamblea nacional de 1919: Discursos oficiales pronunciados en las sesiones de instalación y juramento, por el presidente de la república sr. d. Augusto B. Leguía y por el presidente de la asamblea Dr. d. Mariano H. Cornejo.* Lima: Imprenta Torres Aguirre, 1919.

República Peruana. *Boletín del Ministerio de Fomento, agosto 1922-1925: Sección de asuntos indígenas.* Lima: Imprenta Torres Aguirre, 1926.

República Peruana. *Presidentes del senado, comisiones directivas y señores senadores, 1829-1960.* Lima: Talleres Gráficos del Senado, 1961.

————. *Reglamento del patronato de la raza indígena.* Lima: Imprenta Americana, 1922.

República Peruana. Ministerio de Fomento. Dirección General del Ramo. Sección de Asuntos Indígenas. *Recopilación de leyes, decretos y resoluciones que se relacionan con la raza indígena, y recomendaciones para la organización de expedientes de reconocimiento e inscripción oficial y de levantamiento de planos de conjunto de las tierras de las comunidades de indígenas.* Lima: Imprenta y Librería del Gabinete Militar, 1935.

BOOKS AND PAMPHLETS

Abarca Arias, José Luis. *Proyecto de ley tutelar de la raza indígena.* Arequipa: n.p., 1919.

Adams, Richard N. *A Community in the Andes: Problems and Progress in Muquiyauyo.* Seattle: University of Washington Press, 1959.

Aguilar, Luis F. *Cuestiones indígenas.* Cuzco: Tipografía de El Comercio, 1922.

Aguirre Gamio, Hernando. *Liquidación histórica del Apra y del colonialismo neoliberal.* Lima: Ediciones Debate, 1962.

Alayza Paz-Soldán, Francisco. *El problema del indio en el Perú: Su civilización e incorporación a la nacionalidad.* Lima: Editorial Imprenta Americana, 1928.

Alayza Paz-Soldán, Luis, et al. *Homenaje a Sánchez Cerro, 1933-1953.* Lima: Editorial Huascarán, 1953.

Alexander, Robert J. *Prophets of the Revolution: Profiles of Latin American Leaders.* New York: Macmillan, 1962.

Almanza, J. Antonio. *También el indio ruge: Ensayos psico-sociológicos del indio.* Cuzco: Casa Editora H. G. Rozas Sucesores, 1930.

Alvarez Beltrán, Carlos M. *Estatuto de comunidades de indígenas del Perú (concordado y comentado).* Trujillo: Editorial Escolar "Cabrera," 1964.

Aprismo. Lima: n.p., n.d.

Argüedas, José María. *Las comunidades de España y del Perú.* Lima: Imprenta de la Universidad Nacional Mayor de San Marcos, 1968.

———. *Evolución de las comunidades indígenas.* Lima: C.I.P., 1957.

Aspíllaga, Antero. *Programa de gobierno presentado a la consideración del país por Antero Aspíllaga candidato proclamado a la presidencia de la república por la asamblea general extraordinaria del Partido Civil, 10 diciembre de 1911.* Lima: Tip. de "El Lucero," 1911.

Ayarza, Víctor E. *Reseña histórica del senado del Perú, 1821-1921.* Lima: Imprenta Torres Aguirre, 1921.

Baeza Flores, Alberto. *Haya de la Torre y la revolución constructiva de las Américas.* Buenos Aires: Editorial Claridad, 1962.

Balta, José. *Exposición doctrinaria y programa del Partido Liberal del Perú.* Lima: Empresa Editora "Perú," 1934.

Barra, Felipe de la. *La abolición del tributo por Castilla y su repercusión en el problema del indio peruano.* Lima: Ministerio de Guerra, Servicio de Prensa, Propaganda y Publicaciones Militares, 1956.

———. *El indio peruano en las etapas de la conquista y frente a la república: Ensayo histórico-militar-sociológico y con proposiciones para la solución del problema indio peruano.* Lima: Talleres Gráficos del Servicio de Prensa, Propaganda y Publicaciones Militares, 1948.

Basadre, Jorge. *Introducción a las bases documentales para la historia de la república del Perú con algunas reflexiones.* 2 vols. Lima: Ediciones P. L. Villanueva, 1971.

————. *Los fundamentos de la historia del derecho: Teoría y técnica de la historia del derecho; la profundidad del derecho en el tiempo; los elementos jurídicos llegados al Perú a partir del siglo XVI; sus orígenes históricos; Los carácteres originales de la historia del derecho peruano.* Lima: Librería Internacional del Perú, 1956.

————. *Historia de la república del Perú.* 5th ed., enlarged and corrected. 11 vols. Lima: Talleres Gráficos P. L. Villanueva, 1961-68.

————. *Materiales para otra morada: Ensayos sobre temas de educación y cultura.* Lima: Librería "La Universidad" Editorial, 1960.

————. *Meditaciones sobre el destino histórico del Perú.* Lima: Editorial Huascarán, 1947.

————. *La multitud, la ciudad, y el campo en la historia del Perú.* 2d ed. Lima: Editorial Huascarán, 1947.

————. *Perú, problema y posibilidad: Ensayo de una síntesis de la evolución histórica del Perú.* Lima: Librería Francesa Científica y Casa Editorial E. Rosay, 1931.

Belaúnde, Víctor Andrés. *La crisis presente, 1914-1939.* Lima: Ediciones "Mercurio Peruano," 1940.

————. *El debate constitucional.* Lima: Talleres Gráficos P. L. Villanueva, 1966.

————. *Meditaciones peruanas.* 2d ed. Lima: Talleres Gráficos P. L. Villanueva, 1963.

————. *Memorias.* Vo.l. 1, *Arequipa de mi infancia* (1960). Vol. 2, *Mi generación en la universidad* (1961). Vol. 3, *Planteamiento del problema nacional* (1962). Lima: Imprenta Lumen.

Belaúnde Terry, Fernando. *Peru's Own Conquest.* Lima: American Studies Press, 1965.

Benavides, Oscar R. *El General Benavides a la nación: Mensaje del 25 de marzo de 1939.* Lima: Imprenta C.V.L., 1939.

————. *Mensaje presentado al Congreso del Perú por el señor General de División don Oscar R. Benavides presidente constitucional de la república.* Lima: Talleres Gráficos "Carlos Vásquez L.," 1939.

————. *Mensaje del Gral. Oscar R. Benavides presidente constitucional de la república, 8 de diciembre de 1936.* Lima: C.I.P., 1936.

————. *Mensaje del sr. presidente de la república General de División don Oscar R. Benavides al pueblo peruano, Lima diciembre 9 de 1937.* Lima: Editorial "América Unida," 1937.

————. *El General Benavides a la nación: Mensaje del 8 de diciembre de 1937.* Lima: Empresa Periodística, 1937.

————. *Mensaje del presidente de la república General de División Oscar R. Benavides, presentado al Congreso del Perú el 8 de diciembre de 1939.* N.p., n.d.

————. *Mensaje que s.e. presidente de la república presenta al Congreso Ordinario de 1914.* Lima: Imprenta Americana, 1914.

_____. *Mensaje que s.e. el presidente de la república excmo. señor General Oscar R. Benavides presenta al Congreso Ordinario de 1915.* Lima: Imprenta Americana, 1915.

Benvenutto, Neptalí. *Parlamentarios del Perú contemporáneo.* 3 vols. Vol. 1 (1904-21), Lima: Imprenta Malatesta-Rivas, 1921. Vol. 2 (1904-23), Lima: Imprenta Maletesta-Rivas, 1923. Vol. 3 (1904-25), Lima: Imprenta "Lux" de E. L. Castro, 1925.

Beteta B., A. Eduardo. *Apuntes: Socio-económicos del Perú y Latino-América.* Lima: Offset La Confianza, n.d. (1959-60?).

Billinghurst, Guillermo E. *Discurso programa de s.e. el presidente de la república don Guillermo E. Billinghurst, en el acto de asumir el mando supremo de la nación, 24 de setiembre de 1912.* Lima: Imprenta de "La Acción Popular," 1912.

_____. *Mensaje de s.e. el presidente de la república.* Lima: n.p., 1912.

_____. *Mensaje que s.e. el presidente de la república presenta al Congreso Ordinario de 1913.* Lima: Gil, 1913.

_____. *El presidente Billinghurst a la nación.* Part 1. Santiago: La Imprenta Diener, 1915.

Bonilla, José E., ed. *El siglo de Leguía, 1903-1928.* Lima: T. Scheuch, 1928.

Bourricaud, Francois. *Ideología y desarrollo: El caso del Partido Aprista peruano.* Mexico: El Colegio de México, 1966.

_____. *Poder y sociedad en el Perú contemporáneo.* Translated by Roberta Bifio. Buenos Aires: Editorial SUR, 1967.

Breña Pacheco, Leonor, and Cáceres A., Nelson, comps. and eds. *Legislación de yanaconaje: Contiene todas las leyes, reglamentos y ejecutorias supremas hasta la fecha.* Lima: Editorial "Jolay," 1951.

Bustamante Cisneros, Ricardo. *Condición jurídica de las comunidades de indígenas en el Perú.* Thesis, Universidad Nacional Mayor de San Marcos, Facultad de Jurisprudencia. Lima, 1918.

Bustamante y Rivero, José Luis. *Mensaje al Perú, y "Perú, estructura social."* Lima: Editorial Universitaria, 1960.

_____. *Mensaje del presidente de la república doctor José L. Bustamante y Rivero correspondiente a 1946.* N.p., n.d.

_____. *Mensaje presentado al Congreso Nacional al inaugurarse la Legislatura Ordinaria de 1947 por el señor presidente de la república doctor don José Luis Bustamante y Rivero.* Lima: Imprenta del Colegio Militar Leoncio Prado, 1947.

_____. *Mensaje del señor presidente de la república doctor don José Luis Bustamante y Rivero dirigido a la nación el 29 de febrero de 1948.* Lima: Imprenta del Colegio Leoncio Prado, 1948.

_____. *Mensaje presentado al Congreso por el doctor don J. L. Bustamante y R. presidente constitucional de la república.* Lima: Tipografía Peruana, 1946.

_____. *Tres años de lucha por la democracia en el Perú.* Buenos Aires: Artes Gráficas Bartolomé U. Chiesino, 1949.

Bustamante Robles, Carlos E. *Apellido símbolo Leguía y Salcedo.* Lima: Talleres Gráficos de "La Revista," 1928.

Calderón, Serapio. *Mensaje que el segundo vicepresidente de la república encargado del poder ejecutivo presenta al Congreso Ordinario de 1904.* Lima: Imprenta de Gmo. Stolte, 1904.

Capuñay, Manual A. *Leguía: Vida y obra del constructor del gran Perú.* Lima: Compañía de Impresiones y Publicidad, Enrique Bustamante y Ballivián, Sucesor, 1952.

Carrillo, Francisco. *Clorinda Matto de Turner y su indigenismo literario.* Lima: Ediciones de la Biblioteca Universitaria, Editorial Jurídica, 1967.

Castilla, Ramón. *Ideología.* Lima: Ediciones Hora del Hombre, 1948.

Castillo Delgado, Luis M. *El procedimiento en la administración de justicia indígena.* Cuzco: Editorial H. G. Rozas, 1966.

Castro Arenas, Mario. *La novela peruana y la evolución social.* 2d. ed. corrected and enlarged. Lima: Talleres Gráficos de Iberia, n.d. (1967?).

Castro Pozo, Hildebrando. *Del ayllu al cooperativismo socialista.* Lima: P. Barrantes Castro, 1936.

―――――. *Nuestra comunidad indígena.* Lima: Tipografía "El Lucero," 1924.

―――――, ed. *El yanaconaje en las haciendas piuranas.* Lima: Compañía de Impresiones y Publicidad, 1947.

Chang-Rodríguez, Eugenio. *La literatura política de González Prada, Mariátegui y Haya de la Torre.* Mexico, D.F.: Ediciones de Andrea, Colección Studium 18, 1957.

Chávez León, Fernando Luis. *Legislación social del Perú: Un estudio de la legislación social peruana, recopilada, comentada, anotada y concordada. Apéndice con las ejecutorias del fuero privativo del trabajo y de los tribunales de justicia.* Lima: Empresa Editorial "Rimac," 1937.

Chira C., Magdaleno. *Observaciones e indicaciones básicas de legislación indígena: Elevadas a la comisión parlamentaria respectiva de la honorable asamblea constituyente de 1931 por . . . .* Lima: Imprenta "Hispano-América," 1932.

Chirinos Soto, Enrique. *Cuenta y balance de las elecciones de 1962.* Lima: Ediciones Perú, 1962.

Comisión de Historia. *Próceres del Perú: Felipe Santiago Estenós.* Buenos Aires: Ediciones del Instituto Peruano de Sociología, 1955.

Congreso Indigenista Interamericano, II, Cuzco, 1949. *Anales.* Lima: Editorial Lumen, 1949.

Cornejo, Cirilo A. *Visión objetiva del problema indígena: Planteamiento y solución inmediata.* Lima: Ediciones Continente, 1959.

Cornejo Bouroncle, Jorge. *Las "comunidades" indígenas: La explotación del trabajo de los indios.* Cuzco: H. G. Rozas Sucs., 1948.

―――――. *Tierras ajenas: Estampas de la vida andina.* Cuzco: Ediciones Inca, 1959.

―――――. *Tupac Amaru: La revolución precursora de la emancipación continental.* 2d ed. enlarged. Cuzco: Editorial H. G. Rozas, 1963.

Cornejo Foronda, David. *Don Manuel Pardo y la educación nacional.* Lima: Pontífica Universidad Católica del Perú, 1953.

Cossío, Félix. *La propiedad colectiva del ayllu.* Cuzco: Imprenta "El Trabajo," 1915.

Cossío del Pomar, Felipe. *Haya de la Torre, el indoamericano.* Lima: Editorial Nuevo Día, 1946.

Dávalos y Lissón, Pedro. *Diez años de historia contemporánea del Perú, 1899-1908: Gobiernos de Piérola, Romaña, Candamo, Calderón y Pardo.* Lima: Librería e Imprenta Gil, 1930.

Deustua, Alejandro O. *La cultura nacional.* 2d ed. Lima: Empresa Editora de "El Callao," 1937.

Dobyns, Henry F. *The Social Matrix of Peruvian Indigenous Communities.* Cornell Peru Project Monograph. Ithaca, N.Y.: Cornell University, Department of Anthropology, 1964.

Echegaray, Mariano N., and Silva S., Ramón. *Legislación del trabajo y previsión social: Leyes, decretos y resoluciones concernientes al capital y el trabajo. Disposiciones que favorecen al obrero, la mujer, y el niño. Ley del empleado. Disposiciones que favorecen a los indígenas.* Lima: Imprenta Torres Aguirre, 1925.

Editorial Guillermo Kraft. *Perú: Obra de gobierno del presidente de la república dr. Manuel Prado, 1939-1945.* Buenos Aires: Editorial Guillermo Kraft, 1945.

Eguiguren, Luis Antonio. *En la selva política: Para la historia.* Lima: Sanmarti y Cía., Editores, 1933.

Encinas, José Antonio. *El alcoholismo en la raza indígena.* Lima: n.p., 1915.

———. *Causas de la criminalidad indígena en el Perú: Ensayo de psicología experimental.* Lima: E. E. Villarán, 1919.

———. *Contribución a una legislación tutelar indígena.* Lima: C. F. Southwell, 1918.

Enock, C. Reginald. *Peru: Its Former and Present Civilization, History and Existing Conditions, Topography and Natural Resources, Commerce and General Development.* London: T. Fisher Unwin, 1910.

Enríquez, Luis Eduardo. *Haya de la Torre: La estafa política más grande de América.* Lima: Ediciones del Pacífico, 1951.

La evolución del Perú en el quinquenio, 1919-1924. Lima: Talleres Tipográficos de La Prensa, 1924.

Fajardo, J. V. *Legislación indígena del Perú.* Lima: Editorial Mercurio, n.d. (1961?)

Ford, Thomas R. *Man and Land in Peru.* Gainesville: University of Florida Press, 1955.

Frisancho Macedo, José. *Del jesuitismo al indianismo y otros ensayos.* Lima: Impresión y Fotograbados C. F. Southwell, 1928.

García, José Uriel. *El nuevo indio: Ensayos indianistas sobre la sierra surperuana.* 2d ed., corrected. Cuzco: Editorial H. G. Rozas, Sucesores, 1937.

García Calderón, Francisco. *Diccionario de la legislación peruana. 2a. ed. corr. y aum. con las leyes y decretos dictados hasta 1877.* 2 vols. Nancy, France: Typographie G. Crepin-Leblond, 1879.

González Prada, Adriana Verneuille de. *Mi Manuel.* Lima: Editorial Cultura Antártica, 1947.

González Prada, Manuel. *Bajo el oprobio.* Paris: Tipografía de Louis Bellenand et Fils, 1933.

_____. *Baladas peruanas.* Foreword by Luis Alberto Sánchez. Santiago de Chile: Editorial Ercilla, 1935.

_____. *Figuras y figurones: Manuel Pardo, Piérola, Romaña, José Pardo.* Paris: Tipografía de Louis Bellenand et Fils, 1938.

_____. *Horas de lucha.* Lima: Fondo de Cultura Popular, Ediciones "Futuro," 1964.

_____. *Páginas libres.* 2 vols. Lima: Fondo de Cultura Popular, 1966.

_____. *Prosa menuda.* Buenos Aires: Ediciones Imán, 1941.

Graciano Maita, Víctor. *Política agraria: Bases para una ley agraria y un estatuto de comunidades indígenas.* Lima: Librería y Editorial Mario Campos y Campos, 1963.

Gridilla, P. Alberto, O.F.M. *Un año en el Putumayo: Resúmen de un diario.* Lima: Colección Descalzos, 1943.

Guevara, J. Guillermo. *Rijchari Perú, despierta Perú.* Lima: C.I.P., 1965.

Gutiérrez-Noriega, Carlos, and Zapata Ortiz, Vicente. *Estudios sobre la coca y la cocaína en el Perú.* Lima: Ministerio de Educación Pública, Ediciones de la Dirección de Educación y Extensión Cultural, 1947.

Hardenburg, W. E. *The Putumayo, the Devil's Paradise: Travels in the Peruvian Amazon Region and an Account of the Atrocities Committed upon the Indians Therein.* London: Fisher Unwin, 1912.

Haya de la Torre, Víctor Raúl. *¿A dónde va indoamérica?* 2d ed. Santiago de Chile: Ediciones Ercilla, 1935.

_____. *El antimperialismo y el Apra.* Santiago de Chile: Ediciones Ercilla, 1936.

_____. *Cartas de Haya de la Torre a los prisioneros apristas, recopiladas y anotadas por Carlos Manuel Cox.* Lima: Editorial Nuevo Día, 1946.

_____. *Construyendo el aprismo: Artículos y cartas desde el exilio (1924-1931).* Buenos Aires: Editorial Claridad, 1933.

_____. *La defensa continental.* 4th ed. Lima: Editorial Imprenta "Amauta," 1967.

_____. *Espacio-tiempo-histórico: Cinco ensayos y tres diálogos.* Lima: Ediciones La Tribuna, 1948.

_____. *Haya de la Torre responde al General Benavides.* Incahuasi, Peru: n.p., 1938.

_____. *Pensamiento político de Haya de la Torre.* 5 vols. Vol. 1, *Indoamérica,* Vol. 2, *Ideología aprista.* Vol. 3, *Aprismo y filosofía.* Vol. 4, *El plan de acción,* Vol. 5, *Nuestra América y el mundo.* Lima: Ediciones Pueblo, 1961.

———. *Política aprista.* 2d ed. Lima: Editorial-Imprenta Amauta, 1967.

———. *Por la emancipación de América Latina: Artículas, mensajes, discursos (1923-1927).* Buenos Aires: M. Gleizer-Editor, 1927.

———. *Trienta años de aprismo.* Mexico, D.F.: Fondo de Cultura Económica, 1956.

———. *Y después de la querra aue?* Lima: Editorial PTCM, 1946.

———, and Ingenieros, José. *Teoría y táctica de la acción renovadora y antimperialista de la juventud en América Latina.* Buenos Aires: Editorial Gleizer Publicación del C. E. de C. Económicas, 1928.

Hernández Urbina, Alfredo. *Compendio de sociología peruana.* Lima: Ediciones Raíz, 1963.

———. *Nueva política nacional.* Trujillo, Peru: Ediciones Raíz, 1962.

———. *Los partidos y la crisis del Apra.* Lima: Ediciones Raíz, 1956.

Herrera, Bartolomé. *Escritos y discursos.* 2 vols. Lima: Librería Francesa Científica y Casa Editorial E. Rosay, 1929, 1934.

Heysen, Luis E. *El comandante del Oropesa.* Cuzco: n.p., 1931.

Hidalgo, Alberto. *Por que renuncié al Apra.* Buenos Aires: Imprenta "Leomir," 1954.

———. *Sánchez Cerro o el excremento.* Buenos Aires: n.p., 1932.

Hooper López, René. *Leguía: Ensayo biográfico.* Lima: Ediciones Peruanas, 1964.

Itolararres, José T. *La trinidad del indio o costumbres del interior. Novela.* Lima: n.p., 1885.

Jochamowitz, Alberto. *Mi vida profesional: Apuntes autobiográficos, 1900-1930.* 2 vols. Lima: n.p., 1931.

Johnson, John J. *Political Change in Latin America: The Emergence of the Middle Sectors.* Stanford, Calif.: Stanford University Press, 1958.

Kantor, Harry. *The Ideology and Program of the Peruvian Aprista Movement.* 2d ed. Washington, D.C.: Savile Books, 1966.

Kelley, Hank, and Dot. *Dancing Diplomats.* Albuquerque: University of New Mexico Press, 1950.

Kubler, George. *The Indian Caste of Peru, 1795-1940: A Population Study Based upon Tax Records and Census Reports.* Washington, D.C.: U.S. Government Printing Office, 1952.

Kuczynski Godard, Máxime H. *La condición social del indio y su insalubridad: Miradas sociográficas del Cuzco.* Lima: Ministerio de Salud Pública y Asistencia Social, 1945.

———, and Paz Soldán, Carlos Enrique. *Disección del indigenismo peruano: Un examen sociológico y médico social.* Lima: Instituto de Medicina Social, 1948.

Larrabure y Correa, Carlos. *Perú y Colombia en el Putumayo: Réplica a una publicación aparecida, con fecha 27 de mayo último, en el suplemento sudamericano del Times de Londres.* Barcelona: Imprenta Viuda de Luis Tasso, 1913.

Leguía, Augusto B. *A la nación: Manifiesto del presidente de la república, 1925.* Lima: Tip. "Lima," 1925.

————. *Discursos, mensajes y programas.* Vol. 1. Lima: Editorial Garcilaso, 1924.

————. *Discursos, mensajes y programas.* Vol. 2. Lima: Editorial Garcilaso, 1925.

————. *Discursos, mensajes y programas.* Vol. 3. Lima: Editorial Garcilaso, 1926.

————. *Discursos programa con que el señor Augusto B. Leguía, asumió por tercera vez la presidencia de la república, el 12 de octubre de 1924.* Lima: Imprenta "Garcilaso," 1924.

————. *Discursos pronunciados por el señor don Augusto B. Leguía, presidente de la república y doctor C. Manchego Muñoz, ministro de fomento, al hacer entrega de los albums que el cuerpo directivo de este ministerio preparó como homenaje a la labor ejecutada en los nueve años de la patria nueva, de 1919 a 1928.* Lima: Imprenta Torres Aguirre, 1928.

————. *Leguía: Colección de discursos pronunciados por el presidente de la república, señor don Augusto B. Leguía, durante el año 1928.* Lima: Editorial "Cahuide," 1929.

————. *Leguía: Colección de discursos pronunciados por el presidente de la república, señor don Augusto B. Leguía, sobre la realización de su programa de gobierno, en orden a la política vial y ferroviaria, a las industrias agrícola y minera, a las obras públicas y a la asistencia social.* Lima: Editorial "Cahuide," 1927.

————. *Leguía: Selección de discursos pronunciados por el presidente de la república, señor don Augusto B. Leguía, durante el año 1927.* Lima: Editorial "Cahuide," 1928.

————. *Mensaje presentado al Congreso Ordinario de 1909 por el presidente de la república.* Lima: Talleres Tipográficos de "La Revista," 1909.

————. *Mensaje que s.e. el presidente de la república presenta al Congreso Ordinario de 1910.* Lima: Oficina Tipográfica de "La Opinión Nacional," 1910.

————. *Mensaje que s.e. el presidente de la república presenta al Congreso Ordinario de 1911.* Lima: Imprenta Americana, 1911.

————. *Mensaje que s.e. el presidente de la república presenta al Congreso Ordinario de 1912.* Lima: Imprenta de "La Acción Popular," 1912.

————. *Mensaje presentado al Congreso Ordinario de 1920 por el presidente de la república sr. Augusto B. Leguía.* Lima: Imprenta Torres Aguirre, 1920.

————. *Mensaje presentado al Congreso Ordinario de 1921 por el presidente de la república sr. Augusto B. Leguía.* Lima: C. F. Southwell, 1921.

————. *Mensaje presentado al Congreso Ordinario de 1922 por el presidente de la república.* Lima: C. F. Southwell Imprenta, 1922.

————. *Mensaje presentado al Congreso Ordinario de 1924 por el presidente de la república.* Lima: Imprenta "Garcilaso," 1924.

————. *Mensaje presentado al Congreso Ordinario de 1925 por el presidente de la república don Augusto B. Leguía.* Lima: Imprenta "Garcilaso," 1925.

————. *Mensaje presentado al Congreso Ordinario de 1926 por el presidente*

de la república señor don Augusto B. Leguía. Lima: Imprenta "Garcilaso,"
1926.

———. *Mensaje presentado al Congreso Ordinario de 1927 por el presidente
de la república*. Lima: Imprenta "Garcilaso," 1927.

———. *Mensaje presentado al Congreso Ordinario de 1928 por el presidente
de la república don Augusto B. Leguía*. Lima: Imprenta "Garcilaso," 1928.

———. *Mensaje presentado al Congreso Ordinario de 1929 por el presidente
de la república*. Lima: Imprenta Torres Aguirre, 1929.

———. *Mensaje presentado al Congreso Ordinario de 1930 por el presidente
de la república sr. d. Augusto B. Leguía*. Lima: Imprenta Torres Aguirre,
1930.

———. *Yo tirano, yo ladrón (memorias del presidente Leguía)*. Lima: Editorial "Ahora," n.d.

Leguía, Jorge Guillermo. *Estudios históricos*. Santiago de Chile: Ediciones
Ercilla, 1939.

Lewin, Boleslao. *La rebelión de Túpac Amaru y los orígenes de la emancipación
americana*. Buenos Aires: Librería Hachette, 1957.

Liga de Hacendados, Arequipa. *Memorial relativo a la cuestión indígena que
la Liga de Hacendados eleva al supremo gobierno, aprobado por su comité
ejecutivo en sesión de 15 de mayo de 1922 y sancionado por la asamblea
general de 10 de junio del mismo año*. Arequipa: Tip. S. Quiroz, 1922.

Llosa P., Jorge Guillermo. *En busca del Perú*. Lima: Ediciones del Sol, 1962.

López de Romaña, Eduardo. *Discurso inaugural de excmo. señor Eduardo
L. de Romaña al ser investido con el mando supremo de la república por el
Congreso Ordinario de 1899*. Lima: Imprenta del Estado, 1899.

———. *Mensaje del presidente de la república en la instalación del Congreso
Ordinario de 1900*. Lima: Imprenta del Estado, 1900.

———. *Mensaje del presidente de la república en la instalación del Congreso
Ordinario de 1901*. Lima: Imprenta del Estado, 1901.

———. *Mensaje del presidente de la república en la instalación del Congreso
Ordinario de 1902*. Lima: Imprenta del Estado, 1902.

———. *Mensaje del presidente de la república en la instalación del Congreso
Ordinario de 1903*. Lima: Imprenta del Estado, 1903.

Mac-Lean Estenós, Roberto. *Indios de América*. Mexico, D.F.: Universidad
Nacional Autónoma de México, Instituto de Investigaciones Sociales,
1962.

———. *Sociología del Perú*. Mexico, D.F.: Universidad Nacional Autónoma
de México, Instituto de Investigaciones Sociales, 1959.

Maguiña, Alejandrino. *Informe sobre los indígenas de Chucuito*. Lima: El
Diario, 1909.

Maldonado, Emilio C. *Apuntes acerca del liberalismo del Partido Liberal en
el Perú: Opúsculo no. 1. Instrucción especial para el pueblo*. Ica: Imprenta
de la Regeneración, 1904.

Malpica S. S., Carlos. *Crónica del hambre en el Perú*. Lima: Francisco Moncloa
Editores, 1966.

Mariátegui, José Carlos. *Defensa del marxismo: Polémica revolucionaria.* Lima: Biblioteca Amauta, 1964.

──────. *Siete ensayos de interpretación de la realidad peruana.* 10th ed. Lima: Biblioteca Amauta, 1965.

Martínez, Héctor; Cameo C., Miguel; and Ramírez S., Jesús. *Bibliografía indígena andina peruana (1900-1968).* 2 vols. Lima: Ministerio de Trabajo y Comunidades, Instituto Indigenista Peruano, 1968.

Martínez de la Torre, Ricardo. *Apuntes para una interpretación marxista de historia social del Perú.* 4 vols. Vols. 1, 2, 3, Lima: Empresa Editorial Peruana, 1947, 1948, 1949. Vol. 4, Lima: Compañía Peruana, 1949.

Martínez G., S. *Para la consulta popular: Elecciones de 1963.* Lima: Ediciones Martínez, n.d.

Matto de Turner, Clorinda. *Aves sin nido.* Cuzco: Universidad Nacional del Cuzco, 1948.

Mayer de Zulen, Dora. *Un debate importantisimo en el patronato de la raza indígena.* Lima: n.p., 1930.

──────. *Estudios sociológicos.* Callao: Imprenta del H. Concejo Provincial, 1907.

──────. *Estudios sociológicos de actualidad.* Callao: Imprenta Colegio Militar Leoncio Prado, 1950.

──────. *La historia de las sublevaciones indígenas en Puno.* Publicación mensual doctrinaria, 48, 49. Lima: El Deber Pro-Indígena, 1917.

──────. *El indígena peruano a los cien años de república libre e independiente.* Lima: Imprenta Peruana de E. Z. Casanova, 1921.

──────. *El indígena y los congresos panamericanos.* 3 vols. Lima: Imprenta "Lux," 1938.

Miró Quesada Laos, Carlos. *Autopsia de los partidos políticos.* Lima: Ediciones Páginas Peruanas, Imprenta "Minerva," 1961.

──────. *Pueblo en crisis.* Buenos Aires: Emecé Editores, 1946.

──────. *Radiografía de la política peruana.* Lima: Ediciones "Páginas Peruanas," 1959.

──────. *Sánchez Cerro y su tiempo.* Buenos Aires: Librería "El Ateneo" Editorial, 1947.

Monge Medrano, Carlos. *La vida en las altiplanicies andinas: Procesos ecológicos.* Lima: Ministerio de Trabajo y Asuntos Indígenas, 1963.

More, Federico. *Una multitud contra un pueblo: Etiología diagnóstico terapéutica de una sicosis política.* Lima: Editorial Todo el Mundo, 1934.

──────. *Zoocracia y canibalismo.* Lima: Editorial "Llamarada," 1933.

Moreyra y Paz Soldán, Carlos. *Bibliografía regional peruana (colección particular).* Lima: Librería Internacional del Perú, Editores, 1967.

Niles, Blair. *Peruvian Pageant: A Journey in Time.* New York: Bobbs-Merrill Company, 1937.

Oficina del Periodismo, ed. *La obra de Leguía no ha concluido.* Lima: Empresa Editorial Cervantes, 1926.

Olaechea, Guillermo U. *La constitución del Perú dada por la Asamblea*

Nacional de 1919. Comentada, anotada y concordada con las leyes plebiscitarias y decretos que tienen fuerza de ley. Leyes orgánicas, decretos, reglamentos y resoluciones referentes a ellas hasta 1922. Lima: Imprenta Americana, 1922.

Oyague y Calderón, Carlos. *La conscripción vial ó servicio obligatorio de caminos: Ideas generales y argumentos que pueden servir de base para el estudio de una ley.* Lima: Imprenta del Centro Editorial, 1915.

Pan American Union. *Constitution of the Republic of Peru, 1933.* Washington, D.C., 1965.

Pardo, José. *Mensaje presentado al Congreso Ordinario de 1905 por el presidente de la república.* Lima: Imprenta del Estado, 1905.

———. *Mensaje presentado al Congreso Ordinario de 1906 por el presidente de la república.* Lima: Imprenta del Estado, 1906.

———. *Mensaje presentado al Congreso Ordinario de 1907 por el presidente de la república.* Lima: Imprenta del Estado, 1907.

———. *Mensaje presentado al Congreso Ordinario de 1908 por el presidente de la república.* Lima: Imprenta del Estado, 1908.

———. *Mensaje presentado al Congreso Ordinario de 1916 por el presidente de la república.* Lima: Imprenta del Estado, 1916.

———. *Mensaje presentado al Congreso Ordinario de 1917 por el presidente de la república.* Lima: Imprenta del Estado, 1917.

———. *Mensaje presentado al Congreso Ordinario de 1918 por el presidente de la república.* Lima: Imprenta del Estado, 1918.

———. *Perú: Cuatro años de gobierno constitucional.* New York: n.p., 1919.

Pareja Paz-Soldán, José. *Derecho constitucional peruano.* 4th ed., enlarged. Lima: Ediciones Librería Studium, 1966.

———. *Geografía del Perú.* 2 vols. Lima: Librería Internacional del Perú, 1950.

———, ed. *Las constituciones del Perú (Exposición, crítica y textos): Recopilación y estudio preliminar de José Pareja Paz-Soldán.* Madrid: Ediciones Cultura Hispánica, 1954.

———. *Visión del Perú en el siglo XX.* 2 vols. Lima: Librería Studium, 1962, 1963.

Partido Aprista Peruano. *Los crímenes del Sancho-Civilismo: La revolución de Huaráz.* Buenos Aires: Editorial Claridad, 1933.

———. *40 preguntas y 40 respuestas sobre el Partido Aprista Peruano por el buró de redactores de "Cuaderno Aprista."* Incahuasi: Editorial Indoamericana, 1941.

———. *El proceso Haya de la Torre.* Guayaquil: n.p., 1933.

———. *Programa mínimo o plan de acción inmediata, dictado por el primer Congreso Nacional del partido, reunido en Lima, en 1931.* Lima: Editorial Imprenta Minerva, 1931.

Partido Constitucional Renovador del Perú. *Programa del Partido Constitucional Renovador del Perú.* Lima: n.p., 1935.

Partido Demócrata. *Doctrinas de don Nicolás de Piérola: Declaración de principios, bases de organización del partido, anexo histórico.* Lima: n.p., 1950.

Partido Liberal del Perú. *Proyecto del programa de reformas políticas, sociales y económicas, sancionado por el comité central directivo reorganizador en sesión del 4 de marzo de 1931.* Lima: Imprenta Americana, 1933.

Partido Social Nacionalista. *Nuestro partido.* Lima: Empresa Editora Peruana, 1944.

Partido Social Nacionalista del Perú. *Partido Social Nacionalista del Perú.* Lima: Imprenta "Minerva," 1935.

Patria nueva, 1919-4 de julio-1928. Lima: n.p., n.d.

Patronato de la Raza Indígena, Huánuco. *Memoria del patronato de la raza indígena de Huánuco, años de 1927 y 1928.* Huánuco: n.p., 1929.

Paz Soldán, Mariano Felipe. *Biblioteca peruana.* Lima: Imprenta Liberal, 1879.

Peláez Bazán, Mario. *De la provincia al aprismo.* Lima: Talleres Gráficos EETSA, 1961.

Peña Prado, Mariano. *El dominio del estado en el Perú.* Lima: "Editorial Minerva," 1934.

El pierolismo y compañía; el gobierno Pardo; la candidatura Leguía. Lima: Imprenta Prince, 1908.

Pike, Fredrick B. *The Modern History of Peru.* London: Weidenfeld and Nicolson, 1967.

Poblete Troncoso, Moisés. *Condiciones de vida y de trabajo de la población indígena del Perú.* Ginebra: Oficina Internacional de Trabajo, 1938.

Porras Barrenechea, Raúl, ed. *Fuentes históricas peruanas.* Lima: J. Mejía Baca y P. L. Villanueva, Editores, 1954.

Portal, Magda. *¿Quiénes traicionaron al pueblo?* Lima: Empresa Editora "Salas é Hijos," Cuadernos de Divulgación Popular "Flora Tristán," 1950.

Prado, Jorge del. *Mariátegui y su obra.* Lima: Ediciones "Nuevo Horizonte," 1946.

Prado, Manuel. *Un año de gobierno: Discursos de Manuel Prado, 1939-8 de diciembre de 1940.* Lima: El Universal, 1941.

———. *Un año de gobierno: Resumen del mensaje presentado al Congreso por el señor doctor don Manuel Prado presidente constitucional de la república del Perú.* Lima: Guillermo Kraft, 1944.

———. *Mensaje presentado al Congreso por el señor doctor don Manuel Prado presidente constitucional de la república.* Lima: n.p., 1940.

———. *Mensaje presentado al Congreso por el señor doctor don Manuel Prado presidente constitucional de la república.* Lima: n.p., 1941.

———. *Mensaje presentado al Congreso por el señor doctor don Manuel Prado presidente constitucional de la república.* Lima: n.p., 1942.

———. *Mensaje presentado al Congreso por el señor doctor don Manuel Prado presidente constitucional de la república.* Lima: n.p., 1943.

———. *Mensaje presentado al Congreso por el señor doctor don Manuel Prado presidente constitucional de la república.* Lima: n.p., 1944.

_____. *Mensaje presentado al Congreso por el señor doctor don Manuel Prado presidente constitucional de la república.* Lima: n.p., 1945.

Programa de gobierno del comandante Luis M. Sánchez Cerro, candidato a la presidencia de la república del Perú. Lima: n.p., 1931.

Quiroga, Manuel A. *Proyecto de legislación indígena, presentado por el diputado por la provincia de Chucuito, al Congreso Regional del Sur, 1920.* Arequipa: n.p., 1920.

Reaño García, José. *Historia del leguiísmo: Sus hombres y sus obras.* Edited by Ernesto E. Bacarezo Pinillos. Lima: T. Scheuch, 1928.

Reinaga, César Augusto. *El indio y la tierra en Mariátegui. (Contribución al análisis económico.)* Cuzco: Editorial H. G. Rozas, 1959.

René-Moreno, Gabriel, ed. *Biblioteca peruana: Apuntes para un catálogo de impresos. Libros y folletos peruanos de la biblioteca del instituto nacional y notas bibliográficas.* 2 vols. Santiago de Chile: Biblioteca del Instituto Nacional, 1896.

Rey de Castro, Carlos. *Los escándalos del Putumayo.* 2 vols. Vol. 1, *Carta abierta dirigida a Mr. Geo. B. Michell, y diversos documentos.* Vol. 2, *Carta al director del Daily News and Leader, de Londres, y diversos documentos.* Barcelona: Imprenta Viuda de Luis Tasso, 1913.

Ricketts, Carlos A. *Ensayos de legislación pro-indígena: Párrafos epilogales de Francisco Mostajo.* Arequipa: Tip. Cuadros, 1936.

Ritter, Ulrich Peter. *Comunidades indígenas y cooperativismo en el Perú.* Bilbao, Spain: Ediciones Deusto, 1965.

Robuchon, Eugenio. *En el Putumayo y sus afluentes.* Lima: Imprenta La Industria, 1907.

Roca Sánchez, Pedro Erasmo. *Por la clase indígena: Exposición y proyectos para una solución del aspecto legal del problema indígena, presentado a la constituyente por el autor, en su calidad de representante por el departamento de Ancash.* Lima: Pedro Barrantes Castro, Editor, 1935.

Roel Pineda, Virgilio L. *La economía agraria peruana hacia la reforma de nuestro agro.* 2d ed. 2 vols. Lima: Talleres de Grafcolor, 1961.

_____. *El sendero de un pueblo.* Lima: Editorial "Garcilaso," 1955.

Romero, Emilio. *Historia económica del Perú.* 2d ed., 2 vols. Lima: Editorial Universo, 1968.

_____. *Monografía del departamento de Puno.* Lima: Imprenta Torres Aguirre, 1928.

Rouillon, Guillermo. *Bio-bibliografía de José Carlos Mariátegui.* Lima: Imprenta de la Universidad Nacional Mayor de San Marcos, 1963.

Saco, Alfredo. *Síntesis aprista (una exposición completa de la ideología del aprismo).* Lima: Librería e Imprenta "San Cristóbal," Editorial Atahualpa, 1934.

Saco Miró Quesada, Alfredo. *Programa agrario del aprismo.* Lima: Ediciones Populares, 1946.

Sáenz, Luis N. *La coca: Estudio médico-social de la gran toxicomanía peruana.* Lima: Imprenta de la E. de la G. C. y P., 1938.

Sáenz, Moisés. *Sobre el indio peruano y su incorporación al medio nacional.* Mexico, D.F.: Secretaría de Educación Pública, 1933.

Sainte Marie S., Darío, ed. *Perú en cifras, 1944-1945.* Lima: Talleres de la Empresa Gráfica Scheuch, 1945.

Salazar Bondy, Augusto. *Historia de las ideas en el Perú contemporáneo: El proceso del pensamiento filosófico.* 2 vols. Lima: Francisco Moncloa Editores 1965.

Salazar Bondy, Sebastián; Salazar Bondy, Augusto; Roel Pineda, Virgilio; and Matos Mar, José. *La encrucijada del Perú.* Montevideo, Uruguay: Ediciones ARCA, 1963.

Sánchez, Luis Alberto. *Don Manuel.* 3d ed., corrected. Santiago: Ediciones Ercilla, 1937.

———. *Haya de la Torre y el Apra: Crónica de un hombre y un partido.* Santiago de Chile: Editorial del Pacífico, 1955.

———. *El Perú: Retrato de un país adolescente.* 2d ed. Lima: Imprenta de la Universidad Nacional Mayor de San Marcos, 1963.

———. *Raúl Haya de la Torre o el político: Crónica de una vida sin tregua.* Santiago de Chile: Editorial Ercilla, 1934.

———. *Testimonio personal: Memorias de un peruano del siglo XX.* 3 vols. Lima: Ediciones Villasán, 1969.

Sánchez Cerro, Luis A. *Manifiesto a la nación, 22 de agosto de 1930.* Lima: La Imprenta Peruana, 1930.

San Cristóbal-Sebastián, Antonio. *Economía, educación y marxismo en Mariátegui.* Lima: Ediciones Studium, 1960.

San Cristóval, Evaristo. *Manuel Pardo y Lavalle, su vida y su obra.* Lima: Editorial Gil, 1945.

Secretaría General del Episcopado del Perú. *Exigencias sociales del catolicismo en el Perú: Primera semana social del Perú, 1 al 9 de Agosto de 1959.* Lima: Talleres Gráficos Mercagraph, 1959.

Silva Villacorta, Pablo. *A dónde van las ideas de Haya de la Torre: Una nueva visión sobre las ideas que conforman la doctrina del Apra.* Lima: Talleres de la Imprenta E.R.V., 1966.

Sivirichi, Atilio. *Derecho indígena peruano: Proyecto de código indígena.* Lima: Ediciones Kuntur, 1946.

———. *Historia del senado del Perú.* Lima: Cámara de Senadores, 1955.

Solís, Abelardo. *Ante el problema agrario peruano.* Lima: Editorial "Perú," 1928.

———. *Once años.* Lima: Talleres Gráficos Sanmarti y Cía, 1934.

Steward, Julian H., ed. *Handbook of South American Indians.* 6 vols. Washington, D.C.,: Smithsonian Institution, 1946-50.

Tapia Olarte, Eulogio. *Cinco grandes escritores cuzqueños en la literatura peruana.* Lima: Imprenta D. Miranda, 1946.

Tauro, Alberto. *Amauta y su influencia (síntesis de los 32 números.)* Lima: Biblioteca Amauta, 1960.

———. *Bibliografía peruana de historia, 1940-1953.* Lima: Talleres Gráficos

P. L. Villanueva, 1953.

_____. *Bibliografía peruana de historia (primer suplemento)*. Lima: n.p., 1958.

_____, ed. *Diccionario enciclopédico del Perú*. 3 vols. Lima: Editorial Juan Mejía Baca, 1966-67.

Tezanos Pinto, Víctor de. *Dos necesidades urgentes*. Paris: Imprenta Artística "Lux," 1923.

Tudela y Varela, Francisco. *Socialismo peruano: Estudio sobre las comunidades indígenas*. Lima: Imprenta La Industria, 1905.

Tupac Amaru, Juan Bautista. *Las memorias de Tupac Amaru*. Lima: Fondo de Cultura Popular, 1964.

Ugarteche, Pedro. *Sánchez Cerro, papeles y recuerdos de un presidente del Perú*. 4 vols. Lima: Editorial Universitaria, 1969-70.

_____and San Cristóval Evaristo, eds. *Mensajes de los presidentes del Perú*. 2 vols. Vol. 1, *1821-1867*, Vol. 2, *1869-1899*. Lima: Librería e Imprenta Gil, 1943, 1945.

Ulloa Cisneros, Abel. *Escombros (1919-1930)*. Lima: C.I.P., 1934.

Valcárcel, Carlos A. *El proceso del Putumayo y sus secretos inauditos*. Lima: Imprenta "Comercial" de Horacio La Rosa y Co., 1915.

Valcárcel, Daniel. *La rebelión de Tupac Amaru*. Mexico, D.F.: Fondo Cultura Económica, 1965.

Valcárcel, Luis E. *Ruta cultural del Perú*. 4th ed. Lima: Ediciones Nuevo Mundo, 1966.

_____. *Tempestad en los andes*. Lima: Populibros Peruanos, n.d.

_____. et el. *Estudios sobre la cultura actual del Perú*. Lima: Universidad Nacional Mayor de San Marcos, 1964.

Valdez de la Torre, Carlos. *Evolución de las comunidades indígenas*. Lima: Editorial Euforión, 1921.

Vara Cadillo, N. Saturnino. *La trata de indios en la construcción de la carretera Huánuco-Pucalpa: Documentos parlamentarios*. Lima: Partido Socialista del Perú, 1936.

Varallanos, José. *El cholo y el Perú: Introducción al estudio sociológico de un hombre y un pueblo mestizo y su destino cultural*. Buenos Aires: Imprenta López, 1962.

_____. *Historia de Huánuco: Introducción para el estudio de la vida social de una región del Perú, desde la era prehistórica a nuestros días*. Buenos Aires: Imprenta López, 1959.

_____. *Legislación indiana republicana: Compilación de leyes, decretos, jurisprudencia judicial, administrativa y demás vigentes sobre el indígena y sus comunidades*. Lima: C.I.P., 1947.

Vásquez, Mario C. *Hacienda, peonaje y servidumbre en los andes peruanos*. Lima: Editorial Estudios Andinos, 1961.

Vega, Juan José. *La emancipación frente al indio peruano; la legislación indiana del Perú en la iniciación de la república, 1821-1830: Contribución al estudio del derecho peruano*. Lima: "Editorial San Marcos," Universidad Nacional Mayor de San Marcos, 1958.

_____. *José Gabriel Tupac Amaru*. Lima: Editorial Universo, 1969.

Velasco Núñez, Manuel D. *Compilación de la legislación indigenista concordada.* Lima: Editora Médica Peruana, 1959.

Vidalón Menéndez, Cesáreo. *El problema indígena: Breve estudio histórico-sociológico-legal de la materia.* Lima: Imprenta Peruana de E. Z. Casanova, 1920.

Villanueva, Víctor. *La tragedia de un pueblo y un partido (páginas para la historia del Apra). 2d ed.* Lima: Talleres Gráficos "Victory," 1956.

Villarán, Manuel Vicente. *Anteproyecto de constitución de 1931: Exposición de motivos.* Lima: Talleres Gráficos P. L. Villanueva, 1962.

———. *Páginas escogidas,* prólogo de Jorge Basadre. Lima: Talleres Gráficos P. L. Villanueva, 1962.

Wiesse de Sabogal, María Jesús. *José Carlos Mariátegui: Etapas de su vida y los ensayos de Benjamin Carrión, Jesualdo Sosa, Baldomero Sanín Cano, Medardo Vitier, Jorge Falcón, y Rubén Sardón.* Lima: Biblioteca Amauta, 1959.

Yarlequé, Manuel. *La raza indígena: Artículos y documentos interesantes. Las comunidades indígenas implorando el amparo y protección de Wilson.* Lima: Sanmarti y Cía Impresores, 1920.

Yarlequé de Marquina, Josefa. *El maestro ó democracia en miniatura.* Lima: Librería e Imprenta J. Alvarez A., 1963.

Yépez Miranda, Alfredo. *Signos del Cuzco.* Lima: Imprenta D. Miranda, 1946.

Yépez de la Torre, Julio Oscar. *Apoteosis de Leguía: Conferencia pronunciada por . . . en los teatros ideal y municipal, en las fiestas organizadas por el concejo provincial de Trujillo conmemorando las bodas de plata de la vida política del presidente de la república señor don Augusto B. Leguía y Salcedo, el 8 de setiembre de 1928.* Trujillo: Tipografía "Olaya," 1928.

Yrigoyen, Pedro. *El conflicto y el problema indígenas [sic].* Lima: Sanmarti y Cía., 1922.

Zumaeta, Pablo. *Las cuestiones del Putumayo.* 2 vols. Vol. 1, *Memorial.* Vol. 2, *Segundo memorial.* Barcelona: Imprenta Viuda de Luis Tasso, 1913.

ARTICLES

Arciniegas, Germán. "González Prada, Mariátegui, Haya de la Torre." *Cuadernos americanos 93, no. 3 (May-June 1957): 203-11.*

Argüedas, José María. "El complejo cultural en el Perú y el primer congreso de peruanistas. (Lo indio, lo occidental y lo mestizo. Los prejuicios culturales, la segregación social y la creación artística.)" *América indígena 12* (April 1952): 131-40.

Bermejo, Vladimiro. "La ley y el indio en el Perú." *América indígena 4* (April 1944): 107-12.

Castro Pozo, Hildebrando. "Las comunidades indígenas del Perú." In *Perú en cifras, 1944-1945,* edited by Darío Sainte Marie S. Buenos Aires: Ediciones Internacionales, 1945. Pp. 158-74.

———. "Social and Economic-Political Evolution of the Communities of Central Perú." In *The Andean Civilizations,* edited by Julian Steward. Vol.

2 of *Handbook of South American Indians.* Washington, D.C.: Government Printing Office, 1946. Pp. 483-500.

Cornejo Bouroncle, Jorge. "Las comunidades indígenas." *Revista universitaria* (Universidad Nacional de Cuzco) 38, no. 95 (1948): 67-129.

Cossío del Pomar, F. "Apuntes sobre el indio peruano y su vida." *Cuadernos americanos 18,* no. 6 (November-December, 1944): 161-74.

Davies, Thomas M., Jr. "The *Indigenismo* of the Peruvian Aprista Party: A Reinterpretation." *Hispanic American Historical Review* 51, no. 4 (November 1971): 626-45.

Díaz Rozzotto, Jaime. "José Carlos Mariátegui y las posibilidades del desarrollo no capitalista de la comunidad indígena peruana." *Cuadernos americanos* 25, no. 3 (1966), pp. 173-205.

Faron, Louis. "La formación de dos comunidades indígenas en un valle de la costa peruana." In Luis E. Valcárcel, et al., *Estudios sobre la cultura actual del Perú.* Lima: Imprenta de la Universidad Nacional Mayor de San Marcos, 1964. Pp. 37-63.

Klinge, Gerardo. "La agricultura en el Perú." In *Perú en cifras, 1944-1945,* edited by Darío Sainte Marie S. Buenos Aires: Ediciones Internacionales, 1945. Pp. 65-94.

Kubler, George. "The Quechua in the Colonial World." In *The Andean Civilizations,* edited by Julian Steward. Vol. 2 of *Handbook of South American Indians.* Washington, D.C.: Government Printing Office, 1946. Pp. 331-410.

Mariátegui, José Carlos. "La conscripción vial." *Mundial* (Lima), año 6, no. 299 (March 5, 1926).

Mead, Robert G. "Bibliografía crítica de José Carlos Mariátegui." *Revista hispánica moderna* (New York) 27, no. 2 (April 1961): 138-42.

Mendoza R., General Juan. "El ejército peruano en el siglo XX." In *Visión del Perú en el siglo XX,* edited by José Pareja Paz-Soldán. Vol. 1. Lima: Librería Studium, 1962. Pp. 291-349.

Mishkin, Bernard. "The Contemporary Quechua." In *The Andean Civilizations,* edited by Julian Steward. Vol. 2 of *Handbook of South American Indians.* Washington, D.C.: Government Printing Office, 1946. Pp. 411-70.

Pike, Fredrick B. "The Old and the New APRA in Peru: Myth and Reality." *Inter-American Economic Affairs* 18 (Autumn 1964): 3-46.

Pinilla Sánchez Concha, Antonio. "Los núcleos escolares rurales en el Perú." *América indígena* 12, no. 3 (July 1952): 225-34.

Rodríguez Pastor, Carlos. "Derecho peruano del trabajo." In *Perú en cifras, 1944-1945,* edited by Darío Sainte Marie S. Buenos Aires: Ediciones Internacionales, 1945. Pp. 364-76.

Roel Pineda, Virgilio. "La agricultura en la economía peruana." In Sebastián Salazar Bondy, et al., *La encrucijada del Perú.* Montevideo: Ediciones ARCA, 1963. Pp. 29-53.

Rowe, John Howard. "Inca Culture at the Time of the Spanish Conquest." In *The Andean Civilizations,* edited by Julian Steward. Vol. 2 of *Handbook of*

South American Indians. Washington, D.C.: Government Printing Office, 1946. Pp. 183-330.

———. "The Incas under Spanish Colonial Institutions." *Hispanic American Historical Review* 37 (February 1957): 155-99.

Sánchez, Luis Alberto, and Saco, Alfredo M. "Aprista Bibliography: Books and Pamphlets." *Hispanic American Historical Review* 23 (August 1943): 555-85.

DISSERTATIONS

Chavarría, Jesús. "José Carlos Mariátegui, Revolutionary Nationalist: The Origins and Crisis of Modern Peruvian Nationalism, 1870-1930." Ph.D. dissertation, University of California at Los Angeles, 1967.

Davies, Thomas M., Jr. "Indian Integration in Peru: A Half Century of Experience, 1900-1948." Ph.D. dissertation, University of New Mexico, 1970.

Karno, Howard L. "Augusto B. Leguía and the Modernization of Peru, 1870-1930." Ph.D. dissertation, University of California at Los Angeles, 1970.

Klarén, Peter F. "Origins of the Peruvian Aprista Party: A Study of Social and Economic Change in the Department of La Libertad, 1870-1932." Ph.D. dissertation, University of California at Los Angeles, 1969.

Acknowledgments

Lack of adequate space precludes mention of all the persons who aided this study, but several individuals and organizations stand out.

The Henry L. and Grace Doherty Charitable Foundation awarded me a grant to study in Peru from October, 1966, to October, 1967, during which time I did the bulk of my research. The University of Texas at Austin awarded me a Post-Doctoral Fellowship for the academic year 1969-70, and the San Diego State University Foundation awarded me summer grants for 1971 and 1972. Government agencies in both Peru and the United States contributed measurably to my research. Special thanks are due to the staffs of the Sala de Investigaciones of the Biblioteca Nacional of Lima, the Biblioteca Central of the Ministerio de Trabajo y Comunidades, the Instituto Indigenista Peruano, the Biblioteca of the Ministerio de Relaciones Exteriores, and the United States National Archives.

I wish to express my deep appreciation to the late Professor Allan R. Holmberg of Cornell University, who proposed the topic and offered many helpful suggestions. His death in the fall of 1966 was a great loss to all students of Peru and Latin America. I am also indebted to Professors Henry F. Dobyns and Paul L. Doughty, whose extensive knowledge of Peruvian Indians aided me in the initial stages of my research.

Numerous Peruvian scholars likewise gave generously of their time and knowledge. I am particularly grateful to Drs. Jorge Basadre, Pedro Ugarteche, Julio Cotler, Mario C. Vázquez, Ella Dunbar Temple, and Evaristo San Cristóbal. Dr. Félix Denegri Luna provided insights into Peruvian politics and allowed me to work in his superb library.

I also want to acknowledge my appreciation to numerous Peruvian politicians who granted me interviews. Foremost on the list are Víctor Raúl Haya de la Torre, Deputy Luis Llanos de la Mata, and Luis Bedoya Reyes. Manuel Bustamante de la Fuente not only answered my questions, but granted me free access to his private archive.

Words are insufficient to express my gratitude to the family of Ing. Luis N. Mansilla, with whom I lived from October, 1966, until June of 1968. By taking me into their home and accepting me as a member of the family, Lucho, Betty, Lidia, and Miguel provided me with a rare opportunity to experience the warmth and loyalty of the Peruvian people.

To my father-in-law, General José Monzón Linares, who, through countless hours of conversation, shared with me his more than thirty years of experience in the Guardia Civil, I owe a special debt of gratitude.

Señora Elvira Horna de Dávila spent long hours transcribing notes during my stay in Lima. Her assistance and friendship and that of her husband, Aurelio, helped make this work possible.

Mrs. Marjorie Bray, through her extensive knowledge of Peruvian and Latin American history and her outstanding abilities as an editor, contributed to the style and readability of the text and also caught many errors. Mr. William Hermiston of the Department of Geography at California State University at San Diego is responsible for the three very excellent maps. Mrs. Marion Leitner has patiently typed and retyped the manuscript. Mr. Michael T. Argüello helped me with the index.

Many colleagues have read the manuscript and offered invaluable suggestions and criticisms. I would like to express my appreciation particularly to Professors Jesús Chavarría, Warren Dean, Troy Floyd, Howard Karno, Michael Meyer, Martin Needler, and Stanley Ross. Professor Edwin Lieuwen, who aided and encouraged me through three years of research and writing, deserves a special measure of thanks. All responsibility for interpretations and errors is of course mine alone.

Finally, for my wife, Eloísa Monzón de Davies, I reserve my deepest gratitude. Without her knowledge and insight into Peruvian affairs, her editorial assistance and painstaking proofreading of all Spanish words and titles, and her constant companionship and support through many difficult months, this study could not have been written.

Index

Abarca Arias, José Luis, 71
Acho bullring in Lima: Haya's speech at, 103; Manuel Prado's speech at, 130
Acoria, comunidad of, 119
Agricultural Board of Peru, 147
Aguirre Morales, Augusto, 93
Alberto Sánchez, Luis, 97, 97 n
Alcalde de Vara, 72
Alcanzadores, 91
Alexander, Robert J., 100 n
Alianza Popular Revolucionaria-Americana (APRA), 103, 105, 107, 108, 128; and Civilistas, 108-9; clandestine period, 112-13, 128, 139, 158; critics of, 100 n, 101, 101 n; dissident Apristas, 139 n, 149; election of 1931, 105-6, 106 n, 112; election of 1936, 125; election of 1945, 139; followers of (Apristas), 105, 108, 108 n, 120, 121, 126, 154; founding of, 100; Indian legislation of, 141, 142, 146, 147, 149; *indigenismo* of, 101, 107-8, 112, 112 n, 113, 139, 140, 150, 154, 158; land-reform policy of, 141, 144, 145; middle-class orientation of, 106, 109, 150, 158; National Bureau for Campesinos and Barriadas, 150 n; and Odría (La Coalición), 149-50; revolt in Trujillo, 120; suppression by Benavides, 113, 121, 129; suppression by Sánchez Cerro, 113, 157
Alvariño, Francisco, 78
Alva y Alva, Felipe, 144-45
Alzamora, Isaac, 35
Amat, Humberto Eduardo de, 133

Amauta, 93
Amazon Basin, 2, 56, 58
Ancahuasi, hacienda of, 143
Ancash, department of: Indian population of, 3; Indian uprisings in, 4, 34, 60
Anchorena, José Dionisio, 32
Andoque Indians. *See* Indian tribes
Andrés Belaúnde, Víctor, 116-17
Antapongo, hacienda of, 143
Aparcería. See Exploitive labor systems
APRA. *See* Alianza Popular Revolucionaria Americana
Apra Rebelde, 149
Aprismo. *See* Alianza Popular Revolucionaria Americana
Apristas. *See* Alianza Popular Revolucionaria Americana
Apurímac, department of, 51; Indian Schools in, 131
Aramburu, Gonzalo, 109 n
Arana, Julio C., 56, 57; and Brothers, company of, 56
Araníbar, José M., 71
Arca Parró, Alberto, 143; and Constituent Congress of 1931, 115
Arequipa, city of, 2; 1931 revolt against Sánchez Cerro, 99
Artola del Pozo, Armando, 123
Atacama Desert, 33
Atahualpa, 113, 118, 140
Atusparia, Pedro Pablo, 34
Aves sin nido, 41; Chang-Rodríguez on, 41 n
Ayacucho, Battle of, 20

195